Acing the Certified Kubernetes Administrator Exam

CHAD M. CROWELL

MANNING
SHELTER ISLAND

For online information and ordering of this and other Manning books, please visit
www.manning.com. The publisher offers discounts on this book when ordered in quantity.
For more information, please contact

> Special Sales Department
> Manning Publications Co.
> 20 Baldwin Road
> PO Box 761
> Shelter Island, NY 11964
> Email: orders@manning.com

 Manning Publications Co.
20 Baldwin Road
PO Box 761
Shelter Island, NY 11964

Development editor:	Connor O'Brien
Technical editor:	Curtis Bates
Review editor:	Aleksandar Dragosavljević
Production editor:	Kathleen Rossland
Copy editor:	Kristen Bettcher
Proofreader:	Katie Tennant
Typesetter:	Dennis Dalinnik
Cover designer:	Marija Tudor

ISBN: 9781633439092
Printed and bound by CPI Group (UK) Ltd, Croydon, CR0 4YY

Get the eBook FREE!

(PDF, ePub, Kindle, and liveBook all included)

We believe that once you buy a book from us, you should be able to read it in any format we have available. To get electronic versions of this book at no additional cost to you, purchase and then register this book at the Manning website.

Go to https://www.manning.com/freebook and follow the instructions to complete your pBook registration.

That's it!
Thanks from Manning!

This book is dedicated to my late grandfather, James Crowell,
who introduced me to computers.

brief contents

contents

preface

I started my Kubernetes journey in 2017 while working for a small fintech startup in Austin, Texas. I was asked to migrate servers from Amazon EC2 (Amazon Elastic Cloud Computing) to AKS (Azure Kubernetes Service). I had never heard of Kubernetes before, but the decision from management was firm, and so I was thrown into the fire. I feverishly scrolled through the documentation website, blogs, books, and anything I could find to try to absorb this new technology. I remember feeling afraid to attend standup, as I had only confused myself further and hadn't made any substantial progress. I was stuck and needed some help. I needed someone who was just a little bit ahead of me—someone that knew enough about Kubernetes to get me unstuck.

Shortly after this experience, I made it my goal to help others succeed at learning Kubernetes. It just so happened that this coincided with the very first Certified Kubernetes Administrator (CKA) Exam, which provided a blueprint for the skills one must possess to properly administer Kubernetes. I created my first CKA preparation course in 2018 and have been sharing my knowledge about Kubernetes ever since. Today, I am happy to say that I've helped thousands of people through my courses and content. This book is another medium in which I am excited to share my knowledge and experience.

This book is a complete guide to acing the CKA exam and contains scenarios, exercises, and lessons to help you practice and thoroughly absorb the content. The CKA exam is different from a lot of other exams, which you'll discover in the first chapter. Through persistent practice and effort, you will be well prepared for the CKA exam.

I have held the CKA certification since 2018 and have taken the exam again within the past year to gain recertification and pass the current information on to you, so you have the best chance to receive your certificate as well. I wish you the best of luck on your exam, but you can be certain you'll be prepared after having read this book. You got this!

acknowledgments

Writing a book with Manning has been an incredibly extensive and eye-opening experience. I have a great appreciation and respect for the diligent process Manning takes with each book, and it certainly adds tremendous value to this one. I couldn't have done this without Connor O'Brien, my development editor at Manning. Through his careful inspection and deliberate review, I have learned so much.

My thanks go to Curtis Bates, the technical editor for this book, who has 25 years of experience working as a software architect, systems engineer, and software developer in the distributed computing, cloud, and HPC disciplines.

To all the reviewers—Alessandro Campeis, Amit Lamba, Bradford Hysmith, Dale Francis, Dan Sheikh, David Moravec, Dylan Scott, Emanuele Piccinelli, Ernesto Cárdenas Cangahuala, Frankie Thomas-Hockey, Ganesh Swaminathan, Giampiero Granatella, Giang Châu, Ioannis Polyzos, John Harbin, Joseph Perenia, Kamesh Ganesan, Michael Bright, Michele Adduci, Morteza Kiadi, Roman Levchenko, Shawn Bolan, Simeon Leyzerzon, Simon Tschöke, Stanley Anozie, Swapneelkumar Deshpande, and Tim Sina—thank you, your suggestions helped make this a better book.

I would also like to thank my wife, Georgianne, as she has encouraged me to write and cared for the children many nights and weekends while I hacked away on the keyboard at the nearest coffee shop.

about this book

Who should read this book

This book is for those who are looking to achieve the certification, of course, but it's also for those who would like to follow a validated and endorsed method of learning Kubernetes. By following the exam blueprint, you'll be happy to find this book contains all the necessary components required to be proficient in administering Kubernetes. That said, this is not an introductory Kubernetes book and will require you to know how to navigate the Linux operating system and have a fundamental understanding of Kubernetes and the problems it aims to solve.

Kubernetes experience will help you further your career, as it is increasingly adopted by many Fortune 500 companies. This advanced skill set is in high demand, and having this certification on your resume adds tremendous value, which leads to a great probability of increasing your salary.

How this book is organized: A road map

This is very much a practical book, much like the exam. You should plan on working through the hands-on exercises, for which you do not need any special hardware—a Mac, Windows, or Linux desktop will be fine. We'll set up a local cluster using kind Kubernetes; those setup instructions can be found in appendix A. As you work through the exercises, you will find additional information on how to solve them in appendix D.

The book follows the Cloud Native Computing Foundation (CNCF) exam criteria very closely, as you will want to ensure that all domains are covered, and you're fully prepared for exam day. The book starts with an introduction to the exam, what the exam is, and how to prepare for the exam, and then chapter 2 begins with the CKA exam competencies for cluster architecture, installation, and configuration. The book then progresses to workloads and scheduling, followed by Services and networking, storage, and, finally, troubleshooting.

Chapters 2 and 3 jump into provisioning the underlying infrastructure to deploy a Kubernetes cluster, performing a version upgrade on a Kubernetes cluster using kubeadm, implementing etcd backup and restore, managing role-based access control, and managing a highly available Kubernetes cluster to thoroughly cover the cluster architecture, installation, and configuration exam criteria.

Chapters 4 and 5 build upon the previous chapters by configuring applications that run on top of Kubernetes, using ConfigMaps and Secrets, and continuing to explain how resource limits can affect Pod scheduling. You'll understand how to use manifest management and common templating tools, and the primitives used to create self-healing applications in Kubernetes. You'll then gain an understanding of how to scale applications that run in Kubernetes, as well as how updating Deployments works with rollouts and rollbacks. To round out your knowledge, you'll understand how to create, update, and manage containerized applications that will complete the workloads and scheduling domain of the exam.

Chapter 6 helps with your understanding of how networking works in Kubernetes, including the networking configuration on the cluster nodes and the connectivity between Pods. You'll learn about the types of Services in Kubernetes, including ClusterIP, NodePort, and LoadBalancer. You'll understand how Ingress controllers and Ingress resources work in Kubernetes, as well as how to configure and use CoreDNS. To round out the chapter, you'll be able to choose an appropriate container networking interface plugin, which will complete the services and networking exam criteria.

Chapter 7 explores how volumes and storage work in Kubernetes, including storage classes, persistent volumes, and persistent volume claims. You'll understand volume modes, access modes, and reclaim policies for volumes. You'll also learn how to configure applications with persistent storage, which will round out the storage domain of the exam.

Chapter 8 moves to troubleshooting problems within the Kubernetes cluster. You'll learn how to evaluate cluster and node logging, as well as how to monitor applications running in Kubernetes. You'll also learn how to manage container stdout (standard output) and stderr (standard error) logs and troubleshoot application failure, cluster component failure, and networking. This will completely fulfill the troubleshooting section of the exam criteria.

Chapter 9 is a chapter-by-chapter review, which is meant to serve you for the night before an exam, in case you need to quickly review any material from the book at the last minute. This review can also help with building your confidence, as you can feel better prepared, having checked off each section of chapter 9. Don't forget the exercises that are within each chapter! By the end of the book, you should be confident in managing your own Kubernetes cluster and ready to move on to the exam shortly thereafter.

About the exercises

In each chapter, you'll see various exercises that will test your knowledge about what you just read in the previous sections. I encourage you to go through these on your own, in your local cluster, or if you want to access a free cluster in the browser, visit https://killercoda.com. If you need help, see appendix D for a walk-through of how to solve all the exercises. Practicing these exercises in the terminal, in addition to the main sample scenarios, will be crucial to preparing you for exam day.

About the code

There may be instances where I reference a YAML file or a configuration file, all of which are in the following GitHub repo: https://github.com/chadmcrowell/acing-the-cka-exam. This book contains many examples of source code, which is formatted in a `fixed-width font like this` to distinguish it from ordinary text. In many cases, the original source code has been reformatted; we've added line breaks and reworked indentation to accommodate the available page space in the book, and some listings include line-continuation markers ( ).

You can get executable snippets of code from the liveBook (online) version of this book at https://livebook.manning.com/book/acing-the-certified-kubernetes-administrator-exam. The complete code for the examples in the book is available for download from the Manning website at https://www.manning.com/books/acing-the-certified-kubernetes-administrator-exam and from GitHub at https://github.com/chadmcrowell/acing-the-cka-exam.

liveBook discussion forum

Purchase of *Acing the Certified Kubernetes Administrator Exam* includes free access to liveBook, Manning's online reading platform. Using liveBook's exclusive discussion features, you can attach comments to the book globally or to specific sections or paragraphs. It's a snap to make notes for yourself, ask and answer technical questions, and receive help from the author and other users. To access the forum, go to https://livebook.manning.com/book/acing-the-certified-kubernetes-administrator-exam/discussion. You can also learn more about Manning's forums and the rules of conduct at https://livebook.manning.com/discussion.

Manning's commitment to our readers is to provide a venue where a meaningful dialogue between individual readers and between readers and the author can take place. It is not a commitment to any specific amount of participation on the part of the author, whose contribution to the forum remains voluntary (and unpaid). We suggest you try asking the author some challenging questions lest their interest stray! The forum and the archives of previous discussions will be accessible from the publisher's website as long as the book is in print.

Other online resources

Included in the first chapter are resources you can open during the exam that complement the preparation for the exam. You will be able to use the browser within the virtual machine to access the following documentation and their subdomains: https://kubernetes.io/docs/ and https://kubernetes.io/blog/. This includes all available language translations of these pages (e.g., https://kubernetes.io/zh/docs/). All of these resources will help you prepare for the exam, and it will be helpful to be familiar with these useful tools on exam day. For example, the Kubernetes documentation site has a search function in which you can quickly navigate to resources using certain keywords, which is explained in more depth in chapter 9.

about the author

CHAD M. CROWELL is a DevSecOps engineer at Raft and a Microsoft Certified Trainer. Chad has released eight courses on DevOps and Kubernetes with companies such as A Cloud Guru and INE. Currently, he leads a community called KubeSkills, where he's helping people learn Kubernetes and containers via coaching and cohorts. You can find Chad posting inside the KubeSkills community at https://community.kubeskills.com. He is also on YouTube at https://YouTube.com/@kubeskills and on Twitter as @chadmcrowell.

about the cover illustration

The figure on the cover of *Acing the Certified Kubernetes Administrator Exam* is "Tehinguise ou Danseuse Turcque," or "Turkish Dancer," taken from a collection by Jacques Grasset de Saint-Sauveur, published in 1788. Each illustration is finely drawn and colored by hand.

In those days, it was easy to identify where people lived and what their trade or station in life was just by their dress. Manning celebrates the inventiveness and initiative of the computer business with book covers based on the rich diversity of regional culture centuries ago, brought back to life by pictures from collections such as this one.

First steps

This chapter covers

- Introducing the Certified Kubernetes Administrator Exam
- Defining a Kubernetes administrator
- Meeting Kubernetes and the problems it solves
- Introducing the Kubernetes API
- Kubernetes components and Services, and Linux backend services
- Declarative and imperative commands

Welcome to *Acing the Certified Kubernetes Administrator Exam*. If you've purchased this book, chances are you've already researched the exam, know what it's about, and perhaps even have it scheduled. If not, don't worry; we'll talk about what the exam is and how to get signed up as soon as possible. For those of you who want to get right down to it, go ahead and skip this section, as it will most likely be review for you. You can skip to section 2, where we get into the meat and potatoes of the exam curriculum.

For those who are still being introduced to the CKA exam, let's go over what the exam is and what it entails. First, let me start by stating that I'm glad you've decided to come along with us on this journey to get certified in Kubernetes. Achieving the Certified Kubernetes Administrator (CKA) certification is quite an accomplishment and will help advance your career in a very big way. Also, you'll be part of a large group of individuals who hold this certification, including over 32,000 people worldwide. You might be asking yourself if it's worth it, and to that, I would say yes, and here's why:

- Kubernetes and distributed systems are going to be around for a long time.
- Kubernetes skills are in high demand.
- Getting certified will help solidify your understanding and show that you are well rounded and versed in Kubernetes.

1.1 Introducing the CKA exam

Now, let's get into what the exam is all about. The CKA exam is a competency test like no other. Instead of multiple-choice or fill-in-the-blank questions, this exam is entirely executed from within a Linux terminal (Ubuntu XFCE) in a remote desktop environment provided by PSI Services (the exam provider). Yes, that's right; they'll give you a set of tasks to complete, and you'll execute the solutions by typing the commands inside the terminal within the provided remote desktop environment. This is the entire exam experience, and you will have two hours to complete 15–20 tasks of this nature. Once complete, you are graded on the outcome of your tasks, no matter which path you took to achieve the outcome. This means that there may be more than one way to solve a given task. Throughout this book, you will learn different ways of obtaining the same results, giving you more tools in your tool belt, to achieve a passing grade on this exam, which is 66% or higher. You can also receive partial credit on any task, so that will help your success rate as well.

Throughout this book, we'll address tips and tricks available for each topic within each chapter. This will tie in nicely with applying your lessons and give you the necessary skills to approach the exam with confidence. These exam tips, in combination with your determination and repeated practice, will lead to success in passing the CKA exam. I can't emphasize enough how much muscle memory and putting in the practice will help your brain retain and access the appropriate Kubernetes commands when the time comes for the exam. Acing the CKA is truly an exercise, so if you're determined to pass the exam, you shouldn't take long breaks between study sessions, especially if you aren't working with Kubernetes daily. Don't let this deter you, though; we're going to do this Kubernetes workout together!

The CKA exam is provided by the Linux Foundation, and Kubernetes is maintained by the Cloud Native Computing Foundation (CNCF). The exam costs US$375 as of the writing of this book, but check the updated pricing sheet for current prices and prices in other currencies by visiting the Linux Foundation website at https://training.linuxfoundation.org. This price may be a bit higher than similar certifications of its class, but they do allow one free retake, as well as one additional browser tab, opened to the following sites and their subdomains during the exam:

- https://helm.sh/docs/
- https://kubernetes.io/docs/
- https://github.com/kubernetes/
- https://kubernetes.io/blog/

To take the exam, you will need a computer running Windows 8.1, Windows 10, Windows 11, macOS 10.15, macOS 11, macOS 12, Ubuntu 18.04, or Ubuntu 20.04 that has the Chrome web browser installed (all browsers are supported, but PSI highly recommends Chrome). When you begin the exam, you'll be instructed to download and install a new PSI-secured browser, which will automatically grant you access to the PSI proctoring platform, called *PSI Bridge*, which is the remote desktop environment. The remote desktop environment will include links to open the terminal as well as the provided Firefox browser (you must use Firefox) so you can browse to the authorized sites listed earlier. You will also need a webcam that has at least 640 × 480 pixel resolution, as they will require a 360 view of the room (external camera required for desktops) and will be monitoring you for the duration of the exam. Your computer screen must be 1368 x 769 pixel resolution or higher (dual monitors are not supported), you must have a functional microphone, and your internet bandwidth speed must be at least 300 Kbps to download and upload. The room where you take the exam must be quiet and well lit. Public spaces such as coffee shops or stores are not allowed. Your desk must be cleared of all papers and other electronics, and you must be seen clearly in the center frame of your webcam.

On exam day, you'll sit down at your desk with your computer, make sure it's plugged in, then go to the Linux Foundation portal to start your exam. Before you click the Begin Exam button, make sure that all browser tabs are closed and no other applications are running in the background (the proctor will check this as well). Once you click on the button to begin the exam, you'll immediately be introduced to an exam proctor. This exam proctor will check your environment to make sure that your desk is cleared and there aren't any papers or unauthorized electronics around. So, using your camera, you'll pan around the room to get a full 360 view, and you'll wait for their approval. They'll also periodically check your hands and wrists. The proctor will first check your hands and wrists before you start the exam, then they'll also stop you at frequent intervals in the middle of your exam and ask you to show both sides of your hands and wrists. Before they release the exam to you, they will also ask you for your government-issued ID, which you must hold up to the camera. Once the proctor is done verifying your identity and checking your workspace, they will release the exam, which means they will allow you to enter the exam and view the first question. You'll notice that each question has a similar format, including the context you must use and the task(s) that you must execute via the command line to solve the problem. If you come to a question that you can't answer, my advice is to skip it; you can flag it and come back to it at any time during the exam. It will be clear how to flag a question for review, as they show you in a brief automated walk-through at the beginning of the exam. For each task, you will also see the percentage of points that the task is worth. If you're stumped on something, look at how much it's worth. If it's worth, let's say, 5%, then go ahead and skip it.

> **EXAM TIP**   If you are copying and pasting text back and forth from the Firefox browser and the terminal, use the keyboard shortcut CTRL-SHIFT-C to copy and CTRL-SHIFT-V to paste.

The core competencies on which you will be tested are cluster architecture, installation and configuration; workloads and scheduling; Services and networking; storage; and troubleshooting. We'll cover all these areas in this book. Within the cluster architecture competency, which will comprise 25% of the questions on the exam, you will be tested on role-based access control, using kubeadm to add features and update a Kubernetes cluster, and backing up and restoring the etcd datastore. In the workloads and scheduling competency, which will comprise 15% of the questions on the exam, expect to be tested on performing rolling updates and rollbacks, as well as scaling applications and using ConfigMaps and Secrets. In the Services and networking competency, which comprises 20% of the questions on the exam, you'll be tested on creating and updating various Services in Kubernetes, using Ingress, DNS, and the container network interface in Kubernetes. In the storage competency, which comprises 10% of the questions on the exam, you'll need to understand storage classes, persistent volumes, and volume modes in Kubernetes. Then, in the troubleshooting competency, which is 30% of the questions on the exam, you will be expected to know how to get the logs from a Kubernetes cluster, as well as monitor and repair core cluster components. Table 1.1 outlines these domains and their competencies.

Table 1.1   Exam competencies and their percentages of the exam

Cluster architecture, installation, and configuration—25%
■ Manage role-based access control (RBAC).
■ Use kubeadm to install a basic cluster.
■ Manage a highly available Kubernetes cluster.
■ Perform a version upgrade on a Kubernetes cluster using kubeadm..
■ Implement etcd backup and restore.

Workloads and scheduling—15%
■ Understand Deployments and how to perform rolling updates and rollbacks.
■ Use ConfigMaps and Secrets to configure applications.
■ Know how to scale applications.
■ Understand the primitives used to create robust, self-healing application Deployments.
■ Understand how resource limits can affect Pod scheduling.
■ Awareness of manifest management and common templating tools.

Table 1.1 Exam competencies and their percentages of the exam *(continued)*

Services and networking—20%
▪ Understand host networking configuration on the cluster nodes.
▪ Understand connectivity between Pods.
▪ Understand ClusterIP, NodePort, and LoadBalancer Service types and Endpoints.
▪ Know how to use Ingress controllers and Ingress resources.
▪ Know how to configure and use CoreDNS.
▪ Choose an appropriate container network interface plugin.

Storage—10%
▪ Understand storage classes and persistent volumes.
▪ Understand volume and access modes and reclaim policies for volumes.
▪ Understand persistent volume claims primitive.
▪ Know how to configure applications with persistent storage.

Troubleshooting—30%
▪ Evaluate cluster and node logging.
▪ Understand how to monitor applications.
▪ Manage container stdout and stderr logs.
▪ Troubleshoot application failure.
▪ Troubleshoot cluster component failure.
▪ Troubleshoot networking.

You will have six clusters available during the exam that you will be required to switch between depending on the question. Usually, each question will ask you to perform the task on a different cluster than the previous question. They will provide instructions for how to switch between clusters, so don't worry too much about memorizing the cluster names and commands to switch between clusters.

The exam will also have the alias for `kubectl` set to `k`. An *alias* is a command you run that pertains to another command. For example, a common alias that exists for most Linux operating systems is `l='ls -lah'`, which means when you type the command `l`, it's the same thing as typing `ls -lah`. Similarly for the CKA exam, when you type the command `k`, it's the same as the command `kubectl`. From the command line on your computer, you can type `alias` to list all the existing aliases on your computer. All six clusters will have only one control plane node, and two clusters will have only one worker node, with one out of those two missing a worker node. They will all have a container network interface (CNI) installed and are named `k8s`, `hk8s`, `bk8s`, `wk8s`, `ek8s`, and `ik8s`, as shown in figure 1.1.

So many people have registered for the CKA exam that it has become one of the most popular Linux Foundation certifications to date. This partially speaks to the demand for the certification but also to the credibility of the certification once

CLUSTER	NODES	CNI
k8s	1 control plane, 2 workers	Flannel
hk8s	1 control plane, 2 workers	Calico
bk8s	1 control plane, 1 worker	Flannel
wk8s	1 control plane, 2 workers	Flannel
ek8s	1 control plane, 2 workers	Flannel
ik8s	1 control plane, 1 orphaned (missing node)	Loopback

Figure 1.1 Cluster configuration for all six clusters in the exam environment

received. The certificate is valid for three years, and the process to recertify is the same process that you went through the first time you took the exam.

I suggest scheduling your exam now, so you have an end goal and a deadline for completing it. This will keep you motivated to finish this book and will provide the necessary timeline to keep your knowledge top of mind and appropriately prepared to sit for the exam. If you are currently working with Kubernetes at your job, and you are typing `kubectl` commands daily, then schedule your exam for one month from today.

If you are just approaching the topic of Kubernetes, having never heard of it before, go ahead and schedule your exam for the furthest date the exam scheduler will allow (usually this is three months, but it may be less.) You can always reschedule, but the point is to give yourself two things: (1) a deadline so that you can take this exam seriously and achieve your intended result and (2) daily practice to incorporate into your prefrontal cortex (where memories are stored). This is exactly what you'll need to stay fresh and ready for the exam.

1.2 *What's in store*

Throughout this book, I'll be inserting exercises and exam-like scenarios for you to practice `kubectl` commands and prepare you for the exam. To make practice as easy as possible, I've included instructions for creating your local cluster. In appendix A, I'll walk you through the steps to create a Kubernetes cluster using kind. Kind Kubernetes (https://kind.sigs.k8s.io/) is a free, lightweight, and easy-to-use tool for creating a cluster right on your existing laptop or desktop computer. The only requirement is Docker, and with one command, you'll have a cluster up and running in seconds. This eliminates the barrier to entry for practicing for the CKA. I advise you to utilize this method, as you can waste a lot of time trying to build a cluster manually; and because the exam will have clusters already prepared for you, I believe this is the best way to study and follow along with this book. There are other methods to create a local cluster that you are welcome to use, such as minikube or MicroK8s. The idea is similar, but those tools might not align directly with the scenarios in this book. For example, in chapter 5, we'll prepare a cluster with a missing node. The steps to stage the environment are unique to kind, so reproducing the environment in minikube will be different.

Within each chapter of this book, there will be a scenario that resembles the real exam, which we'll work through together, followed by additional practice exercises that you can complete on your own. In appendix D, you can review hints for solving these practice exercises. You can use these to both test your knowledge of the book's content and to gauge your readiness for the CKA exam.

Before we begin, I'd like to clarify some points and let you know what this book is and what it isn't. This book is not an introduction to Kubernetes, so I expect that you have a background in containers and an understanding of what problem Kubernetes solves, as these will not be covered in this book. The CKA exam is not introductory; therefore, it will require quite a bit of experience with using and navigating the Linux operating system. People who understand cgroups and namespaces, which provide containers in Linux, will have an easier time following this book and subsequently passing the exam. Also, most who sit for this exam are already working with the technology in their job today, by either being introduced to it via a new project or by already using cluster administration as a primary function within their role. I'm not saying that people who are not working with Kubernetes won't pass the exam, but getting direct exposure to real-world scenarios, using your knowledge in a daily, hands-on fashion is more likely to lead to success.

1.2.1 What is a Kubernetes administrator?

The role of a Kubernetes administrator is twofold. A Kubernetes administrator knows the inner workings of Kubernetes and how to translate that into value for the end users. Here's what a job posting for a Kubernetes administrator might look like: "The responsibility of a Kubernetes administrator is to ensure that the company's services meet the needs of the customers within the desired levels of reliability, performance, and availability by developing continuous improvements, tools, and automation. You must know how to install, configure, deploy, update, and patch each of the components of the Kubernetes infrastructure to ensure that services and underlying systems are properly monitored and have adequate observability. This includes identifying and monitoring proper KPIs (key performance indicators) to ensure service health, minimizing MTTA (mean time to acknowledge) and MTTR (mean time to repair)."

Let's not sugarcoat it; the difficulty level of the exam remains high, hence the need for this book. But you will start to realize the complexities of Kubernetes after reading this book—not only how to envision the complexities and how they relate to what you already know about engineering and technology, but also how to dig through the complexities to troubleshoot and determine the root cause for the actions within a Kubernetes cluster.

1.3   *Meeting Kubernetes*

That brings me to the next point—the Kubernetes cluster. What is it? The Kubernetes cluster is called a *cluster* because it is a RESTful API of machines working together, in conjunction, as in figure 1.2. Just like a server farm, the machines are interconnected and housed within the same facility or network. But the key difference in Kubernetes is that the connected servers not only distribute load appropriately but also easily exchange data to eliminate a single point of failure. If one of the nodes fails, it doesn't bring down the entire cluster. Throughout this book, we'll call servers *nodes*. *Node* is a term that's specific to clusters, which tend to indicate that the server is a part of a larger system. We'll talk more about the anatomy of a cluster in chapter 2.

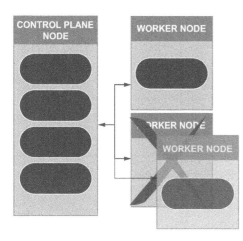

Figure 1.2   Servers (called nodes) working together in a cluster. When one fails, it takes itself out of the cluster to be repaired.

NOTE   Kubernetes is often referred to as K8s for short (pronounced kates), where the 8 between the K and the S represents the number of characters between those letters ("ubernete" = 8 characters).

Kubernetes is nothing more than a piece of software that you interact with via a REST API. A RESTful API is a well-defined, highly scalable, loosely coupled application architecture that favors communication over a network—and, more importantly, the act of transferring the state of a resource over a network. I can't stress enough how important it is to remember that Kubernetes is behind an API (a RESTful one, which is a collection of resources that can be manipulated through that API). *Resources* is the keyword here. Resources are how we address objects in Kubernetes. Sometimes in the Kubernetes community, we use the words *resources* and *objects* interchangeably, but there is a fundamental difference. Objects can have more than one resource address; for example, Deployments can have multiple URIs (uniform resource identifiers) based on the API version or based on the Deployment name, as you can see in figure 1.3. *Deployments* in Kubernetes are objects that offer more automated control over Pods and ReplicaSets that comprise your application running on Kubernetes. ReplicaSets are another type of object in Kubernetes that provides a control loop running a specified number of Pods (i.e., Pod replicas). You can list all available API resources with the command `kubectl api-resources` from any Kubernetes cluster.

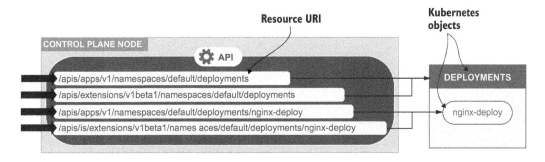

Figure 1.3 Kubernetes addresses objects by their resource URI, where multiple URIs can point to a single object.

We commonly interact with the Kubernetes API, and the objects within, by using a command-line tool called `kubectl`. We will solely be using `kubectl` throughout this book, as this is the command-line tool used on the exam to interface with the Kubernetes API. Having the `kubectl` command-line tool, in addition to a certificate, is needed to create, read, update, and delete Kubernetes resources. Depicted in figure 1.4 is a certificate that provides us with the role-based access that we need to perform certain operations in the Kubernetes cluster.

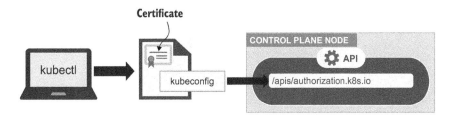

Figure 1.4 `kubectl` is the tool used to access Kubernetes objects, given a valid certificate inside the kubeconfig.

1.3.1 Cluster architecture, installation, and configuration

As previously mentioned, the architecture of a cluster is comprised of nodes, and on those nodes are running Pods. A Pod is the smallest deployable unit in Kubernetes and contains one or more containers. In an abstraction of the API, resources like Deployments are created that are comprised of *ReplicaSets*, which in turn are running one or more Pods across multiple nodes. In Kubernetes, there are two types of nodes—the *control plane node* and the *worker node*. The control plane node runs the API server, DNS, the controller manager, the scheduler, kube-proxy, and etcd datastore. All these parts and their relationships are shown in figure 1.5.

Communication to the control plane happens through the API, on the control plane node. The worker nodes, by way of the kubelet, get instructions from the control plane to fulfill their duty to not only run the containers themselves but to report on the health, providing a constant status to the control plane. The workers carry the brunt of the load, which makes their role very important for running applications in Kubernetes.

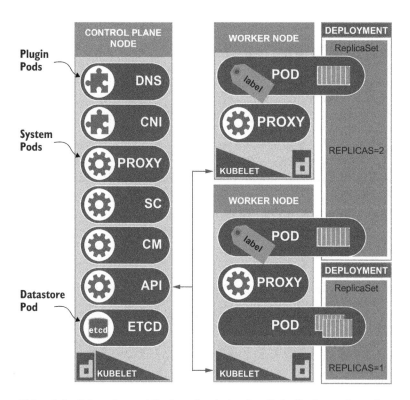

Figure 1.5   Kubernetes architecture showing nodes, Pods, Deployments, and ReplicaSets

1.3.2   *Workloads and scheduling*

Resources like ReplicaSets (`rs`) and Deployments (`deploy`) are essential to developing stateless application workloads running on Kubernetes. Without them, we wouldn't be able to automatically scale Pods, which provides load balancing, making our applications more readily available when running on Kubernetes. We call the process of deploying these applications to Kubernetes *scheduling*. The term *scheduling* comes from the *scheduler*, which is a component of the control plane. We'll talk more about the control plane components later in this chapter. Historically, if you had to create an application that runs on hardware, it had to be maintained and updated from time to time. This can cause outages and/or limitations to what that hardware can do (it gets old). Kubernetes (the application) abstracts this hardware away and creates a common interface (an API) between it and everything else (hardware alike). This allows you to switch out hardware on the fly, as well as incorporate hardware from different vendors and mix and match.

My favorite way of driving home this point is to look at an example to get a solid understanding of resources inside of an API. Let's look at an API that's been rendered through the browser at https://swapi.dev. If you go to SWAPI (*Star Wars* API), you'll see how to request different facts about *Star Wars* movies. You make this request via a GET request to the API. Because the API is built on top of the HTTP protocol, we can perform HTTP methods to take action on the API Endpoints. Those actions can be create, read, update, or delete, usually designated by an acronym: *CRUD*. In this case, though, the purpose of the SWAPI is to make a request to the API and "GET" back some data. So, in the request field, type people/1/, and down below you should see the results, shown in figure 1.6.

Figure 1.6   The SWAPI website allows you to access objects the same way that Kubernetes does.

The result is "Luke Skywalker", but the result doesn't really matter; the point is that you just received data (in JSON format) from the API. The data that you received is the resource URI we've been talking about. The object located at that URI was "Luke Skywalker", and that object contains data such as height, hair color, eye color, etc.

Relating this to Kubernetes, the `people` object in SWAPI is much like the Deployment object in Kubernetes. And you can similarly access the Kubernetes API. The Kubernetes Dashboard even offers the API rendered through a browser, just like SWAPI. Figure 1.7 shows some Kubernetes resource URIs.

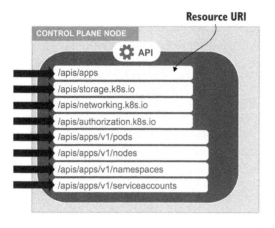

Figure 1.7   Objects in Kubernetes accessed according to their resource URI. Nodes, for example, are located in `/apis/apps/v1/nodes`.

There are different API calls (called *HTTP methods*) that perform certain actions against the API (given you have already authenticated to the API). They are GET, POST, PATCH, PUT, and DELETE. A GET HTTP method is exactly what we've been doing with the SWAPI, which is to retrieve or view information about the resources in our API. A POST HTTP method is used to create a new resource in the API. A PATCH HTTP method is used to update existing resources, and a PUT HTTP method is used to replace existing resources in the API. Finally, a DELETE HTTP method is used to delete a resource from the API.

1.3.3   *Services and networking*

To have the end user interact with your application running on Kubernetes, we create an object called a *Service*. These Services provide a load-balancing feature to the Pods they serve. They also provide a single IP address and DNS name, which we'll review in later chapters. Speaking of DNS, there's a component in Kubernetes called CoreDNS that provides names for IP translations. This means that resources in Kubernetes can talk to each other using common names as opposed to IP addresses. The three types of Services are ClusterIP, NodePort, and LoadBalancer.

An Ingress resource is another Kubernetes object that provides path-based routing to a Service in Kubernetes. For example, you would create an Ingress resource to offer a layer-7 (application layer) route to a Service based on a URL path.

1.3.4   *Storage*

While managing ephemeral objects such as Pods in Kubernetes, you can't rely on storage to be tied to a single Pod. Storage is the data that an application uses to store and organize files in a filesystem such as NTFS, XFS, or ext4. A filesystem is the act of the organization of storage that takes place in an operating system such as Linux. In Kubernetes, there's a concept of persistent volumes that aren't tied to an individual Pod but instead to an NFS, EFS, or iSCSI volume. Having the storage decoupled from the ephemeral applications creates that persistence of data.

In addition, from a developer's perspective, you no longer have to manage the underlying storage. To Kubernetes, it seems like just one large storage layer. The developer can utilize an object called a *persistent volume claim* to reserve a persistent volume, so it cannot be used for other applications running in Kubernetes. This still requires the persistent volume to exist, so in the case that it doesn't, the developer may access storage dynamically using an object called *storage class*. Storage class pertains to the different classes that volumes come in—for example, slow versus fast.

Volumes can also be used by multiple Pods at the same time as well as reused, specifying certain access modes and certain reclaim policies, respectively. The access modes allow the read and write capability of a volume to one or many Pods. The reclaim policy will allow or deny access from other Pods in a Kubernetes cluster.

1.3.5 Troubleshooting

Kubernetes clusters aren't perfect; they can become quite complex the more resources and objects are created in them. Troubleshooting when problems arise is essential to limit the downtime of running applications and also to detect problems to optimize and have Kubernetes performing at its best. Being able to decipher logs from a running container, analyze failures, and propose a solution to that failure is key to becoming a great Kubernetes administrator. Logs are time-based behavioral data sent via text to a directory on the filesystem to give you verbose information about a problem that's occurring. All the redundancy in the world will not fix a cluster that has been poorly constructed and not well maintained.

Applications running on Kubernetes also have an added maintenance responsibility. They contain logs from stdout and stderr that are important for detecting when communication problems arise or application failure is imminent.

1.4 Control plane node

The Services and components on the control plane that make it the control plane are as follows:

- Controller manager
- API server
- Scheduler
- etcd datastore

The controller manager is a control loop, responsible for matching the current state to the desired state. For example, the controller manager will automatically scale a Deployment if the Pods do not match the desired number of replicas. The controller manager also creates the default accounts and API access tokens for new namespaces. That's why you'll see when we create a Kubernetes cluster in the next chapter that there's a default namespace, Service Account, and secret already created for you to start deploying your resources (applications) into. This makes it easy to start running containerized applications on Kubernetes right away. When referring to a namespace, think of it as a dedicated virtual environment for your Kubernetes resources. The default namespace will be isolated within the scope of that namespace and can have its own grouping of Kubernetes resources.

The API server is exactly what it sounds like: it's the component that exposes the Kubernetes API (the RESTful API that we talked about earlier). It's the entry point for the cluster, so all communication to the cluster passes through it to access the cluster components. Think of it like a gate that will open only if opened with the right key using authentication, as in figure 1.8. We'll talk more about authentication in chapter 3.

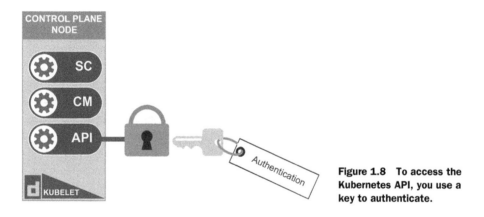

Figure 1.8   To access the Kubernetes API, you use a key to authenticate.

The scheduler is the component that selects the nodes on which the Pods run. You will probably hear the word *scheduling* a lot throughout this book, so from here on when I say "scheduling," it just means that the Pods are being placed (scheduled) on the nodes for running them. If multiple nodes already have Pods running on them, then the scheduler is going to place the Pods on a different node, taking into consideration the available resources and other rules/specifications that have been placed on that node.

There are certain Services (called *daemons*) that run on the control plane and are critical for the Kubernetes cluster to operate. They are so critical, in fact, that in a production scenario, they are replicated for high availability. Replicating the control plane components is beyond the scope of this book and the exam because the Kubernetes clusters on the exam are not going to have more than one control plane node. In general, replicating the control plane works by performing two functions. First, replication ensures that the control plane components have only one instance-receiving request at a time. This is achieved by electing a leader. The leader will act as the primary control plane and relay its status to the other followers. Second, because the control plane relies on etcd for storing all the Kubernetes configuration data (the state of resources and how they are running in Kubernetes), you'll create multiple redundant copies of etcd. If you want to learn more about replicating the control plane for high availability in Kubernetes, you can read more here: http://mng.bz/5wz7.

The etcd datastore is one of those critical control plane components we addressed earlier. Etcd stores all the Kubernetes configuration data (the state of Kubernetes). Etcd is a consistent, distributed key-value store designed to hold small amounts of data that can fit entirely in memory. This is important because data can be retrieved more quickly than other traditional databases (see figure 1.9). The most important thing to remember about the etcd datastore is that losing it (etcd failure) is catastrophic, as it contains all the configuration information for resources running inside a Kubernetes cluster, so making sure it's backed up is extremely important. You may come across questions on the exam about backing up etcd, so we'll cover how to do this in the next chapter.

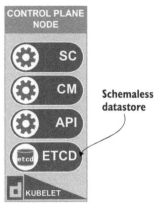

Figure 1.9   The etcd datastore resides in a Kubernetes Pod on the control plane node.

1.5 Worker nodes

Now that we've talked about the control plane components in great detail, let's review the components that reside on a worker node, as shown in figure 1.10. The components that run on a worker node are different from the components on the control plane because the worker nodes play a different role in the Kubernetes landscape. You will

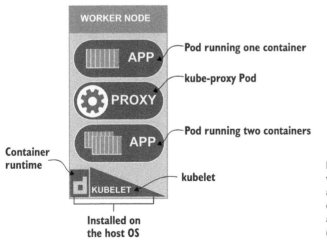

Figure 1.10   The role of the worker node is to run the application workloads. It also contains kubelet, kube-proxy, and the container runtime (e.g., containerd).

most certainly have more than one node inside of a Kubernetes cluster, and each one of the following components is installed on each node:

- The kubelet
- kube-proxy
- The container runtime

The kubelet service that runs on each worker node makes sure that containers are running in a Pod. However, although it's not aware of containers that aren't managed by the scheduler, kubelet can detect when a container (within a Pod) is failing and take corrective action to ensure that the container restarts in the way that is specified in the YAML manifest, the set of instructions for configuring a Pod in YAML (YAML isn't markup language) format. It's like a set of declarative instructions (with the end state in mind) for the kubelet to follow to maintain high availability for the application running on Kubernetes. If the kubelet can't make the container run, it will report the status of the Pod and container to the Kubernetes API server, and you can see it in the Pod events by performing the command `kubectl describe po nginx` (nginx is the name of the Pod). A similar output is shown here:

```
$ kubectl describe po nginx
Name:         nginx
Namespace:    default
Priority:     0
Node:         host01/172.17.0.33
Start Time:   Tue, 01 Feb 2022 16:49:36 +0000
Labels:       run=nginx
Annotations:  <none>
Status:       Running
IP:           192.168.0.4
IPs:
  IP:   192.168.0.4
Containers:
  nginx:
    Container ID:   containerd://4de3efffd3a6f1ec49c968d7fde95e8eae4ae0c25574
      e8055cca33a1974998
➥ 79
    Image:          nginx
    Image ID:
➥ docker.io/library/nginx@sha256:2834dc507516af02784808c5f48b7cbe38b8ed5d
➥ 0f4837f16e78d00deb7e7767
    Port:           <none>
    Host Port:      <none>
    State:          Running
      Started:      Tue, 01 Feb 2022 16:49:44 +0000
    Ready:          True
    Restart Count:  0
    Environment:    <none>
    Mounts:
      /var/run/secrets/kubernetes.io/serviceaccount from kube-api-access-
➥ 5ffvj (ro)
Conditions:
```

```
Type                   Status
 Initialized           True
 Ready                 True
 ContainersReady       True
 PodScheduled          True
Volumes:
 kube-api-access-5ffvj:
   Type:               Projected (a volume that contains injected
➥ data from multiple sources)
   TokenExpirationSeconds:  3607
   ConfigMapName:      kube-root-ca.crt
   ConfigMapOptional:  <nil>
   DownwardAPI:        true
QoS Class:             BestEffort
Node-Selectors:        <none>
Tolerations:           node.kubernetes.io/not-ready:NoExecute
➥ op=Exists for 300s

                       node.kubernetes.io/unreachable:NoExecute
➥ op=Exists for 300s
Events:
 Type    Reason     Age   From              Message
 ----    ------     ----  ----              -------
 Normal  Scheduled  17s   default-scheduler Successfully assigned
➥ default/nginx to host01
 Normal  Pulling    16s   kubelet           Pulling image "nginx"
 Normal  Pulled     9s    kubelet           Successfully pulled image
➥ "nginx" in 6.993614669s
 Normal  Created    9s    kubelet           Created container nginx
 Normal  Started    9s    kubelet           Started container nginx
```

When you look at the events after describing the Pod, you see that there are different states of a container (shown as the status), including waiting, running, and terminated. You will also see the state of the container by running the command kubectl get po.

The kube-proxy Service running on each worker node is the communication mechanism of a Kubernetes Service. A Service is another resource type in Kubernetes and is responsible for allocating traffic to the various Pods within that Service. We'll review Services in depth in chapter 6. These are basic network rules for the node to follow if traffic needs to get to the Pods in Kubernetes. There's a fascinating video that describes this in greater detail called "Life of a Packet." I highly encourage you to watch it here: https://youtu.be/0Omvgd7Hg1I.

Finally, running on each node in the Kubernetes cluster is the container runtime. This is a necessary component for Kubernetes to work, as it is the engine that runs the containers themselves. Interestingly, though, it is an external dependency, meaning that it's one of the only components necessary to a Kubernetes cluster that Kubernetes doesn't apply or install itself. This means that you have choices when it comes to container engines that you have to install. Kubernetes supports any container runtime time that follows the CRI requirements (http://mng.bz/6D0R). The common options are either Docker (https://docs.docker.com/engine/), containerd (https://containerd .io/docs/), or CRI-O (https://cri-o.io/#what-is-cri-o). Chances are you've heard of

Docker, but did you know that Docker uses containerd as the container runtime under the hood while using a feature called dockershim to get to containerd? Docker is also not CRI compliant (http://mng.bz/o1nD). So, containerd, implied by the last sentence, is the stripped-down (so it's lightweight and portable) container runtime that is also CRI compliant. CRI-O is another lightweight container runtime that supports the open container initiative (OCI). So, it's a community-driven, open source project that supports multiple image formats, including Docker images.

1.6   *API model and PKI*

We'll talk more about RBAC and identity management in Kubernetes in chapter 3, but for now, let's just talk about the public key infrastructure that comprises the client-to-server relationship in Kubernetes. As we have seen, to manipulate objects in Kubernetes, we need two things. The first is the command-line tool `kubectl`. The second is a client certificate, as you can see in figure 1.11.

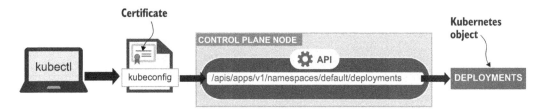

Figure 1.11   To manipulate Kubernetes objects, we must authenticate with a client certificate.

Public key infrastructure (PKI) is a very common client–server communication pattern, and it is the usual way our computers securely communicate with websites via web servers. At a high level, PKI enables secure communication over the web by ensuring that the website you're visiting is the website that you intended to visit (via cryptographic signature). This ensures that you're visiting the right website (not an imposter's website), but also ensures that nobody is snooping or intercepting the traffic back and forth. If you think about accessing your bank over the web, this PKI infrastructure is critical to ensuring that bank accounts are safe, that the people accessing them are indeed the owners of the accounts, and that the bank you are accessing is indeed the correct bank.

The fundamental pieces of the PKI include three elements, which are shown in figure 1.12. First and foremost is the certificate authority (CA). The CA is the source of truth and signs the server certificate (in the case of one used with the API), and subsequently, the client can determine if the server is valid. On the web, for example, the common certificate authorities are DigiCert, Symantec, and Thawte and are already trusted by the browser (the client) as a way for your browser to quickly verify a website's identity (e.g., whether google.com is actually Google). The second and third pieces of the PKI puzzle are the server and client, both relying on the CA—the client trying to verify the identity of the server, and the server trying to authenticate and prove to the CA that they are who they say they are. Just like the PKI for the web, the same PKI model is applied to Kubernetes.

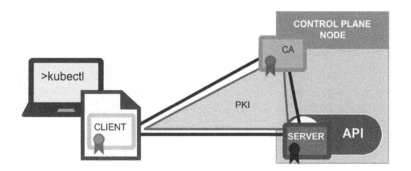

Figure 1.12 The control plane node serves as the certificate authority (CA), which signs the certificate and provides authentication to client and server communication.

Taking the same three pieces of the PKI puzzle and applying them to Kubernetes, Kubernetes is its own CA and will be the source of truth for the other components within a Kubernetes cluster. The clients in Kubernetes (the ones checking whether the servers are who they say they are) are the kubelet, the scheduler, the controller manager, and the etcd datastore. The same Kubernetes component can be a client and a server at the same time. The servers in Kubernetes (the ones trying to prove their identity to the CA) are the kubelet, the Kubernetes API, and the etcd datastore (see figure 1.13).

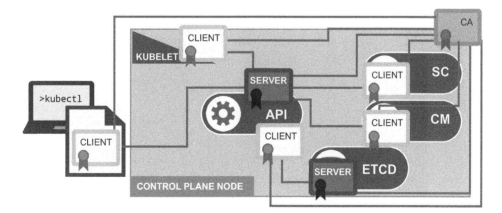

Figure 1.13 The Kubernetes API has multiple responsibilities in the PKI infrastructure of both client and server. The CA is generating certificates, and servers are proving their identity (http://mng.bz/mV68).

Luckily, you don't have to worry about creating a CA, client, or server certificate. Kubeadm will do all of this for you. Kubeadm is another command-line tool like `kubectl`, but its purpose is for creating the necessary components that make up our Kubernetes cluster (including the CA and other certificates); sometimes we call this *bootstrapping the cluster*. We'll talk more about kubeadm and the location of all of these certificates in chapter 3.

1.7   *Linux system services*

With all this talk about Services and components to both the control plane and the worker nodes, I thought it pertinent to mention Linux system services. Linux system services are a grouping of files on the Linux operating system that provides a software program that constantly runs in the background. If you remember, I referred to certain services that run on the control plane as daemons. Daemons have been used in the Linux world for ages, not to be confused with a DaemonSet in Kubernetes, which makes sure the daemon is running on each node as a Pod in the Kubernetes cluster at all times, as shown in figure 1.14. If you are more familiar with Windows computers, this same concept is called a *service*.

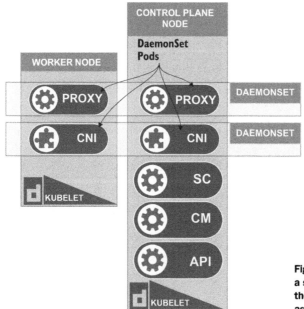

Figure 1.14   **DaemonSets ensure that a single Pod is running on each node in the cluster. kube-proxy and CNI both run as DaemonSets.**

For that matter, the control plane components that we spoke about earlier are a good example of that. You can have a DaemonSet running on each node that provides the kube-proxy component, for example. See for yourself by running the command `kubectl get ds -A`.

```
$ kubectl get ds -A
NAMESPACE       NAME              DESIRED   CURRENT   READY   UP-TO-DATE
  AVAILABLE     NODE SELECTOR               AGE
kube-system     kube-flannel-ds   1         1         1       1
    1                             <none>                18m
kube-system     kube-proxy        1         1         1       1
    1                             kubernetes.io/os=linux  19m
```

There is one service, however, that you don't want Kubernetes to manage (as a DaemonSet), and that is kubelet. kubelet is one of the only services in the context of Kubernetes that will be located on the Linux system itself (as a Linux system service). You must know this for the exam. Why? Because the Linux service may be down, presenting a scenario on the exam for you to repair it. Knowledge about where this service is and how to repair it will come in handy. To see a list of all services on your Linux system, type the command `sudo systemctl list-unit-files --type service --all | grep kubelet -a6`.

```
$ sudo systemctl list-unit-files --type service --all | grep kubelet -a6
ip6tables.service                    enabled        enabled
iptables.service                     enabled        enabled
irqbalance.service                   enabled        enabled
keyboard-setup.service               enabled        enabled
kmod-static-nodes.service            static         enabled
kmod.service                         static         enabled
kubelet.service                      enabled        enabled
logrotate.service                    static         enabled
lvm2-lvmpolld.service                static         enabled
lvm2-monitor.service                 enabled        enabled
lvm2-pvscan@.service                 static         enabled
lvm2.service                         masked         enabled
man-db.service                       static         enabled
```

You will see a list of services that will show the unit file (the service name) and the state of the service (enabled/disabled/masked/static). In this list, you will see `kubelet.service` as one of these. Once you've identified that the kubelet service is running on your system, you can do one of three things. If it has stopped, you can start it by typing `systemctl start kubelet`. If you notice that the service does not start when the node is rebooted, then you can enable it with the command `systemctl enable kubelet` so that it automatically starts up when the node starts up (or restarts). Finally, if you simply want to check the status of the service to see if it's active or inactive, you can run the command `systemctl status kubelet`.

Within the list of services, you may have noticed the `systemd.journald` service. If you didn't, go ahead and run the following command to show it: `sudo systemctl list-unit-files --type service --all | grep journald.service`.

```
$ systemctl list-unit-files --type service --all | grep journald.service
systemd-journald.service             static         enabled
```

Journald (another Linux system service) is used to collect logs about the kubelet service on each node. Journalctl is a command-line utility for viewing logs on a Linux system collected by systemd, which is the primary daemon in Linux that controls all processes. This logging mechanism can prove very useful during the exam. You may find yourself digging through the logs to find out why the kubelet service is failing, for example. Use the commands `sudo journalctl -u kubelet` and `sudo journalctl -u containerd` as a reference.

You can check the `/var/log/pods` directory for Pod logs; however, you can also retrieve these in the exact same fashion with the `kubectl logs` command (e.g., `kubectl logs kube-controller-manager-server1 -n kube-system`). More on troubleshooting and collecting these logs in chapter 8. For now, just know that these Linux system services are important for collecting valuable information about Kubernetes and that some services exist on the Linux system (the node) and some Services exist within the confines of Kubernetes (in a Pod).

1.8 Declarative syntax

Now that you have a good idea of the composition of a Kubernetes cluster and its underlying Services, I would be remiss not to mention the primary purpose of Kubernetes, which is to run applications. Yes, once you have the foundation (which we've talked about thus far in this chapter) of your control plane components, worker node components, and Linux system services, and the cluster is functioning as a loosely coupled unit (remember the API model?), it's time to run your applications. After all, this is the primary function and the reason why we're using Kubernetes in the first place. As far as running these applications on Kubernetes, you can run a Java application on Kubernetes, just the same as a .NET application.

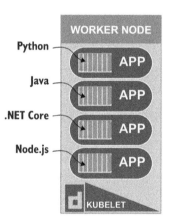

Figure 1.15 In a true microservices architecture, each microservice is decoupled from other services; therefore, it can be built in the language that suits the service best.

Kubernetes doesn't care at all about the language or about how the application runs, as depicted in figure 1.15. It will run your containers the same way in every instance and does so by keeping that same foundational benefit to containers, which inherently run the same way on every machine because the application binaries and libraries are packaged up along with the container.

So, if Kubernetes doesn't care about the language or the framework of the application, how are applications deployed on Kubernetes? This brings us to a very important word in DevOps and cloud native—*declarative*. You will find that building applications on Kubernetes in a declarative way is far better than imperative. Why? Imperative is nothing more than running a series of commands in a specific sequence. This makes it hard to track these commands and detect if a command failed during the execution

of those imperative commands in sequential order. Declarative is more descriptive
and succinct and has the following major benefits:

- Describing your configuration via YAML file, which can be checked into version
  control
- Building with the end state in mind, without considering order or specific commands to run
- Having the efficiency and speed to get up and running through parallel actions

YAML is a human-readable language, also rendered for machines, so creating this configuration file is fairly simple. Most resources follow the same pattern and structure for
YAML and how it's made. Here's an example of a file named `my-pod-manifest.yaml`:

```
apiVersion: v1
kind: Pod
metadata:
  labels:
    run: nginx
  name: nginx
spec:
  containers:
  - image: nginx
    name: nginx
```

These YAML files (called *manifests*) can be referred to years later, which is a good form
of documenting how the application was built. Checking it into version control will
allow you to track changes and work in teams to develop and enhance the configuration over time. You have the freedom to build applications running on Kubernetes
with the end in mind. This is called *goal seeking*. You don't have to be concerned about
the path to reach that end state; you simply submit the YAML file to the Kubernetes
API, and the API chooses the best path to complete your build.

Interestingly enough, submitting your file to the API is the same as performing a
POST request to the API. Because everything running in your cluster is visible to the
API, actions can be processed in parallel and will reach your end state faster. Here's an
example of running an imperative command (using `kubectl`) to create a Pod via the
YAML file declaratively:

```
$ kubectl create -f my-pod-manifest.yaml
pod/nginx created
```

There are three different ways you can submit this file to the Kubernetes API using
`kubectl`—by using the command `kubectl create -f my-pod-manifest.yaml`, the command `kubectl apply -f my-pod-manifest.yaml`, or the command `kubectl replace -f
manifest.yaml`. The `create` command expects that no resource has been created yet,
and if otherwise, it will throw an error. The `apply` command, on the other hand, can
be used to either create or update an existing resource. The `replace` command will
delete the resource if it's there and create an entirely new one as if you deleted the

resource manually and then created a new one. Using the replace command on a Deployment, for example, will trigger a new rollout, where the Pods within that Deployment will be gracefully terminated and new Pod replicas will be spun up. We'll talk about Deployments in more detail in chapter 4 and rollouts in chapter 5.

Idempotent is another important word to remember. The benefit of working with the Kubernetes API is that the state of the resources within will remain unchanged, no matter how many times the same call is made to the API. This creates consistency in your environment, and you know what to expect as your infrastructure and applications get increasingly complex over time.

Now that we've talked about Kubernetes to exhaustion and discussed the complexities and complications that we may or may not run into, let's dive into the next chapter and get more hands-on with our approach to learning Kubernetes. After all, you'll have your hands on the keyboard for the exam, so why not dive into practicing and simulating the exam experience? Roll up your sleeves!

1.9   *Exam exercises*

1 Perform the command to list all API resources in your Kubernetes cluster. Save the output to a file named `resources.csv`.
2 List the services on your Linux operating system that are associated with Kubernetes. Save the output to a file named `services.csv`.
3 List the status of the kubelet service running on the Kubernetes node, output the result to a file named `kubelet-status.txt`, and save the file in the `/tmp` directory.
4 Use the declarative syntax to create a Pod from a YAML file in Kubernetes. Save the YAML file as `chap1-pod.yaml`. Use the `kubectl create` command to create the Pod.
5 Using the `kubectl` CLI tool, list all the Services created in your Kubernetes cluster across all namespaces. Save the output of the command to a file named `all-k8s-services.txt`.

Summary

In this chapter, you've met Kubernetes. You now know what Kubernetes looks like inside and out and what it's commonly used for. You should also know the following:

- Kubernetes is an application that runs other applications and is built much like other RESTful web apps. The API is the central hub for authentication, authorization, and communication in the Kubernetes cluster.
- A cluster has many different components, including two main parts: a control plane, which is handled by the control plane nodes, and the worker nodes, which are responsible for running the workloads (i.e., the containerized applications running on top of Kubernetes).
- Linux system services are important in Kubernetes because they are responsible for keeping Kubernetes running on the host itself.

- You can access the cluster in two ways, programmatically or using a tool called `kubectl`, which both require a certificate to authenticate. This certificate is common in a PKI (public key infrastructure) system that checks in with the CA (certificate authority) to ensure that the certificate is valid and that communication can happen between components in the Kubernetes cluster.

- Kubernetes was built with microservices in mind, meaning that large microservice applications can run more efficiently in Kubernetes, being that each service is decoupled from the overall application.

- Running Services on Kubernetes is more efficient via a declarative approach. This way, we can describe what we want the end state to be, as opposed to running a set of imperative commands to achieve the same result.

Kubernetes cluster

This chapter covers
- Control plane and worker node components in a multinode cluster
- Upgrading control plane components with kubeadm
- Investigating Pod and node networking
- Backing up and restoring etcd
- Taints and tolerations

The Kubernetes cluster architecture is almost impossible to grasp without getting inside a running cluster and discovering the components firsthand. No matter how you look at it, as Kubernetes administrators, we have to know what's happening under the hood. When you finish this chapter, you will feel comfortable accessing all the components in a Kubernetes cluster, upgrading components when needed, and backing up the cluster configuration.

The cluster architecture, installation, and configuration

This chapter reviews part of the cluster architecture, installation, and configuration domain of the CKA curriculum. This domain covers the elements of a Kubernetes cluster, including key components and how to maintain a healthy Kubernetes cluster. The chapter encompasses the following competencies.

Competency	Chapter section
Provision underlying infrastructure to deploy a Kubernetes cluster.	2.1
Perform a version upgrade on a Kubernetes cluster using kubeadm.	2.1
Implement etcd backup and restore.	2.2
Manage a highly available Kubernetes cluster.	2.2

2.1 Kubernetes cluster components

The control plane Pods work together to form the control plane. Those components are the API server, the controller manager, the scheduler, and etcd. In the Kubernetes clusters that you will face on exam day, these components exist as Pods running on the control plane node. You can see the cluster components by viewing the Pods running in the `kube-system` namespace. You can view those Pods with the command `kubectl get po -n kube-system`, and you'll see output similar to figure 2.1. We first run the command `docker exec -it kind-control-plane bash` to get a shell to the control plane node.

In the coming sections of this chapter, you'll learn how to manage these components, including how to access them, modify their configuration, back them up, and upgrade them. Now, let's get our hands dirty working in the terminal.

2.1.1 Kubernetes version upgrade

The CKA exam will test your knowledge of maintaining a Kubernetes cluster. This includes upgrading the control plane components to a certain version. For example, the exam question will say something like the following.

> **EXAM TASK** There's a need for company X to upgrade the Kubernetes controller to version 1.24 or higher, due to a bug that affects Pod scheduling. Perform the update with minimal downtime and loss of service.

Knowing that you should use kubeadm to do so will allow you to breeze through that task on the exam and feel confident you're heading toward a passing score.

If you don't already have access to an existing Kubernetes cluster, creating a Kubernetes cluster with kind is explained in appendix A. As soon as your kind cluster is built, use

Get a Bash shell inside the container   **View running Pods in the**
named kind-control-plane.   **kube-system namespace.**

```
$ docker exec -it kind-control-plane bash
root@kind-control-plane:/# kubectl get po -n kube-system
NAME                                         READY  STATUS    RESTARTS       AGE
coredns-64897985d-gqbcl                      1/1    Running   2 (24m ago)    24d
coredns-64897985d-s2gxz                      1/1    Running   2 (24m ago)    24d
etcd-kind-control-plane                      1/1    Running   0              23m
kindnet-6qktm                                1/1    Running   9              24d
kindnet-l9snz        ─ Pod for each node     1/1    Running   9              24d
kindnet-stx7d                                1/1    Running   9 (24m ago)    24d
kube-apiserver-kind-control-plane            1/1    Running   0              23m
kube-controller-manager-kind-control-plane   1/1    Running   2 (24m ago)    24d
kube-proxy-n27nd                             1/1    Running   2 (24m ago)    24d
kube-proxy-rq2xs     ─ Pod for each node     1/1    Running   2 (24m ago)    24d
kube-proxy-xz9tn                             1/1    Running   2 (24m ago)    24d
kube-scheduler-kind-control-plane            1/1    Running   2 (24m ago)    24d
```

Figure 2.1   The Pods in the `kube-system` namespace

the `kubectl` tool preinstalled on the control plane node. You can get a Bash shell to the control plane node by typing the command `docker exec -it kind-control-plane bash` and following along. Having a cluster that is built with kubeadm means we can also use kubeadm to view the versions of our control plane components, as shown in figure 2.2, and upgrade the cluster. Using the command `kubeadm upgrade plan` from the control plane shows a list of control plane components and displays the current version in the CURRENT column, as well as the version to which you can upgrade in the TARGET column.

> **NOTE** The TARGET column doesn't show the latest release of Kubernetes. This is because we can only update to the current version of kubeadm. If kubeadm was at version 1.26.0, the TARGET column would show v1.26.3. To upgrade kubeadm from 1.26.0 to 1.26.3, run the command `apt update; apt install -y kubeadm=1.26.3-00`.

If you must upgrade kubeadm to the latest release, first download the GPG key and add kubeadm to your local `apt` packages (still in a shell on the control plane node). To download the GPG key, run the command `curl -fsSLo /etc/apt/keyrings/kubernetes-archive-keyring.gpg https://packages.cloud.google.com/apt/doc/apt-key.gpg`. To add kubeadm to your local `apt` packages, run the command `echo "deb [signed-by=/etc/apt/keyrings/kubernetes-archive-keyring.gpg] https://apt.kubernetes.io/kubernetes-xenial main" | tee /etc/apt/sources.list.d/kubernetes.list`. Having done that, rerun the command `apt update; apt install -y kubeadm=1.26.3-00` to

**Get the current version of the control plane components
and see which version they can be upgraded to.**

```
root@kind-control-plane:/# kubeadm upgrade plan
[upgrade/config] Making sure the configuration is correct:
[upgrade/config] Reading configuration from the cluster...

Upgrade to the latest version in the v1.25 series:


COMPONENT                    CURRENT    TARGET
kube-apiserver               v1.25.0    v1.25.8
kube-controller-manager      v1.25.0    v1.25.8
kube-scheduler               v1.25.0    v1.25.8
kube-proxy                   v1.25.0    v1.25.8
CoreDNS                      v1.9.3     v1.9.3
etcd                         3.5.4-0    3.5.4-0


You can now apply the upgrade by executing the following command:

        kubeadm upgrade apply v1.25.8
```

**Control plane
components**

Figure 2.2   View the control plane components and how to upgrade them, if necessary.

upgrade kubeadm to version 1.26.3. When you run the `kubeadm upgrade plan` command again, you'll notice that your `TARGET` column has a higher version of 1.24.3 to which you can upgrade. See the abbreviated output from this command in figure 2.3.

```
root@kind-control-plane:/# curl -fsSLo /etc/apt/keyrings/kubernetes-archive-keyring.gpg https://packages.cloud.googl
e.com/apt/doc/apt-key.gpg

root@kind-control-plane:/# echo "deb [signed-by=/etc/apt/keyrings/kubernetes-archive-keyring.gpg] https://apt.kubern
etes.io/ kubernetes-xenial main" | tee /etc/apt/sources.list.d/kubernetes.list

root@kind-control-plane:/# apt update; apt install -y kubeadm=1.26.3-00

Upgrade to the latest stable version:

COMPONENT                 CURRENT   TARGET
kube-apiserver            v1.25.0   v1.26.3
kube-controller-manager   v1.25.0   v1.26.3
kube-scheduler            v1.25.0   v1.26.3
kube-proxy                v1.25.0   v1.26.3
CoreDNS                   v1.9.3    v1.9.3
etcd                      3.5.4-0   3.5.6-0

You can now apply the upgrade by executing the following command:

        kubeadm upgrade apply v1.26.3
```

**Get gpg key
for Kubernetes.**

**Copy the
sources
into local
apt repository.**

**Install version 1.26.3
of kubeadm.**

**The target version has changed because
the kubeadm version has changed.**

Figure 2.3   When you upgrade kubeadm, you can upgrade your control plane components as well.

Congratulations! You've successfully upgraded the control plane components of a Kubernetes cluster, also known as "upgrading Kubernetes."

2.1.2 *The control plane*

The control plane and worker nodes have different responsibilities. Worker nodes carry the application workload and run the Pods that contain those application containers, whereas the control plane runs an initial set of Pods, comprised of the control plane components we just saw when we upgraded the cluster. We refer to them as *system Pods* because they contain the necessary structure around the running of the entire Kubernetes system. The `kube-apiserver`, `kube-controller-manager`, `kube-scheduler`, and `etcd` all run as system Pods on the control plane node. These system Pods will exist regardless of where your Kubernetes cluster resides or how it was built, as they are essential to the core of Kubernetes. You can see the system Pods by running the command `k get po -o wide -A --field-selector spec.nodeName=kind-control-plane`, which will show output similar to figure 2.4.

**Select only Pods on the
control plane node.**

```
root@kind-control-plane:/# k get po -o wide -A --field-selector spec.nodeName=kind-control-plane
NAMESPACE           NAME                                        READY  STATUS    RESTARTS        AGE   IP           NODE
SS GATES
kube-system         coredns-64897985d-gqbcl    System Pods      1/1    Running   6 (102s ago)    49d   10.244.0.3   kind-control-plane
kube-system         coredns-64897985d-s2gxz                     1/1    Running   6 (102s ago)    49d   10.244.0.4   kind-control-plane
kube-system         etcd-kind-control-plane                     1/1    Running   0               90s   172.18.0.6   kind-control-plane
kube-system         kindnet-stx7d                               1/1    Running   16 (102s ago)   49d   172.18.0.6   kind-control-plane
kube-system         kube-apiserver-kind-control-plane           1/1    Running   0               92s   172.18.0.6   kind-control-plane
kube-system         kube-controller-manager-kind-control-plane  1/1    Running   2 (102s ago)    5d4h  172.18.0.6   kind-control-plane
kube-system         kube-proxy-n27nd                            1/1    Running   6 (102s ago)    49d   172.18.0.6   kind-control-plane
kube-system         kube-scheduler-kind-control-plane           1/1    Running   2 (102s ago)    5d4h  172.18.0.6   kind-control-plane
local-path-storage  local-path-provisioner-5ddd94ff66-jxzcx     1/1    Running   87 (61s ago)    49d   10.244.0.2   kind-control-plane
```

Figure 2.4   System Pods that reside on the control plane node

CoreDNS is also a Pod that runs on the control plane node, but it's considered a plugin, not a core system Pod. In addition, the kube-proxy Pod will run on all nodes, regardless of whether it's a control plane node or a worker node. Let's focus on the core components of a control plane node, as illustrated in figure 2.5.

Each Pod plays a specific role in the operation of Kubernetes. The controller manager Pod maintains cluster operations, ensuring Deployments are running the correct number of replicas. The scheduler Pod is responsible for detecting available resources on a node, so you can place a Pod on that node. The act of assigning a Pod to a node is called *scheduling*; from now on, when I say "a Pod is scheduled to a node," I mean that a new Pod has been started on that node. The API server Pod will expose the API interface and is the communication hub for all other components, including those components on a worker node and control plane node. Finally, the etcd Pod is the

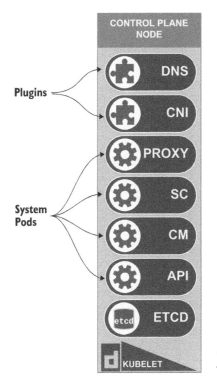

**Figure 2.5   System Pods and plugins on
the Kubernetes control plane node.**

etcd datastore for storing cluster configuration data, as we've discussed in this chapter as well as the previous chapter.

2.1.3 Taints and tolerations

By default, application Pods will not run on the control plane node. Why is that? Well, the control plane has a special attribute assigned to it called a *taint*. A taint will repel work, meaning it will disable scheduling to that node unless a certain specification exists in the YAML spec called a *toleration*. Let's see what a taint looks like on our control plane node (`docker exec -it kind-control-plane bash`) by typing the command `kubectl describe no | grep Taints`:

```
root@kind-control-plane:/# kubectl describe no | grep Taints
Taints:              node-role.kubernetes.io/master:NoSchedule
Taints:              <none>
Taints:              <none>
```

As we can see, a taint has been applied to our control plane node as part of the cluster creation process, and the taint is `node-role.kubernetes.io/master:NoSchedule`. The taint has three parts: a key, an effect, and a value. A taint doesn't need to have a value but must have a key and an effect. So, in this case, the key is `node-role.kubernetes.io` and the effect is `NoSchedule`. This means that unless there is a toleration for that taint, the Pod will not get scheduled to that node with that taint. In figure 2.6, you'll see a demonstration of this, as the Pod doesn't have a toleration for the taint, so it's not scheduled to that node.

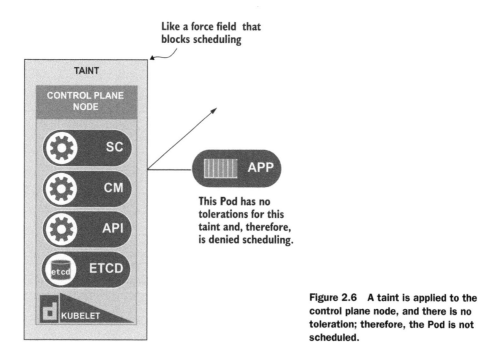

Figure 2.6   A taint is applied to the control plane node, and there is no toleration; therefore, the Pod is not scheduled.

Let's apply a taint to one of our worker nodes and see what a taint with a key, effect, and value looks like, using the command `kubectl taint no kind-worker decdi-cated=special-user:NoSchedule`. This command is deconstructed in figure 2.7 to show which item is the key versus which item is the value and effect.

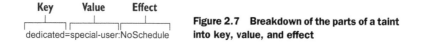

Figure 2.7   Breakdown of the parts of a taint into key, value, and effect

A full taint (key, value, and effect) is appropriate when you want to be more specific about the qualification a Pod must have to "get past" a taint. Yes, there's a way to schedule a Pod to a node even though that node may have a taint applied. This is called a toleration. This is important to remember because tolerations do not mean that you are selecting that particular node; they mean that the scheduler may choose to schedule the Pod there if the conditions are right among all the other nodes. This is how Pods like the DNS Pod run on the control plane. These Pods have toleration for the taint. To view the tolerations within the Pod YAML, run the command kubectl get po coredns-558bd4d5db-7dmrp -o yaml -n kube-system | grep tolerations -A14. This command will get the YAML output of the Pod, named core-dns-64897985d-4th9h, in the kube-system namespace, and then use the grep tool to filter the results and give us 14 lines after the result. The output will be similar to figure 2.8, which you can compare to the taint that's placed on the control plane node.

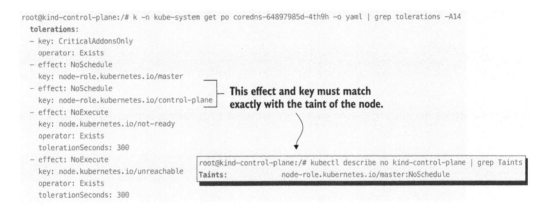

Figure 2.8   Comparison between how the taint is set and the toleration for it in the CoreDNS Pod

As we see in the YAML spec for this CoreDNS Pod, within the list of tolerations, the key node-role.kubernetes.io/master and the effect NoSchedule match our taint. This is how the CoreDNS Pod was able to be scheduled to the control plane node. Remember that your CoreDNS Pod will have a different name, so you'll want to replace core-dns-64897985d-4th9h with the name of your CoreDNS Pod. If you don't know the name of the Pod, you can get the name by typing kubectl get po -A.

As we see in this case, the toleration must match the key and the effect exactly. If it's off by even a little, then the Pod will not be scheduled to the intended node. So, as you can imagine, having more loosely defined rules for tolerations makes it easier to define a toleration when you're writing the YAML. In figure 2.8, you may also notice other fields like operator and tolerationSeconds. operator, if not defined explicitly, like in the toleration for the node-role of the control plane taint, will default to Equal of the two possible values of Exists or Equal. Because the operator was not defined for the node-role taint toleration, it defaulted to Equal.

A toleration matches a taint if the keys and effects are the same and the operator is equal. If there is a value, then the toleration matches a taint if the keys, effects, and values all match exactly and the operator is Equal. If the operator is Exists, no value should be specified, but the key and the effect must match. Referring to the command output in figure 2.8, the effect `NoExecute` and key `node.kubernetes.io/not-ready` must match exactly because the operator is `Exists`. The `tolerationSeconds` is an optional parameter that allows you to specify how long the Pod will stay bound to the node after the taint is added, in this case, 300 seconds. There is an example of this in figure 2.9, where the toleration matches the taint of the node; therefore, it's successfully scheduled to the node.

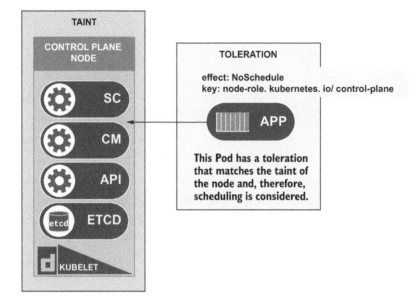

Figure 2.9   The toleration applied to the Pod ensures that it can be scheduled to the tainted node.

Now let's create a Pod that has a toleration for the taint that we applied to `kind-worker`. This taint had an effect of `NoSchedule`, a value of `special-user`, and a key named `dedicated`. This means that we must match all of those while using the default operator `Equal`. Let's start with building out a Pod template with the command `k run pod-tolerate --image=nginx --dry-run=client -o yaml > pod-tolerate.yaml`:

```
root@kind-control-plane:/# k run pod-tolerate --image=nginx --dry-
➥ run=client -o yaml > pod-tolerate.yaml
root@kind-control-plane:/# cat pod-tolerate.yaml
apiVersion: v1
kind: Pod
metadata:
  creationTimestamp: null
  labels:
    run: pod-tolerate
  name: pod-tolerate
spec:
```

```
  containers:
  - image: nginx
    name: pod-tolerate
    resources: {}
  dnsPolicy: ClusterFirst
  restartPolicy: Always
status: {}
```

NOTE We build this Pod template with the `dry-run` flag and send the output of the command to a file, which is much easier than typing out the file from scratch.

Let's open the file `pod-tolerate.yaml` using the Vim text editor with the command `vim pod-tolerate.yaml`. We can add the tolerations we need to match the taint that's applied to our worker node. We see in figure 2.10 in the output of the command `kubectl describe no kind-worker | grep Taints` that the key is `dedicated`, the value is `special-user`, and the effect is `NoSchedule`. With the file still open, in line with the word `containers`, insert `tolerations:`. Just below that, insert the line `- key: "dedicated"`, followed by `value: "special-user"`, and on the next line, `effect: "NoSchedule"`. You can see exactly what it should look like in figure 2.10.

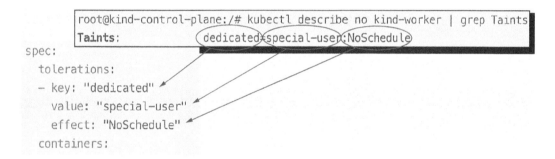

Figure 2.10   How tolerations for a taint are applied to effectively schedule a Pod

Once you've added the toleration to the Pod YAML manifest, you can save and close the file. Then you can submit the YAML to the API server with the command `kubectl create -f pod-tolerate.yaml`, and the Pod will be created in the default namespace. You can see which node the Pod is running on with the command `kubectl get po -o wide`:

```
root@kind-control-plane:/# kubectl create -f pod-tolerate.yaml
pod/pod-tolerate created
root@kind-control-plane:/# k get po -o wide
"[CA]"
NAME           READY   STATUS    RESTARTS   AGE   IP
⇒ NODE          NOMINATED NODE   READINESS GATES
pod-tolerate   1/1     Running   0          6s    10.244.2.6
⇒ kind-worker   <none>           <none>
```

You'll see from the wide output that the Pod is running on the `kind-worker` node, but it could have just as easily been scheduled to the `kind-worker2` because tolerations don't explicitly select which node the scheduler should choose. If you're still having trouble creating the Pod, you can run this command, which already has the YAML intact, then you can compare and see where you went wrong. Just type the command `k apply -f https://raw.githubusercontent.com/chadmcrowell/k8s/main/manifests/ pod-tolerate.yaml`.

Next, we'll talk about node selectors and node names you can add to your Pod YAML that will make such explicit statements to the scheduler. Node selectors, as the name implies, allow you to select a node to which a Pod is scheduled based on that node(s) label. Many labels are applied to a node by default. You can see a list of labels by performing the command `k get no --show-labels`. Labels don't change the operation of the node but can be used to query the nodes with a particular label or to schedule Pods to that node using its label (which we'll discuss in the coming sections of this chapter). Labels can also be applied to Pods. You can see Pod labels on Pods in the `kube-system` namespace using the command `k get po -n kube-system --show-labels`. The output will be similar to figure 2.11.

Figure 2.11   The default labels applied to nodes and Pods when a Kubernetes cluster is created

Node names allow you to select a single node by its hostname. Let's keep the taint applied to the node so we can work through this together and better visualize how these node selectors are applied in Kubernetes.

2.1.4   *Nodes*

kind stands for *Kubernetes in Docker*. kind creates a cluster's Kubernetes node inside of a Docker container. Depicted in figure 2.12, the container exists inside the Pod, which is inside the node, which, in this case (with kind), is also a container comprised of a Kubernetes cluster in Docker.

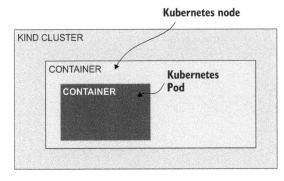

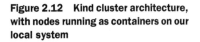

Figure 2.12 Kind cluster architecture, with nodes running as containers on our local system

Let's start by viewing the Docker container that kind created for us. You can view the Docker container with the command `docker container ls`, and your output will look exactly like this, but with a different container ID:

```
$ docker container ls
⇒ CONTAINER ID    IMAGE                   COMMAND        CREATED
⇒ STATUS          PORTS                     NAMES
c23f3ab00ba3    kindest/node:v1.21.1    "/usr/lo…"    4 days ago   Up 25 hours
⇒    127.0.0.1:59546->6443/tcp    kind-control-plane
```

The container name is `kind-control-plane`, which you may have guessed consists of the control plane components. What about the worker node? Well, because we are using this cluster for testing (and for simplicity's sake), we have combined the control plane and worker components in the same node, but for all other production scenarios, these would be two or more separate nodes. To prevent getting sidetracked and to keep things simple, let's continue. We'll build some multinode clusters later in this chapter, since they will be included on the CKA exam. You can also see the nodes in a Kubernetes cluster using the `kubectl` tool with the command `kubectl get nodes`, as follows:

```
$ kubectl get no
NAME                  STATUS    ROLES                  AGE     VERSION
kind-control-plane    Ready     control-plane,master   4d23h   v1.21.1
```

As you see in table 2.1, we can use shorthand for addressing certain resources in Kubernetes, which will come in handy for the exam as it saves a lot of keystrokes. Also in table 2.1, you can see other abbreviations or shorthand for addressing different Kubernetes resources.

Table 2.1 Kubernetes resource abbreviations and examples of use with `kubectl`

Resource	Abbreviation	Example
Namespace	ns	`k get ns`
Pod	po	`k get po`

Table 2.1   Kubernetes resource abbreviations and examples of use with `kubectl` *(continued)*

Resource	Abbreviation	Example
Deployment	deploy	k get deploy
ReplicaSet	rs	k get rs
Service	svc	k get svc
Service Account	sa	k get sa
ConfigMap	cm	k get cm
DaemonSet	ds	k get ds
Persistent volume	pv	k get pvc
Persistent volume claim	pvc	k get pvc
Storage class	sc	k get sc
Network policy	netpol	k get netpol
Ingress	ing	k get ing
Endpoints	ep	k get ep

You can also see by typing `kubectl get no -o wide` that containerd is in fact used instead of the `dockershim` in our kind Kubernetes cluster. The `-o wide` is a way to retrieve a verbose output from the `get` command. We'll explore this more throughout the rest of this book.

```
$ kubectl get no -o wide
NAME                    STATUS     ROLES                    AGE      VERSION
➥ INTERNAL-IP   EXTERNAL-IP   OS-IMAGE        KERNEL-VERSION
➥ CONTAINER-RUNTIME
kind-control-plane   Ready      control-plane,master    3d23h    v1.21.1
➥ 172.18.0.2     <none>        Ubuntu 21.04    5.10.76-linuxkit
➥ containerd://1.5.2
```

Getting back to our single-node cluster, let's now get a shell inside of the container so we can look inside. We can do this by typing `docker exec -it kind-control-plane bash` into our terminal, and we'll see this exact output, which means that you are operating as root inside the `kind-control-plane` container:

```
$ docker exec -it kind-control-plane bash
root@kind-control-plane:/#
```

From this point forward, we'll perform commands inside the container (after `root@kind-control-plane:/#`), as `kubectl` is already preinstalled and we can view additional information about our cluster. For example, we can use the `crictl` tool to list the control plane components as containers. The `crictl` tool is another command-line utility used to inspect and debug containers that are CRI (container runtime interface) compatible. CRI is a standard for how container runtimes are built and provides the kubelet with a consistent interface for interacting with the container runtime, whether Docker, containerd, or any other container runtime that is CRI compliant. With the command `crictl ps`, you can list the containers running inside of our `kind-control-plane` container:

```
root@kind-control-plane:/# crictl ps
CONTAINER          IMAGE               CREATED            STATE
    ➥               NAME                 ATTEMPT             POD ID
1fec85d809fc4       e422121c9c5f9       26 hours ago       Running
    ➥               local-path-provisioner  2                 6be3b31e9b9eb
1b8372af65cf2       296a6d5035e2d       26 hours ago       Running
    ➥               coredns             1                   0821c481585d6
85c7a1f4305f0       6de166512aa22       26 hours ago       Running
    ➥               kindnet-cni         1                   f7a5090363d9b
fe14d75b82341       296a6d5035e2d       26 hours ago       Running
    ➥               coredns             1                   4ee287bd9f248
76ab2ca16da9d       0e124fb3c695b       26 hours ago       Running
    ➥               kube-proxy          1                   e40195d6d1bed
4198ed634fc67       1248d2d503d37       26 hours ago       Running
    ➥               kube-scheduler      1                   c2aaffa11479c
5aac336ec4338       0369cf4303ffd       26 hours ago       Running
    ➥           etcd                    1                   09c5891be5560
80a672211961d       96a295389d472       26 hours ago       Running
    ➥               kube-controller-manager  1              764b1292d728e
a67abd31ab1ae       94ffe308aeff9       26 hours ago       Running
    ➥               kube-apiserver      1                   1865042cc7955
```

The `local-path-provisioner` is used for persistent storage in our cluster, `coredns` is used for resolving names to IP addresses in our cluster (DNS), and the `kindnet-cni` is used for Pod-to-Pod communication in our cluster. Pods are the smallest deployable unit in Kubernetes and can contain one or many containers. We'll see in future chapters that Pods can run independently or as a part of a Deployment, ReplicaSet, and StatefulSet.

Let's now talk about the components that exist on a worker node. These components will be the same for each node in the cluster, whether you have just one worker node or thousands of worker nodes. They all contain the kubelet, the kube-proxy, and the container runtime. Let's look at the kube-proxy Pods that run on the worker nodes in our cluster with the command `kubectl get po -o wide -A | grep worker`:

```
root@kind-control-plane:/# kubectl get po -o wide -A | grep worker
kube-system          kindnet-fs6jt                               1/1
   ➥ Running    0          22h   172.18.0.2   kind-worker
kube-system          kube-proxy-szr7n                            1/1
   ➥ Running    0          22h   172.18.0.2   kind-worker
```

The kube-proxy creates our iptables rules and makes sure when Services are created that we can get to the Pods associated with that Service, as mentioned previously in the discussion about the kube-proxy on the control plane node. The kindnet Pod that we see there alongside the kube-proxy Pod is for CNI, but again, it is considered a plugin, not part of core Kubernetes.

Next, let's take a look at the container runtime that's installed in each node. For this, we'll run the command `kubectl get no -o wide | grep containerd`:

```
root@kind-control-plane:/# kubectl get no -o wide | grep containerd
kind-control-plane  Ready  22h  v1.26.3  172.18.0.3  Ubuntu 22.04.1 LTS
➥ 5.15.49-linuxkit  containerd://1.6.7
kind-worker  Ready  22h  v1.25.0  172.18.0.2  Ubuntu 22.04.1 LTS  5.15.49-
➥ linuxkit  containerd://1.6.7
```

As we can see in the last column of that output, containerd is the container runtime that's used for our nodes. Containerd is a lightweight daemon for Linux and utilizes cgroups and namespaces to run the containers that are inside of our Pods running in Kubernetes.

Finally, we'll take a look at the kubelet. Because the kubelet is a systemd service running on the node, and because our nodes are really containers in kind, we'll have to get a shell into the container that is our worker node. First type `exit` to exit from the control plane shell. You can now get a shell to the worker node with the command `docker exec -it kind-worker bash`. Now, get the status of the service by running the command `systemctl status kubelet` like so:

```
$ docker exec -it kind-worker bash
root@kind-worker:/# systemctl status kubelet
? kubelet.service - kubelet: The Kubernetes Node Agent
    Loaded: loaded (/etc/systemd/system/kubelet.service; enabled; vendor
➥ preset: enabled)
   Drop-In: /etc/systemd/system/kubelet.service.d
            └─10-kubeadm.conf
    Active: active (running) since Thu 2022-03-03 15:34:52 UTC; 5h 17min
➥ ago
      Docs: http://kubernetes.io/docs/
   Process: 170 ExecStartPre=/bin/sh -euc if [ -f
➥ /sys/fs/cgroup/cgroup.controllers ]; then create-kubelet-cgroup-v2; fi
➥   (code=exited, status=0/SUCCESS)
  Main PID: 176 (kubelet)
     Tasks: 19 (limit: 2246)
    Memory: 38.0M
       CPU: 5min 39.923s
    CGroup: /system.slice/kubelet.service
            └─176 /usr/bin/kubelet --bootstrap-
➥ kubeconfig=/etc/kubernetes/bootstrap-kubelet.conf -
➥ kubeconfig=/etc/kubernetes/kubelet.conf
➥ config=/var/lib/kubelet/config.yaml --container-runtime=remote -
➥ container-runtime-endpoint=unix:///run/containerd/containerd.sock -
➥ fail-swap-on=false --node-ip=172.18.0.2 --node-labels= --pod-infra-
➥ container-image=k8s.gcr.io/pause:3.4.1 --provider-
➥ id=kind://docker/kind/kind-worker --fail-swap-on=false --cgroup-
➥ root=/kubelet
```

```
Mar 03 20:04:49 kind-worker kubelet[176]: W0303 20:04:49.309978    176
➥ sysinfo.go:203] Nodes topology is not available, providing CPU topology
Mar 03 20:09:49 kind-worker kubelet[176]: W0303 20:09:49.100474    176
➥ sysinfo.go:203] Nodes topology is not available, providing CPU topology
```

As you can see, the systemd service is active and running, which is a good thing. There may be a question on the exam where you need to remember how to check if the kubelet service is running. Remember, if the kubelet is not running, your node status will show as `NotReady`. You can even test this by running the command `systemctl stop kubelet`, exiting out of the container shell, and then running the command `kubectl get no`. Go ahead and try it!

```
root@kind-worker:~# systemctl stop kubelet
root@kind-worker:~# exit
$ kubectl get no
NAME                 STATUS     ROLES                  AGE     VERSION
kind-control-plane   Ready      control-plane,master   5h27m   v1.21.1
kind-worker          NotReady   <none>                 5h27m   v1.21.1
kind-worker2         Ready      <none>                 5h27m   v1.21.1
```

> **NOTE** It may take a few seconds for the message that the kubelet service is not running to get back to the API server, so if the node doesn't show `NotReady` right away, don't worry.

To start the kubelet service again, simply get a shell inside the worker node again, then run the command `systemctl start kubelet`:

```
$ docker exec -it kind-worker bash
root@kind-worker:/# systemctl start kubelet
root@kind-worker:/#
```

We'll talk more about troubleshooting Services in chapter 8, but I just couldn't wait to show you this valuable tool for determining if the kubelet service has not started in your Kubernetes cluster. For this next section, we'll exit out of the `kind-worker` shell with the `exit` command.

2.2 Datastore etcd

The datastore etcd contains all of our cluster configuration data, which means information about how many Pods or Deployments are running in our cluster (including historical information), as well as which ports are exposed on which Services. If you didn't have this data, you'd be lost when recreating Kubernetes resources from scratch. Just to be clear, we're not talking about the data associated with your application. We're talking about the configuration of the Kubernetes cluster itself. This is depicted in figure 2.13, where the etcd datastore runs inside of a Pod in the Kubernetes cluster, containing cluster configuration data.

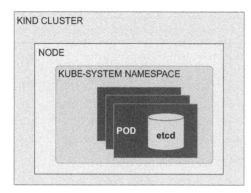

Figure 2.13 Etcd exists as a Pod in the `kube-system` **namespace.**

2.2.1 *Working with etcdctl*

The CKA exam will test your knowledge of both backing up and restoring the etcd database. Luckily, there's a tool preinstalled in the exam terminal called `etcdctl`, which you can use for both of these operations. Knowing this on exam day will be valuable as you are rewarded for answering etcd-related questions correctly, on your way to a passing score. An exam question might look something like the following.

> **EXAM TASK** The cluster k8s has been misconfigured and needs to be restored from a backup located at `/tmp/c02dkjs0-001.db`. Perform the restore and verify that the DaemonSet kube-proxy has been restored to the cluster.

To begin, we'll get a shell to our control plane node with the command `docker exec -it kind-control-plane bash`. To accomplish this task, we must first back up etcd using a command-line utility for etcd called `etcdctl`. We can install `etcdctl` with the command `apt update; apt install -y etcd-client`.

> **NOTE** The `etcdctl` client will be available for you on the exam, so you won't need to know how to install it during the exam.

Once we have `etcdctl` installed, we need to set it to version 3. We can do this with the command `export ETCDCTL_API=3`, which creates an environment variable named `ETCDCTL_API` that sets it to the value 3. The `etcdctl` tool is now set to the correct version, so the command will be available to perform the backup. Run the command `etcdctl -v` to retrieve the version of `etcdctl`, which should now be set to version 3:

```
root@kind-control-plane:/# etcdctl -v
etcdctl version: 3.3.25
API version: 2
```

Now that we have the version set, run the command `etcdctl snapshot save snap-shotdb --cacert /etc/kubernetes/pki/etcd/ca.crt --cert /etc/kubernetes/pki/etcd/server.crt --key /etc/kubernetes/pki/etcd/server.key` to perform a snapshot backup of the etcd datastore. Run `ls | grep snapshotdb` to list the snapshot in the current directory:

```
root@kind-control-plane:/# etcdctl snapshot save snapshotdb --cacert
➥ /etc/kubernetes/pki/etcd/ca.crt --cert
➥ /etc/kubernetes/pki/etcd/server.crt --key
➥ /etc/kubernetes/pki/etcd/server.key
2022-03-02 03:49:00.578988 I | clientv3: opened snapshot stream; downloading
2022-03-02 03:49:00.616108 I | clientv3: completed snapshot read; closing
Snapshot saved at snapshotdb
root@kind-control-plane:/# ls | grep snapshotdb
snapshotdb
```

Now we can check to see if there's any data in that snapshot file using the command `etcdctl snapshot status snapshotdb --write-out=table`:

```
root@kind-control-plane:/# etcdctl snapshot status snapshotdb --write-
➥ out=table+----------+----------+------------+------------+
|   HASH   | REVISION | TOTAL KEYS | TOTAL SIZE |
+----------+----------+------------+------------+
| dac82c4e |  893315  |    1217    |   2.1 MB   |
+----------+----------+------------+------------+
```

Let's go ahead and perform the restore of etcd. To simulate something to restore, delete the DaemonSet that was created for our kube-proxy service, which will allow us to verify that our restore operation was successful after we restore it. To delete the DaemonSet, perform the command

```
kubectl delete ds kube-proxy -n kube-system
$ kubectl delete ds kube-proxy -n kube-system
daemonset.apps "kube-proxy" deleted
```

If we view the DaemonSets in the `kube-system` namespace, we'll notice that there's only the kindnet DaemonSet, and the kube-proxy DaemonSet is no longer there:

```
$ kubectl get ds -A
NAMESPACE     NAME       DESIRED   CURRENT   READY   UP-TO-DATE
➥ AVAILABLE   NODE SELECTOR   AGE
kube-system   kindnet    1         1         1       1
➥ 1             <none>         6d20h
```

EXAM TIP The `-A` at the end of the command is shorthand for `--all-name-spaces`. This is a real time-saver for the CKA exam.

Now that we've modified the cluster state, and the keys inside of our etcd datastore are different than our backup, we can perform the restore. To do this, we'll use the command `etcdctl snapshot restore snapshotdb --data-dir /var/lib/etcd-restore`:

```
root@kind-control-plane:/# etcdctl snapshot restore snapshotdb --data-dir
➥ /var/lib/etcd-restore
2022-03-02 16:01:03.198967 I | mvcc: restore compact to 914490
```

```
2022-03-02 16:01:03.207022 I | etcdserver/membership: added member
⇒ 8e9e05c52164694d [http://localhost:2380] to cluster cdf818194e3a8c32
```

We used the `--data-dir` parameter to specify a format that the cluster can read as well as relocate our backup to a directory that's already in use by Kubernetes. Now that we've prepared the snapshot for use by Kubernetes and stored it in the `/var/lib/etcd-restore` directory, we'll go ahead and change the location where Kubernetes looks for the etcd data. This can be changed in the YAML specification for the API server, which will always be located on the control plane node in the `/etc/kubernetes/manifests` directory. Any YAML files that you place in this directory will automatically schedule the Kubernetes resources within.

The `kind-control-plane` doesn't have Vim installed, so we'll run the command `apt install update; apt install vim` to install it and edit our file. Open the file with the command `vim /etc/kubernetes/manifests/etcd.yaml`. Scroll down to the very bottom and change the path for the volume from `/var/lib/etcd` to `/var/lib/etcd-restore` (make sure to press the I key for insert mode). Here's a snippet from that file, so you can check your work:

```
volumes:
- hostPath:
    path: /etc/kubernetes/pki/etcd
    type: DirectoryOrCreate
  name: etcd-certs
- hostPath:
    path: /var/lib/etcd-restore
    type: DirectoryOrCreate
  name: etcd-data
status: {}
```

> **NOTE** To exit out of Vim, you'll press the Esc key on your keyboard, followed by the colon (`:`) and the letter `w` to write and the letter `q` to quit (`:wq`).

That's all you have to do to complete the restore! It may take a few seconds to get a response from the API server with your new cluster data, but shortly after, you'll be able to run `kubectl get ds -A` and see both the kube-proxy and kindnet DaemonSets back where they should be. Congratulations, you've successfully backed up and restored etcd!

2.2.2   *Client and server certificates*

In the previous section, we talked about etcd needing authentication to the cluster. This method of authenticating between client and server is called PKI (public key infrastructure). PKI is the client-server model that Kubernetes imposes, authenticating any requests that come into the API using a certificate. `kubectl` also uses a certificate to authenticate to the Kubernetes API, and we refer to this as the kubeconfig. However, `kubectl` is not the only tool or object that's trying to access the API. In addition to `kubectl`, the controller manager, the scheduler, and the kubelet all need to use certificates to authenticate to the API. These certificates are all generated by the boot-strap process (via kubeadm). You don't have to manage these certificates, but it is good to know where they reside for the CKA exam. In figure 2.14, you'll see a visual representation of every client or server certification used for every component within a Kubernetes cluster. Let's run the command `ls /etc/kubernetes` to list the contents of that directory and see the client certificates for the kubelet, scheduler, and controller manager:

```
root@kind-control-plane:/# ls /etc/kubernetes
admin.conf  controller-manager.conf  kubelet.conf  manifests  pki  scheduler.conf
```

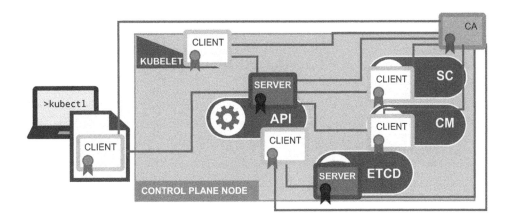

Figure 2.14 Client and server certificate placement in Kubernetes

NOTE You'll still need a shell to the `kind-control-plane`. In case you forgot, here's the command: `docker exec -it kind-control-plane bash`.

You'll see `controller-manager.conf`, `kubelet.conf`, and `scheduler.conf`, which are representative of the kubeconfig used to authenticate to the Kubernetes API. If you view the contents of `kubelet.conf`, for example, you'll see a config similar to your `kubectl` kubeconfig (in `~/.kube/config`). Type the command `cat /etc/kubernetes/kubelet.conf`:

```
root@kind-control-plane:/# cat /etc/kubernetes/kubelet.conf
apiVersion: v1
clusters:
- cluster:
    certificate-authority-data:
  LS0tLS1CRUdJTiBDRVJUSUZJQ0FURS0tLS0tCk1JSUM1ekNDQWMrZ0F3SUJBZ00FURS0tLS
  0tCg==
    server: https://kind-control-plane:6443
  name: kind
contexts:
- context:
    cluster: kind
```

```
    user: system:node:kind-control-plane
  name: system:node:kind-control-plane@kind
current-context: system:node:kind-control-plane@kind
kind: Config
preferences: {}
users:
- name: system:node:kind-control-plane
  user:
    client-certificate: /var/lib/kubelet/pki/kubelet-client-current.pem
    client-key: /var/lib/kubelet/pki/kubelet-client-current.pem
```

Notice the user is the system user, and the client certificate is located on the node in `/var/lib/kubelet/pki/kubelet-client-current.pem`. This will be the case for all nodes in Kubernetes, as all nodes run the kubelet service.

You may have noticed a `pki` directory in `/etc/kubernetes`, and if you list the contents of that directory, you'll find more client and server certificates. Let's take a look with the command `ls /etc/kubernetes/pki`:

```
root@kind-control-plane:/# ls /etc/kubernetes/pki
apiserver-etcd-client.crt  apiserver-kubelet-client.crt  apiserver.crt
↬ ca.crt  etcd                front-proxy-ca.key       front-proxy-
↬ client.key  sa.pub
apiserver-etcd-client.key  apiserver-kubelet-client.key  apiserver.key
↬ ca.key  front-proxy-ca.crt  front-proxy-client.crt  sa.key
```

In this `pki` directory, you'll see another kubelet certificate (`kubelet.crt`), which is a server certificate. Yes, you can have a client and server certificate for the same service in Kubernetes. This is also apparent in the two files named `apiserver.crt` and `apiserver-etcd-client.crt`, a server and client certificate, respectively. And because the kubelet has a server certificate, it must have a client certificate, which is the file named `apiserver-kubelet-client.crt`. The `apiserver.crt` is the server certificate to the client certificates that we looked at in the `/etc/kubernetes` directory just a moment ago.

Finally, there's etcd. In the `/etc/kubernetes/pki/etcd` directory, you'll also see a `server.crt` file, which pertains to the server certificate for etcd. The API server is constantly trying to authenticate to the etcd datastore and obtain the cluster config data. In this way, not just anyone can view or modify the cluster state.

2.3   *Exam exercises*

1 Increase your efficiency with running `kubectl` commands by shortening `kubectl` and creating a shell alias to `k`.

2 Using the `kubectl` CLI tool, get the output of the Pods running in the `kube-system` namespace and show the Pod IP addresses. Save the output of the command to a file named `pod-ip-output.txt`.

3 Use the CLI tool, which allows you to view the client certificate that the kubelet uses to authenticate to the Kubernetes API. Output the results to a file named `kubelet-config.txt`.

4 Using the `etcdctl` CLI tool, back up the etcd datastore to a snapshot file named `etcdbackup1`. Once that backup is complete, send the output of the command `etcdctl snapshot status etcdbackup1` to a file named `snapshot-status.txt`.

5 Using the `etcdctl` CLI tool, restore the etcd datastore using the same `etcdbackup1` file from the previous exercise. When you complete the restore operation, `cat` the etcd YAML and save it to a file named `etcd-restore.yaml`.

6 Upgrade the control plane components using kubeadm. When completed, check that everything, including kubelet and `kubectl`, is upgraded to version 1.24.0

Summary

- The bootstrapping process hides the complexity of creating a Kubernetes cluster, such as the PKI and etcd creation, generating kubeconfigs, and more.
- The kubeconfig is created by kubeadm in the bootstrap process and is how we authenticate with the API using `kubectl`. This file is located in the `~/.kube/config` directory.
- Services are Kubernetes objects, providing load balancing to one or more Pods based on the Pod labels. Services have their own unique IP address and DNS name through which Pods can be reached.
- The client and server certificates in the directory `/etc/kubernetes/pki` allow the control plane and worker nodes to authenticate to the API. Multiple Kubernetes components can have both client and server certificates.
- Etcd is a key-value datastore that contains the cluster configuration, including how many objects exist. To back up etcd, the command `etcdctl snapshot save` is used, and to restore from snapshot, the command `etcdctl snapshot restore` is used.
- The directory `/etc/kubernetes/manifests` contains YAML files for the API server, controller manager, scheduler, and etcd. These files are not detected by the scheduler; therefore, kubelet will automatically pick up and create whatever is in this directory.
- In a multinode cluster, the worker node runs kubelet, kube-proxy, and the container runtime, whereas the control plane also runs the kubelet, controller manager, scheduler, and etcd. To prevent application Pods from running on the control plane, a taint is applied during the bootstrap process.

Identity and
access management

In this chapter, we'll focus on role-based access control, which is within the cluster architecture, installation, and configuration section of the exam curriculum. Now that you know how the Kubernetes API works, it's essential to understand how to authenticate and authorize a user and/or a Service Account for the exam.

The cluster architecture, installation, and configuration domain

This chapter covers part of the cluster architecture, installation, and configuration domain of the CKA curriculum. This domain covers what consists of a Kubernetes cluster and how we configure different aspects of the cluster. It encompasses the following competencies.

Competency	Chapter section
Manage role-based access control (RBAC).	3.1, 3.2
Manage a highly available Kubernetes cluster.	3.3

3.1 Role-based access control

To access the resources within a Kubernetes cluster, you must first be authenticated. If you remember from chapter 2, we used the kubectl tool to interface with the Kubernetes API. We were allowed to do this because we had a client certificate that carried a token with which to authenticate, as depicted in figure 3.1. This is called role-based access control (RBAC) because, based on our Role in Kubernetes, we were able to list the running Pods in the kube-system namespace. There are different ways that we can control these actions and block them if we wish. The authentication and authorization system built into Kubernetes allows us the ability to control access of a given user or machine to a Kubernetes cluster. We'll talk more about this in the following sections of this chapter.

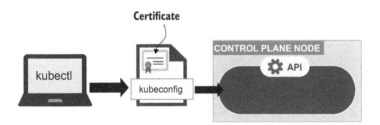

Figure 3.1 Using a certificate and token to access the Kubernetes API

For that matter, you can view resources within their API groups in Kubernetes by using curl and passing in the certificate. Following this paragraph is the location of our Pods and Deployments in the API, which are in the /core and /apps group, respectively. From a Kubernetes cluster built with kubeadm, you can access these resources in the same manner using the following commands, assuming the address of the control plane is 10.0.0.4, which can be retrieved using the command kubectl config view and/or kubectl cluster-info:

```
kubectl create role pod-deploy-reader --verb=get --verb=list --verb=watch -
➥ -resource=pods,deployments

kubectl create rolebinding pod-deploy-reader-binding --role=pod-deploy-
➥ reader --serviceaccount=default:default

TOKEN=$(kubectl get secret -n default -o json | jq -r
➥ '(.items[].data.token)' | base64 --decode | tr -d "\n")

curl -X GET https://10.0.0.4:6443/api/v1/namespaces/default/pods --header
➥ "Authorization: Bearer $TOKEN" --cacert /etc/kubernetes/pki/ca.crt

curl -X GET
➥ https://10.0.0.4:6443/apis/apps/v1/namespaces/default/deployments --
➥ header "Authorization: Bearer $TOKEN" --cacert /etc/kubernetes/pki/ca.crt
```

You can authenticate in different ways via authentication plugins. Some of these plugins come out of the box with Kubernetes, so that's why we didn't need to install them separately. The built-in plugin that we use with `kubectl` is called the certificates plugin. Many other authentication plugins are sources for authentication. Here are some common plugins, also depicted in figure 3.2:

- Static token file (e.g., CSV file)
- Third-party identity service (AWS IAM)
- Basic HTTP authentication (token passed in an HTTP header)

More plugins can be enabled when starting the API server.

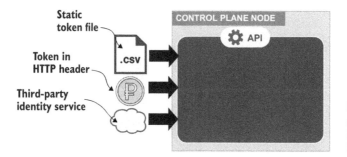

Figure 3.2   Many different authentication plugins can be used to access the Kubernetes API.

When you make a request to the Kubernetes API, all the plugins analyze this request and try to determine if they can read it in sequence. The first plugin able to translate the meaning of the request handles the authentication. This involves determining if the request is coming from a human or a machine. If the request is coming from a human—like when we are using `kubectl`—then the user is authenticated as a specific username, and that name is used for subsequent steps. If the request originates from a machine, it must have a Service Account, and its credentials must be stored as a Secret in Kubernetes.

Both Service Accounts and Secrets are Kubernetes resources, whereas users are not. A Service Account is an identity for processes that run inside of a Pod, providing a method to authenticate and perform actions in the cluster on behalf of a Pod. This allows other access-management systems to easily integrate with Kubernetes via SSO through LDAP (lightweight directory access protocol) or AD (active directory) for authentication.

A Service Account is a Kubernetes resource; therefore, Kubernetes manages this along with other resources like Pods, Deployments, and persistent volumes. Service Accounts are often associated with Pods running in the cluster, which allow applications running inside the Pod (as containers) to access the Kubernetes API and make requests. A token is mounted to each Pod via a Service Account, as depicted in figure 3.3. You can disable this feature, as most of the time you don't need your Pods to talk to the API. We will go through an example of mounting a Service Account in a Pod and preventing Service Accounts from mounting to a Pod later in this chapter.

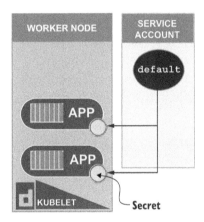

Figure 3.3 A Service Account can be used to mount a token in a Pod, so it can authenticate with the API.

After the authentication phase, the request is passed on to the authorization plugins. RBAC is considered one of the authentication plugins, but there are others like the Node authorization plugin and the WebHook authorization plugin. For the purposes of the CKA exam, we are going to focus solely on RBAC, as you see depicted in figure 3.4. RBAC prevents unauthorized users from viewing or modifying the cluster state through the principle of least privilege. That principle states that administrators can allow explicit access to a single subject in Kubernetes but provide no additional privileges to any other subjects (e.g., permissions to view Pods but not delete them).

The authorization mode in our kind cluster was set to RBAC as well as Node authorization on the Kubernetes API server during the bootstrap process. We can view this setting in the `/etc/kubernetes/manifests` directory in our `kind-control-plane` container. You will see it under `spec`, in the list of container commands, as

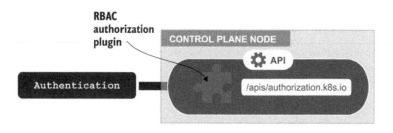

Figure 3.4   The RBAC plugin prevents unauthorized requests from accessing the Kubernetes API.

`--authorization-mode=Node,RBAC`. Let's get the contents of that file and pipe it to `more` with the command `cat /etc/kubernetes/manifests/kube-apiserver.yaml | more`:

```
root@kind-control-plane:/# cat /etc/kubernetes/manifests/kube-
➥ apiserver.yaml | more
apiVersion: v1
kind: Pod
metadata:
  annotations:
    kubeadm.kubernetes.io/kube-apiserver.advertise-address.endpoint:
➥ 172.18.0.4:6443
  creationTimestamp: null
  labels:
    component: kube-apiserver
    tier: control-plane
  name: kube-apiserver
  namespace: kube-system
spec:
  containers:
  - command:
    - kube-apiserver
    - --advertise-address=172.18.0.4
    - --allow-privileged=true
    - --authorization-mode=Node,RBAC
    - --client-ca-file=/etc/kubernetes/pki/ca.crt
    - --enable-admission-plugins=NodeRestriction
    - --enable-bootstrap-token-auth=true
    - --etcd-cafile=/etc/kubernetes/pki/etcd/ca.crt
    - --etcd-certfile=/etc/kubernetes/pki/apiserver-etcd-client.crt
    - --etcd-keyfile=/etc/kubernetes/pki/apiserver-etcd-client.key
    - --etcd-servers=https://127.0.0.1:2379
    - --insecure-port=0
    - --kubelet-client-certificate=/etc/kubernetes/pki/apiserver-kubelet-
➥ client.crt
    - --kubelet-client-key=/etc/kubernetes/pki/apiserver-kubelet-client.key
    - --kubelet-preferred-address-types=InternalIP,ExternalIP,Hostname
    - --proxy-client-cert-file=/etc/kubernetes/pki/front-proxy-client.crt
    - --proxy-client-key-file=/etc/kubernetes/pki/front-proxy-client.key
    - --requestheader-allowed-names=front-proxy-client
    - --requestheader-client-ca-file=/etc/kubernetes/pki/front-proxy-ca.crt
```

```
   - --requestheader-extra-headers-prefix=X-Remote-Extra-
   - --requestheader-group-headers=X-Remote-Group
   - --requestheader-username-headers=X-Remote-User
   - --runtime-config=
--More--
```

We could have opened this file in a text editor just as easily, but we used the cat command instead. This YAML manifest is important to remember, as it contains the cluster configuration for many components in the Kubernetes cluster, such as the advertise address, privileged modes, and all the certificates and keys for etcd and the kubelet.

> **EXAM TIP**   Remember that the manifests for control plane components are in the /etc/Kubernetes/manifests directory. This directory will be located on the control plane server, which you will have to SSH into to view or modify. On the exam, the SSH keys are shared; therefore, you can simply type ssh control-plane-node to get a shell to the control plane node.

When the RBAC authorization plugin receives the request, it determines what action is allowed to be performed by the user or group. Yes, groups are factored into RBAC as well, which simply means a group of users who are all assigned the same level of privilege in Kubernetes. We'll go through creating users and groups later in this chapter.

3.1.1   Roles and Role bindings

So, how does RBAC know what actions are permitted? This is determined by four different types of objects in Kubernetes: the Role, the cluster Role, the Role binding, and the cluster Role binding, as depicted in figure 3.5. Previously we talked about Kubernetes resources that are namespace scoped. Permissions for resources that are inside a

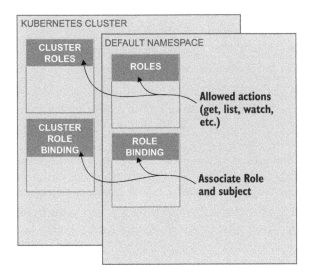

Figure 3.5   Roles and Role bindings define privileges in a namespace, where cluster Roles and cluster Role bindings define cluster-wide privileges.

namespace need to be scoped to that namespace as well. The same goes for resources that are not namespace scoped, such as persistent volumes, nodes, or namespaces themselves. These resources need properly defined cluster Roles (cluster-wide) or Roles (namespaced).

> **NOTE**   It helps to remember which type of user will be accessing namespaced resources versus cluster resources. Application developers will commonly be assigned Roles because they develop applications that exist inside a name-space. Cluster administrators will commonly be assigned cluster Roles because they are updating nodes and creating volumes and other operations outside of the namespace (cluster-wide).

Roles are not only scoped to a namespace but also to a particular resource in Kubernetes (i.e., Pods) and will list the specific actions allowed within that Role. The actions are referred to as *request verbs*. They are like API requests, but because a resource can have multiple Endpoints, a request verb targets a specific Endpoint and uses the lower-cased HTTP method of the request as the verb. So, `get`, `list`, `create`, `update`, `patch`, `watch`, `delete`, and `deletecollection` are all API request verbs, which allow you to perform an action on a resource, as depicted in figure 3.6.

HTTP verb	request verb
POST	create
GET	get, list, watch
PUT	update
PATCH	patch
DELETE	delete

Get a resource.

List a collection of resources.

Watch for streaming updates to a resource.

Figure 3.6   Request verbs correspond roughly with HTTP verbs, as shown here.

Let's look at an example by typing the command `kubectl create role pod-reader --verb=get,list,watch --resource=pods`, and you'll see output similar to figure 3.7. The YAML output from the Role that we just created with the command `kubectl get role pod-reader -o yaml` shows output similar to figure 3.8.

Instead of creating the Role right away, we could have done a "dry run" and saved the contents to a YAML file. This comes in handy if you like to take a more declarative approach and keep your YAML files in a version control system. Let's run the same command to create a Role, but this time we'll perform a dry run and save the output of the command to a file named `role.yaml`. Run the command `kubectl create role pod-reader -verb=get,list,watch -resource=pods -dry-run=client -o yaml > role.yaml`, and you'll see that the file has been created, as in figure 3.9.

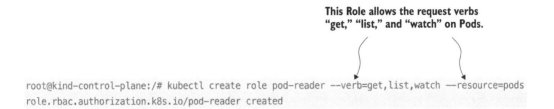

**This Role allows the request verbs
"get," "list," and "watch" on Pods.**

```
root@kind-control-plane:/# kubectl create role pod-reader --verb=get,list,watch --resource=pods
role.rbac.authorization.k8s.io/pod-reader created
```

Figure 3.7   With this imperative command, create a Role and assign request verbs for a resource.

```
root@kind-control-plane:/# kubectl get role pod-reader -o yaml
apiVersion: rbac.authorization.k8s.io/v1
kind: Role
metadata:
  creationTimestamp: "2022-04-07T14:40:03Z"
  name: pod-reader
  namespace: default
  resourceVersion: "1783"
  uid: 54afc1e9-b4ac-4ed3-9e21-c3e20e19ce9c
rules:
- apiGroups:
  - ""
  resources:          The resource that
  - pods              this Role applies to
  verbs:
  - get
  - list              The request verbs
  - watch
```

**Figure 3.8   The `kubectl get role` command shows which resources this Role
applies to and which actions the Role allows.**

**The dry run allows you to
preview the object without
really submitting it.**

**Output the YAML
and save it to a file
named role.yaml.**

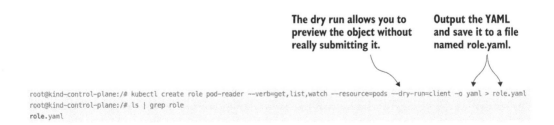

```
root@kind-control-plane:/# kubectl create role pod-reader --verb=get,list,watch --resource=pods --dry-run=client -o yaml > role.yaml
root@kind-control-plane:/# ls | grep role
role.yaml
```

Figure 3.9   Instead of creating a Role, we perform a dry run and then save the contents of the YAML to a file.

In the first chapter, we looked at all the different Kubernetes API resources. Each resource had a path and at the end of that path led you to the object. In the case of Pods, the path is /api/v1/pods, so the API group is within /api/v1/. Deployments are in the API group /apis/apps/v1, which are listed separately in this Role definition, depicted in figure 3.10.

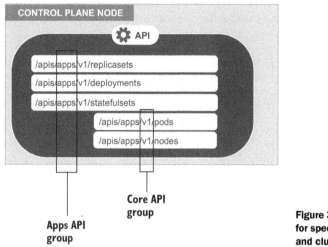

Figure 3.10 The API group is used for specifying the resource in Roles and cluster Roles.

Notice that this Role doesn't indicate permissions for a user at all. That's where Role bindings come in. Role bindings will attach (or bind) a Role to a user, group, or Service Account and will provide that user, group, or Service Account with a Role. Let's create a Role binding now with the command kubectl create rolebinding pod-reader-binding --role=pod-reader --user=carol.

The YAML output of our pod-reader-binding shows the Role reference (roleRef) and the user (subjects). This Role binding is how the user carol will be authorized to access Pods in our Kubernetes cluster.

```
$ kubectl create rolebinding pod-reader-binding --role=pod-reader -
➥ user=carol
rolebinding.rbac.authorization.k8s.io/admin-binding created
$ kubectl get rolebinding pod-reader-binding -oyaml
apiVersion: rbac.authorization.k8s.io/v1
kind: RoleBinding
metadata:
  creationTimestamp: "2022-03-29T04:22:35Z"
  name: pod-reader-binding
  namespace: default
  resourceVersion: "566785"
  uid: 9f7d1036-9123-4288-94cf-ef527aa090d0
roleRef:
  apiGroup: rbac.authorization.k8s.io
  kind: Role
```

```
  name: pod-reader
subjects:
- apiGroup: rbac.authorization.k8s.io
  kind: User
  name: carol
```

There's a really useful tool built into `kubectl` to verify if users can perform certain actions in the Kubernetes cluster without explicitly assuming that user's identity. This command is `kubectl auth can-i`. If you get the help pages for this command, you'll see a plethora of examples you can use to test authorization as a user, group, or Service Account:

```
$ kubectl auth can-i -h
Check whether an action is allowed.

VERB is a logical Kubernetes API verb like 'get', 'list', 'watch',
⮡ 'delete', etc. TYPE is a Kubernetes resource.

Shortcuts and groups will be resolved. NONRESOURCEURL is a partial URL that
⮡ starts with "/". NAME is the name of a
particular Kubernetes resource.

Examples:
  # Check to see if I can create pods in any namespace
  kubectl auth can-i create pods --all-namespaces

  # Check to see if I can list deployments in my current namespace
  kubectl auth can-i list deployments.apps

  # Check to see if I can do everything in my current namespace ("*" means
⮡ all)
  kubectl auth can-i '*' '*'

  # Check to see if I can get the job named "bar" in namespace "foo"
  kubectl auth can-i list jobs.batch/bar -n foo

  # Check to see if I can read pod logs
  kubectl auth can-i get pods --subresource=log

  # Check to see if I can access the URL /logs/
  kubectl auth can-i get /logs/

  # List all allowed actions in namespace "foo"
  kubectl auth can-i --list --namespace=foo
```

Let's check if the user `carol` can list or delete Pods in the default namespace in our Kubernetes cluster using the command `kubectl auth can-i`. Notice the output just says yes or no. What an easy way to verify authorization in Kubernetes!

```
$ kubectl auth can-i get pods -n default --as carol
yes
$ kubectl auth can-i delete pods -n default --as carol
no
```

> **EXAM TIP** I encourage you to use `kubectl auth can-i` on the exam, as it will
> allow you to verify that you've completed the task successfully and save pre-
> cious time.

How you create a cluster Role and cluster Role binding are the same, so we won't go
over this in detail. The `kubectl` commands for creating cluster Roles and cluster Role
bindings are `kubectl create clusterrole` and `kubectl create clusterrolebinding`,
respectively.

> **EXAM TIP** Use the `-h` flag to get a list of examples for running your command
> (e.g., `kubectl create clusterrole -h`). This will save you time on the exam,
> as you can copy the examples without having to type out or remember the
> entire command.

You can also use cluster Roles with Role bindings when you require a resource that is
not scoped to a namespace (e.g., nodes) to be accessible from a user, group, or Service Account that is applied from within a namespace. You *cannot* attach a cluster Role
binding to a Role because permissions from within a namespace (Role permissions)
can't be applied to a subject that is not namespace-scoped, as we see depicted in figure
3.11. One thing you have to keep in mind is that permissions via cluster Roles will
affect all namespaces, current and future. You must keep in mind the principle of
least privilege to be cautious not to assign a Role or cluster Role that gives unfettered
access to your Kubernetes cluster.

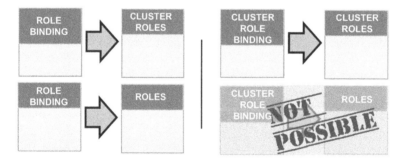

Figure 3.11 **With the exception of cluster Role bindings to Roles, all other
combinations are supported.**

3.1.2   *System Roles and groups*

Now that we know what users, Service Accounts, Roles, and bindings are used for, let's
take a look at the built-in Roles and groups and what user and group we've been using
for our own cluster thus far. The API server creates a set of default cluster Roles and
cluster Role bindings. They are directly managed by the control plane. You will see
they are `cluster-admin`, `admin`, `edit`, and `view` when you run the command `kubectl
get clusterrole | grep -v system`:

```
root@kind-control-plane:/# kubectl get clusterrole | grep -v system
NAME                               CREATED AT
admin                              2022-03-25T17:44:03Z
cluster-admin                      2022-03-25T17:44:03Z
edit                               2022-03-25T17:44:03Z
kindnet                            2022-03-25T17:44:08Z
kubeadm:get-nodes                  2022-03-25T17:44:05Z
local-path-provisioner-role        2022-03-25T17:44:09Z
view                               2022-03-25T17:44:09Z
```

The `cluster-admin` cluster Role is intended to be used cluster-wide and allows read and write access for most objects, including Roles and Role bindings, with the exception of resource quotas, Endpoints, or the namespace itself. The edit cluster Role will not allow you to modify Roles or Role bindings; however, it will allow you to access Secrets and run Pods with any Service Accounts inside the namespace. The view cluster Role is just like it sounds, allowing you to view most namespaced objects except for Secrets because the contents of a Secret contain the credentials for API access.

> **EXAM TIP** Kubernetes allows assigning (binding) a cluster Role to multiple users/groups/Service Accounts via Role or cluster Role binding, so, on the exam, it may save you time to create a Role binding and assign it to an existing Role (i.e., `view`).

Now that we know all the Roles that are created by default, which one do we assume is the user of `kubectl`? For that, we'll have to talk about groups in more detail—more specifically, the built-in groups that are managed by the Kubernetes API server. Like users, groups are not a managed resource in Kubernetes, so the group name is just an arbitrary name. However, these built-in groups are different. They are managed by the API server and cannot be modified. When the API server starts up, it reconciles with any missing permissions and updates the default cluster Role bindings with any missing subjects (i.e., groups). This allows the cluster to automatically repair any misconfigurations and keep the Roles and bindings up to date with new releases of Kubernetes. These built-in default cluster Role bindings are `system:authenticated`, `system:unauthenticated`, and `system:masters`:

- The `system:authenticated` group assigns privileges to users who are successfully authenticated.
- The `system:unauthenticated` group is used when none of the authentication plugins can validate the request.
- The `system:masters` group is used for super users and provides unfettered access to everything in Kubernetes.

The `system:masters` group is the group we have been assuming this entire time. Yikes! We better tread carefully, so as to not misconfigure anything and deem our cluster incapable of running. All joking aside, you should never use this group for normal users, because if it were to fall into the wrong hands, it could be dangerous. To prove that we have unrestricted access to our cluster, we can use the command `kubectl auth can-i --list` to list the actions we can take on each and every object in the cluster:

```
root@kind-control-plane:/# kubectl auth can-i --list
Resources                                       Non-Resource URLs
     Resource Names    Verbs
*.*                                             []                    []
                       [*]
                                                [*]                   []
                       [*]
selfsubjectaccessreviews.authorization.k8s.io   []                    []
                       [create]
selfsubjectrulesreviews.authorization.k8s.io    []                    []
                       [create]
                                                [/api/*]              []
                       [get]
                                                [/api]                []
                       [get]
                                                [/apis/*]             []
                       [get]
                                                [/apis]               []
                       [get]
                                                [/healthz]            []
                       [get]
                                                [/healthz]            []
                       [get]
                                                [/livez]              []
                       [get]
                                                [/livez]              []
                       [get]
                                                [/openapi/*]          []
                       [get]
                                                [/openapi]            []
                       [get]
                                                [/readyz]             []
                       [get]
                                                [/readyz]             []
                       [get]
                                                [/version/]           []
                       [get]
                                                [/version/]           []
                       [get]
                                                [/version]            []
                       [get]
                                                [/version]            []
                       [get]
```

Furthermore, we can run the command `kubectl get clusterrolebinding cluster-admin -o yaml` to see the `clusterrolebinding` that binds the Role `cluster-admin` to our user, who is a part of the `system:masters` group:

```
kubectl get clusterrolebinding cluster-admin -o yaml
apiVersion: rbac.authorization.k8s.io/v1
kind: ClusterRoleBinding
```

```
metadata:
  annotations:
    rbac.authorization.kubernetes.io/autoupdate: "true"
  creationTimestamp: "2022-03-25T17:44:03Z"
  labels:
    kubernetes.io/bootstrapping: rbac-defaults
  name: cluster-admin
  resourceVersion: "141"
  uid: d91f5e22-e179-47b3-b90e-2591f4617b3b
roleRef:
  apiGroup: rbac.authorization.k8s.io
  kind: ClusterRole
  name: cluster-admin
subjects:
- apiGroup: rbac.authorization.k8s.io
  kind: Group
  name: system:masters
```

Finally, we can see the Role, which also shows the actions we can take on cluster resources. You'll notice that the asterisk (*) is a wildcard for everything. So, we have access to all resources in all API groups and are allowed to take any action (get, list, create, delete, update, patch, watch).

EXAM TIP If you are ever stuck on how a cluster Role is formatted, you can send the output of `kubectl` to a file and edit it inline. To do this, use the command `kubectl create clusterrole pod-reader --verb get,list,watch --resource pods --dry-run=client -o yaml > pod-reader.yaml`.

Exam exercises

Create a new Role named `sa-creator` that will allow for creating Service Accounts.

Create a Role binding that is associated with the previous `sa-creator` Role, named `sa-creator-binding`, that will bind to the user Sandra.

3.2 Users and groups

We've uncovered the greatest fear of every security engineer in the world: a back door to our Kubernetes cluster that allows full, unrestricted access to do anything! We can even expose our cluster publicly to anonymous users, inviting anyone and everyone to get into our cluster and do as they please. No, don't do that. Let's allow those security folks to rest easy at night and create a new user that follows the principle of least privilege. Remember carol? We created a Role binding that associates the `pod-reader` Role with the carol user. Let's create the kubeconfig that carol can use to access the cluster, as depicted in figure 3.12.

Because users and groups are arbitrary notations on a certificate and not managed by Kubernetes, let's start by creating a new certificate-signing request. Remember we learned that the Kubernetes API is its own certificate authority? This means that it can

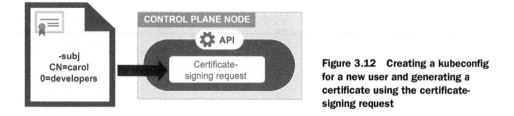

Figure 3.12 Creating a kubeconfig for a new user and generating a certificate using the certificate-signing request

sign certificates for us, rendering them valid authentication mechanisms for the Kubernetes API. How convenient!

First, let's generate a private key using 2048-bit encryption with the command `openssl genrsa -out carol.key 2048`:

```
root@kind-control-plane:/# openssl genrsa -out carol.key 2048
Generating RSA private key, 2048 bit long modulus (2 primes)
..................................................+++++
.....................+++++
e is 65537 (0x010001)
```

Now, let's create a certificate-signing request file, using the private key we just created, that we'll eventually give to the Kubernetes API. It's important here that we specify our user and group in the common name of the certificate-signing request with the command `openssl req -new -key carol.key -subj "/CN=carol/O=developers" -out carol.csr`:

```
root@kind-control-plane:/# openssl req -new -key carol.key -subj
    "/CN=carol/O=developers" -out carol.csr
root@kind-control-plane:/# ls | grep carol
carol.csr
carol.key
```

Let's store the CSR file in an environment variable, as we'll need it later. To do this, use the command `export REQUEST=$(cat carol.csr | base64 -w 0)` to store the Base64 encoded version of the CSR file in an environment variable named `REQUEST`.

Now we have exactly what we need to create our certificate-signing request resource in Kubernetes. We go about creating this resource just like we would with so many other Kubernetes resources and objects (e.g., Deployments, Pods, Service Accounts, etc.), via a YAML file.

> **EXAM TIP** Because you can have an additional tab open during the exam, utilize the search function in Kubernetes docs (https://kubernetes.io/docs). This is allowed and encouraged. Before you click on the search result, hover over the link and ensure it's staying within the `kubernetes.io/docs` subdomain.

We can use the Kubernetes documentation to find a copy of the correct YAML structure for a certificate-signing request resource. You'll need to become familiar with the

Kubernetes documentation for the exam, as it is your lifeline and a great time saver for copying examples (i.e., YAML) and pasting them into your terminal. Let's go to http://mng.bz/vnaa and practice. Copy the YAML for the certificate-signing request—the big long string to the right of the word `request`—and paste it into your terminal, changing three elements: replace it with our `REQUEST` environment variable and change the name and the groups to match the common name in the CSR file. It'll look like this:

```
cat <<EOF | kubectl apply -f -
apiVersion: certificates.k8s.io/v1
kind: CertificateSigningRequest
metadata:
  name: carol
spec:
  groups:
  - developers
  request: $REQUEST
  signerName: kubernetes.io/kube-apiserver-client
  usages:
  - client auth
EOF
```

If you don't want to bother with copying and pasting, or maybe you don't have access to a browser right now, that's fine. You can run the following command, and it will achieve the same result: `kubectl apply -f` https://raw.githubusercontent.com/chadmcrowell/k8s/main/manifests/csr-carol.yaml.

Congratulations, you've successfully submitted a signing request to the Kubernetes API! Because this is an object that Kubernetes manages, we can run the command `kubectl get csr` to see a list of requests. You'll notice that the one we just submitted is named `carol` and its condition is `Pending`:

```
root@kind-control-plane:/# kubectl get csr
NAME    AGE    SIGNERNAME                              REQUESTOR
➥ CONDITION
carol   4s     kubernetes.io/kube-apiserver-client     kubernetes-admin
➥ Pending
```

We can simply approve the request with the command `kubectl certificate approve carol`, and we'll see the condition change from `pending` to `Approved,Issued`:

```
root@kind-control-plane:/# kubectl certificate approve carol
certificatesigningrequest.certificates.k8s.io/carol approved
root@kind-control-plane:/# kubectl get csr
NAME    AGE     SIGNERNAME                              REQUESTOR
➥ CONDITION
carol   2m12s   kubernetes.io/kube-apiserver-client     kubernetes-admin
➥ Approved,Issued
```

Now that it's been approved, we can extract the contents of the signed certificate—namely, the client certificate—Base64, decode it, and store it in a file named `carol.crt` using the command `kubectl get csr carol -o jsonpath='{.status.certificate}' | base64 -d > carol.crt`:

```
root@kind-control-plane:/# kubectl get csr carol -o
    jsonpath='{.status.certificate}' | base64 -d > carol.crt
root@kind-control-plane:/# ls | grep carol
carol.crt
carol.csr
carol.key
```

We have the key (`carol.key`) and client certificate (`carol.crt`) and can add these credentials to our kubeconfig. We can simultaneously embed the certificate and key values into the file (similar to our current kubeconfig) with the command `kubectl config set-credentials carol --client-key=carol.key --client-certificate=carol.crt --embed-certs`.

> **NOTE** If you don't want to embed the certificate and key, you can leave off the `--embed-certs` option. This would list the path to the two files instead of the raw certificate values.

You will now see the credentials for `carol` in the kubeconfig by using the command `kubectl config view`:

```
root@kind-control-plane:/# kubectl config view
apiVersion: v1
clusters:
- cluster:
    certificate-authority-data: DATA+OMITTED
    server: https://kind-control-plane:6443
  name: kind
contexts:
- context:
    cluster: kind
    user: kubernetes-admin
  name: kubernetes-admin@kind
current-context: kubernetes-admin@kind
kind: Config
preferences: {}
users:
- name: carol
  user:
    client-certificate-data: REDACTED
    client-key-data: REDACTED
- name: kubernetes-admin
  user:
    client-certificate-data: REDACTED
    client-key-data: REDACTED
```

To add the user carol to our context, we'll run the command `kubectl config set-context carol --user=carol --cluster=kind`. Once you run this command, you'll notice that the context has been added by running the command `kubectl config get-contexts`:

```
root@kind-control-plane:/# kubectl config set-context carol --user=carol -
➡ cluster=kind
Context "carol" created.
root@kind-control-plane:/# kubectl config get-contexts
CURRENT   NAME                       CLUSTER   AUTHINFO           NAMESPACE
          carol                      kind      carol
*         kubernetes-admin@kind      kind      kubernetes-admin
```

The asterisk in the `current` column on the left indicates which context we are currently using. Before moving forward, let's run the command `kubectl run nginx --image nginx` to create a Pod so we can properly test if the user carol has the appropriate permissions according to the Role `pod-reader`. Then, to switch contexts and use the carol context, run the command `kubectl config use-context carol`. You'll notice the asterisk changed the current context to `carol`. Finally, just like with the `kubectl auth can-i` command, we can verify that carol can list Pods but cannot delete them:

```
root@kind-control-plane:/# kubectl config use-context carol
Switched to context "carol".
root@kind-control-plane:/# kubectl get po
NAME    READY    STATUS    RESTARTS    AGE
nginx   1/1      Running   0           13s
root@kind-control-plane:/# kubectl delete po nginx
Error from server (Forbidden): pods "nginx" is forbidden: User "carol"
➡ cannot delete resource "pods" in API group "" in the namespace "default"
```

Let's take it one step further and bind the Role (using a Role binding) to a group versus a user (which is what we have right now). To switch back to the admin user, type the command `kubectl config use-context kubernetes-admin@kind`. Then, delete the current Role binding with the command `kubectl delete rolebinding admin-binding`, and create a new Role binding with the command `kubectl create rolebinding pod-reader-bind --role=pod-reader --group=developers`. Let's switch back to the user carol with the command `kubectl config use-context carol` and test our authorization (this time via groups) with the command `kubectl get po`:

```
root@kind-control-plane:/# kubectl config use-context kubernetes-admin@kind
Switched to context "kubernetes-admin@kind".
root@kind-control-plane:/# kubectl delete rolebinding admin-binding
rolebinding.rbac.authorization.k8s.io "admin-binding" deleted
root@kind-control-plane:/# kubectl create rolebinding pod-reader-bind -
➡ role=pod-reader --group=developers
rolebinding.rbac.authorization.k8s.io/pod-reader-bind created
root@kind-control-plane:/# kubectl config use-context carol
Switched to context "carol".
root@kind-control-plane:/# kubectl get po
```

```
NAME    READY   STATUS    RESTARTS   AGE
nginx   1/1     Running   0          8m9s
```

We are done testing with the user carol, so let's switch back to the admin user again and continue on to the next topic in this chapter: Service Accounts.

> **Exam exercises**
> Create a new user named Sandra by first creating the private key, then the certificate-signing request, and then using the CSR resource in Kubernetes to generate the client certificate. Add Sandra to your local kubeconfig using the `kubectl config` command.

3.3   *Service Accounts*

Users and groups are great, but what about machines? They need to access the Kubernetes API too, and sometimes we utilize tools like Helm or Jenkins or a load balancer controller—running as Pods in our cluster—that need to communicate with the Kubernetes API to carry out actions (read, write, delete, etc.) as a part of their primary function. We provide them with a similar authentication mechanism—namely, a token—to carry out these actions, as depicted in figure 3.13. Then we can limit their privileges using Roles and Role bindings, again making sure that we are following the principle of least privilege. We don't want a situation in which a Pod in our cluster has unrestricted access like our `system:masters` group had. The good news is that this default group is not applied to Service Accounts in the same way it was to our admin user.

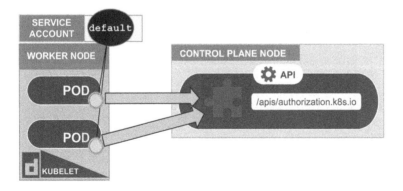

Figure 3.13   Service Accounts mounted to Pods can access the API in the same way users can.

Service Accounts are namespace-scoped resources. You'll find at least one in each namespace, and that one, called the default Service Account, is created automatically each time you generate a new namespace. Let's try it!

```
root@kind-control-plane:/# kubectl create ns web
namespace/web created
root@kind-control-plane:/# kubectl get sa -n web
NAME       SECRETS   AGE
default    1         10s
```

This default Service Account is created automatically; you don't have to do anything
special to make this default behavior happen. If we run the command `kubectl
describe secret -n web`, we can see the token that is also automatically generated
with the Service Account as well:

```
root@kind-control-plane:/# kubectl describe sa -n web
Name:                 default
Namespace:            web
Labels:               <none>
Annotations:          <none>
Image pull secrets:   <none>
Mountable secrets:    default-token-mv8xd
Tokens:               default-token-mv8xd
Events:               <none>
```

Furthermore, you can cat out the token and reveal its value with the command
`kubectl describe secret default-token-mv8xd -n web`:

```
root@kind-control-plane:/# kubectl describe secret default-token-mv8xd -n
   web
Name:          default-token-mv8xd
Namespace:     web
Labels:        <none>
Annotations:   kubernetes.io/service-account.name: default
               kubernetes.io/service-account.uid: b0f4ff77-80be-44ab-85b3-
   b6f662678fff

Type:   kubernetes.io/service-account-token

Data
====
namespace:  3 bytes
token:
```
```
   eyJhbGciOiJSUzI1NiIsImtpZCI6IllyN3NCd1JPOHZMbkhFZ3BLQkVBbUloZGx0eU5JSEF
   kS3JuUFRxS3dwWGsifQ.eyJpc3MiOiJrdWJlcm5ldGVzL3NlcnZpY2VhY2NvdW50Iiwia3V
   iZXJuZXRlcy5pby9zZXJ2aWNlYWNjb3VudC9uYW1lc3BhY2UiOiJ3ZWIiLCJrdWJlcm5ldG
   VzLmlvL3NlcnZpY2VhY2NvdW50L3NlY3JldC5uYW1lIjoiZGVmYXVsdC10b2tlbi1tdjh4Z
   CIsImt1YmVybmV0ZXMuaW8vc2VydmljZWFjY291bnQvc2VydmljZS1hY2NvdW50Lm5hbWUi
   OiJkZWZhdWx0Iiwia3ViZXJuZXRlcy5pby9zZXJ2aWNlYWNjb3VudC9zZXJ2aWNlLWFjY29
   1bnQudWlkIjoiYjBmNGZmNzctODBiZS00NGFiLTg1YjMtYjZmNjYyNjc4ZmZmIiwic3ViIj
   oic3lzdGVtOnNlcnZpY2VhY2NvdW50OndlYjpkZWZhdWx0In0.DoBREFRm9pOUnSfqaI4qe
   mDGFKA5nkXBfXePPQscAm8C-S4an0X6JtcQShRp04WrDQzqGYCQ2nnCldxdxCPd8BPwBV-
   xBzsidL1Cwg-
   iXQTElvJLIx0N6CB9FGpiFBBHFY5GRTtX3LFBcWqoUoqNmyDUqJJnlNEKqGzy5-
   4bjjMNOQ5JYywtjm50cxiGE2flORBjU7FBzZVWmvzo2XhtVR18LWUdomaZ1IwESXFU5HZNe
   sK-1MqcvD4C5wWc9igVBBxFJBoMJ06Z_Afi9vitnCtCYarQHcg66RvOVK-
   xyrc00RtjQbFLIlrjy68F3zG4BrvU9ChQOuMPAbCkG1ay4g
```
```
ca.crt:        1066 bytes
```

Technically, we can use this token (as a user) to authenticate with the Kubernetes API. This is why the default `view` Role doesn't allow viewing the Service Accounts and why we are hesitant to give read access of our Secrets to any user. These tokens can be used outside of the cluster as well.

When we create a Pod, this default Service Account is automatically mounted to the Pod, so the Pod can authenticate to the Kubernetes API. Let's run the command `kubectl get po nginx -o yaml | grep volumeMounts -A14` to list the Service Account within the Pod YAML. You'll see that the default Service Account is, in fact, mounted to the Pod at the path `/var/run/secrets/kubernetes.io/serviceaccount`:

```
root@kind-control-plane:/# kubectl get po nginx -o yaml | grep volumeMounts
➥ -A14
    volumeMounts:
    - mountPath: /var/run/secrets/kubernetes.io/serviceaccount
      name: kube-api-access-nhxf2
      readOnly: true
  dnsPolicy: ClusterFirst
  enableServiceLinks: true
  nodeName: kind-worker2
  preemptionPolicy: PreemptLowerPriority
  priority: 0
  restartPolicy: Always
  schedulerName: default-scheduler
  securityContext: {}
  serviceAccount: default
  serviceAccountName: default
  terminationGracePeriodSeconds: 30
```

If we exec into the Pod, we can view the token in the same manner as we did before by describing the Secret. To get a shell into the Pod's container and `cat` out the token, we can run the command `kubectl exec -it nginx --sh`, followed by `cat /var/run/secrets/kubernetes.io/serviceaccount/token` (# indicates that you have successfully entered a shell inside the container):

```
root@kind-control-plane:/# kubectl exec -it nginx --sh
# cat /var/run/secrets/kubernetes.io/serviceaccount/token
eyJhbGciOiJSUzI1NiIsImtpZCI6IllyN3NCd1JPOHZMbkhFZ3BLQkVBbUloZGx0eU5JSEFFkS3J
➥ uUFRxS3dwWGsifQ.eyJhdWQiOlsiaHR0cHM6Ly9rdWJlcm5ldGVzLmRlZmF1bHQuc3ZjLmN
➥ sdXN0ZXIubG9jYWwiXSwiZXhwIjoxNjgwMTQ0NDMxLCJpYXQiOjE2NDg2MDg0MzEsImlzcy
➥ I6Imh0dHBzOi8va3ViZXJuZXRlcy5kZWZhdWx0LnN2Yy5jbHVzdGVyLmxvY2FsIiwia3ViZ
➥ XJuZXRlcy5pbyI6eyJuYW1lc3BhY2UiOiJkZWZhdWx0IiwicG9kIjp7Im5hbWUiOiJuZ2lu
➥ eCIsInVpZCI6ImRmMzE3OTA3LTgwNTAtNDJmMS05ZWRmLTNhNDY2NzU4M2E5NiJ9LCJzZXJ
➥ 2aWNlYWNjb3VudCI6eyJuYW1lIjoiZGVmYXVsdCIsInVpZCI6ImRkMjlkZWEzLTkyMjMtNG
➥ QyOC1iOGE1LWUwODIxNTU1NGRjZCJ9LCJ3YXJuYWZ0ZXIiOjE2NDg2MTIwMzh9LCJuYmYiO
➥ jE2NDg2MDg0MzEsInN1YiI6InN5c3RlbTpzZXJ2aWNlYWNjb3VudDpkZWZhdWx0Om5lZmF1
➥ bHQifQ.ECeBokD1IbvCbBOIi6yiWtV1VIPABtxwnXmtudiQcRdmglQX06MVBEdCVJ4PT_rb
➥ nS7oB5fNAYFU2-8xU0EcDofeJH6IFEkALaI09TLCcha5YnQ65C6J1aKV-
➥ 58BR2I9aIZDb9uCJ247nyrDc075e2nf5zuBcfX82X5Yl0qAUtuiWDG-
➥ HPIwLfVnWYj9AasiFOMAMVaM_Ydsgru1U2vHwGFi-
➥ 7vo2CITU33X3NoTyDCSuNaNlAcB08_aWJuOYpQFtlAzpHQJR0XqGveIqu7cCMBd4XuD-
➥ m9AQDpkUZY59GOsJINCzkKo0cH1_nWx_PU42-drEwHU8m1HEdGwsAhNRg#
```

If we don't want to automatically mount the token to every Pod that we create, then we can turn this feature off from the serviceAccount itself, or we can dismount the token for certain Pods in the Pod YAML specification, as depicted in figure 3.14. We can even do both in case our team members accidentally forget to address this for the Pods they create.

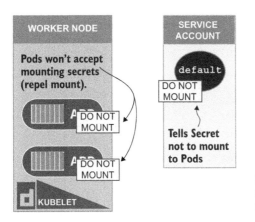

Figure 3.14 You can choose to disable mounting Secrets from the Service Account or the Pod or both.

Let's create a new Service Account and tell the Service Account not to mount the token to the Pod automatically. The quickest way to do this is to create the framework for the Service Account YAML and then modify it in place with the command kubectl create sa nomount-sa --dry-run=client -o yaml > nomount-sa.yaml. Add the automount-ServiceAccountToken: false to the end of the file nomount-sa.yaml with the command echo "automountServiceAccountToken: false" >> nomount-sa.yaml:

```
root@kind-control-plane:/# echo "automountServiceAccountToken: false" >>
  nomount-sa.yaml
root@kind-control-plane:/# cat nomount-sa.yaml
apiVersion: v1
kind: ServiceAccount
metadata:
  creationTimestamp: null
  name: nomount-sa
automountServiceAccountToken: false
```

Now that we have the YAML all set, we can create the Service Account object with the command kubectl create -f nomount-sa.yaml. If we create a new Pod and use this Service Account, we won't see it mounted at all. Let's create a new Pod named no-mount and specify within the YAML to use this new Service Account, much like figure 3.15.

We'll use the same shortcut method of outputting a skeleton of the YAML manifest and modifying it afterward with the command kubectl run no-mount --image nginx --dry-run=client -o yaml > no-mount-pod.yaml.

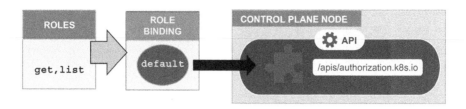

Figure 3.15   A Role subject can be a user, group, or Service Account in authorizing against Kubernetes.

> **NOTE**   If you've created a new kind cluster since the last chapter, you'll need to install Vim so you can edit the file. Use the command `apt update && apt install -y vim`.

Now that we have that file locally, we can edit it using our Vim text editor, so type the command `vim no-mount-pod.yaml` to open it. Just under the spec, indented two spaces, you should add `serviceAccountName: nomount-sa`. It will look like this:

```
apiVersion: v1
kind: Pod
metadata:
  creationTimestamp: null
  labels:
    run: no-mount
  name: no-mount
spec:
  serviceAccountName: nomount-sa
  containers:
  - image: nginx
    name: no-mount
    resources: {}
  dnsPolicy: ClusterFirst
  restartPolicy: Always
status: {}
```

We have explicitly told the Pod to use this Service Account, so let's create the Pod and inspect it with the commands `kubectl create -f no-mount-pod.yaml` and `kubectl get po no-mount -o yaml | grep volumeMounts -A14`. You will notice that the correct Service Account is used, and you don't see any volume mounts. This is a good thing.

```
root@kind-control-plane:/# kubectl get po no-mount -o yaml | grep
⮑  serviceAccount
  serviceAccount: nomount-sa
  serviceAccountName: nomount-sa
root@kind-control-plane:/# kubectl get po no-mount -o yaml | grep
⮑  volumeMounts -A14
root@kind-control-plane:/#
```

When creating yet another Pod, we'll use the default token, which is set to automatically mount tokens to Pods, but we'll explicitly tell it not to during the creation of our

Pod. Create a new Pod YAML file with the command `kubectl run default-no-mount --image nginx --dry-run=client -o yaml > default-no-mount-pod.yaml`. Again, let's open the file with Vim; just below the spec, indented two spaces, insert `auto-mountServiceAccountToken: false`. We don't have to tell the Pod to use the default token, because, if not specified, it will use the default Service Account automatically. This is the case for all Pods by default. The Pod YAML will look like this:

```
apiVersion: v1
kind: Pod
metadata:
  creationTimestamp: null
  labels:
    run: default-no-mount
  name: default-no-mount
spec:
  automountServiceAccountToken: false
  containers:
  - image: nginx
    name: default-no-mount
    resources: {}
  dnsPolicy: ClusterFirst
  restartPolicy: Always
status: {}
```

Let's create the Pod with the command `kubectl create -f default-no-mount-pod.yaml`. We'll see the default Service Account used with the Pod, but no volume mounts, which is what we want.

```
root@kind-control-plane:/# kubectl get po default-no-mount -o yaml | grep
➥ serviceAccount
  serviceAccount: default
  serviceAccountName: default
root@kind-control-plane:/# kubectl get po default-no-mount -o yaml | grep
➥ volumeMounts -A14
root@kind-control-plane:/#
```

Now that we've learned about creating Service Accounts and mounting them to Pods (or explicitly not mounting them to Pods), let's review assigning Roles and Role bindings to Service Accounts. This happens similarly to creating any other Role or Role binding, but the subject is a Service Account instead of a user or a group. Start by creating a Role that will only allow the action `list` for the resource `pods`. To do this, we can run the command `kubectl create role pod-list --verb=list --resource=pods`. We'll create the Role binding named `pod-list-bind` to bind the Service Account to the Role `pod-list` for the Service Account `nomount-sa` by running `kubectl create rolebind-ing pod-list-bind --role=pod-list --serviceaccount=default:nomount-sa`:

```
root@kind-control-plane:/# kubectl create role pod-list --verb=list -
➥ resource=pods
role.rbac.authorization.k8s.io/pod-list created
```

```
root@kind-control-plane:/# kubectl create rolebinding pod-list-bind -
➥ role=pod-list --serviceaccount=default:nomount-sa
rolebinding.rbac.authorization.k8s.io/pod-list-bind created
```

To test that our Role and Role binding worked, we can use the `kubectl auth can-i` command and determine if we can list Pods in this Service Account. To do this, we'll run the command `kubectl auth can-i list pods --as system:serviceaccount :default:nomount-sa`:

```
root@kind-control-plane:/# kubectl auth can-i list pods --as
➥ system:serviceaccount:default:nomount-sa
yes
```

The Service Account is addressed as `system:serviceaccount:default:nomount-sa` because this is the username of the Service Account according to the RBAC plugin. This is the perspective from which we are looking at the Service Account, so we need to address it with the `system:serviceaccount` prefix, followed by the namespace (in our case, it was `default`), and then the Service Account API resource name. Congratulations! You have created a Service Account and assigned it to a Role via a Role binding in Kubernetes!

You can now use this Service Account for multiple Pods at the same time, as long as those Pods exist within the same namespace. You can never use a Service Account from a different namespace for a Pod. Also, to use the `nomount-sa` service account for new Pods, you'll have to specify the Service Account to use in the Pod YAML for each Pod, as we did in the previous example. You might think about deleting the default Service Account, but this is not possible. The Service Account resource has its own controller that automatically creates it when we generate a new namespace.

Exam exercises

Create a new Service Account named `secure-sa`, and create a Pod that uses this Service Account. Make sure the token is not exposed to the Pod.

Create a new cluster Role named `acme-corp-role` that will allow the `create` action on Deployments, replicates, and DaemonSets. Bind that cluster Role to the Service Account `secure-sa` and make sure the Service Account can only create the assigned resources within the default namespace and nowhere else. Use `auth can-i` to verify that the `secure-sa` Service Account cannot create Deployments in the `kube-system` namespace, and output the result of the command plus the command itself to a file and share that file.

Summary

- Anything that tries to access Kubernetes must be authenticated via a certificate carrying a token with which to authenticate.
- The authentication plugin is used in Kubernetes to provide a mechanism to accept or deny user requests.

- Kubernetes has its own certificate-signing request object, which can sign certificates to make them valid for a user or anything trying to access the Kubernetes API.

- A common plugin called role-based access control (RBAC) is used to give permissions to users in a Kubernetes cluster.

- Users and groups are arbitrary meanings in Kubernetes, so there is no user database or directory structure. The certificate is the only thing that's checked, so the user or group can be any name.

- You can assign RBAC permissions via Roles, cluster Roles, Role bindings, and cluster Role bindings, each applied to different use cases.

- All combinations of Roles, cluster Roles, Role bindings, and cluster Role bindings can be used for the exam except for one: cluster Role binding to Roles.

- There are two main subjects in RBAC: the user and Service Accounts. Users are not a managed resource in the Kubernetes API, whereas Service Accounts are.

- When creating a user, the common name inside the certificate-signing request is required. You can generate a client certificate from the Kubernetes API, which is its own certificate authority.

- When creating a Role for the exam, you can use the dry run option and save yourself some time typing the YAML for a Role where values need to be added.

- Built-in groups are different than regular groups in Kubernetes. Built-in groups are managed by the API server and cannot be modified.

- Service Accounts are automatically created when new namespaces are created. The token inside of a Service Account is mounted to a Pod unless otherwise specified in the YAML manifest.

- To prevent the token from automatically mounting to a Pod, you can both add an instruction to your Pod YAML and disable mounting from the Service Account by adding an instruction to your Service Account YAML. You can also disable the mounting of a token when you first create a Service Account.

- A useful tool during the exam is called `kubectl auth can-I`, and it can test permissions for users and Service Accounts.

Deploying applications in Kubernetes

This chapter covers

- Scheduling Pods to nodes
- Creating multiple containers within a Pod
- Using the Helm templating engine
- Requesting and limiting the resources a Pod can take
- Passing configuration data to Pods

In this chapter, we'll shift our focus to the workloads and scheduling part of the exam objectives and focus on the many different aspects of scheduling and their intricacies. You will realize that one size doesn't fit all, which creates freedom to run an application in the environment that's best for containerized applications. This includes the ability to reserve resources from the underlying infrastructure as well as decouple components such as configuration information and sensitive data within.

The workloads and scheduling domain

This chapter covers part of the workloads and scheduling domain of the CKA curriculum. This domain covers how we run applications on Kubernetes. It encompasses the following competencies.

Competency	Chapter section
Use ConfigMaps and Secrets to configure applications.	4.3
Understand how resource limits can affect Pod scheduling.	4.3
Awareness of manifest management and common templating tools.	4.2
Understand the primitives used to create robust, self-healing application Deployments.	4.1

4.1 Scheduling applications

Deploying applications to run on Kubernetes is called *scheduling*, which makes sense when you think of it from the perspective of running a Pod on a node. There are many ways to deploy applications (schedule Pods) to Kubernetes. As we've discovered in previous chapters, the Kubernetes component that controls the assignment of a Pod to a node is called the *scheduler*. The scheduler will not only tell the Pod to run on a specific node, but it will also ensure that the resources are available on the node so that the Pod can run successfully, as depicted in figure 4.1.

The CKA exam will test your knowledge of creating and updating application Deployments. This includes scheduling to certain nodes, according to their labels. For

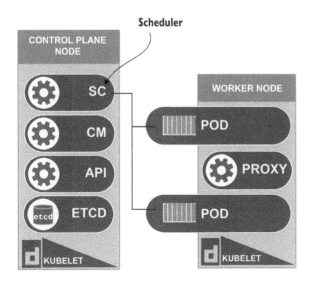

Figure 4.1 The scheduler allows the Pod to run on the worker node after verifying resource availability.

example, an exam prompt might say, "Apply the label 'disk=ssd' to the worker node named 'kind-worker' and schedule a Pod named 'ssd-pod' to the 'kind-worker' node by using node selector." To better approach a task like this when we sit for the exam, let's create a new Pod from YAML with the command k run ssd-pod --image=nginx --dry-run=client -o yaml > ssd-pod.yaml. This command will save the Pod YAML in a file named ssd-pod.yaml. Before we start modifying the YAML, we have to show the existing labels on each node in our cluster with the command k get no --show-labels:

```
root@kind-control-plane:/# k get no --show-labels
NAME                STATUS     ROLES                  AGE    VERSION    LABELS
kind-control-plane  Ready      control-plane,master   13d    v1.23.4
  beta.kubernetes.io/arch=amd64,beta.kubernetes.io/os=linux,kubernetes.io
  /arch=amd64,kubernetes.io/hostname=kind-control-
  plane,kubernetes.io/os=linux,node-role.kubernetes.io/control-
  plane=,node-role.kubernetes.io/master=,node.kubernetes.io/exclude-from-
  external-load-balancers=
kind-worker         Ready      <none>                 13d    v1.23.4
  beta.kubernetes.io/arch=amd64,beta.kubernetes.io/os=linux,kubernetes.io
  /arch=amd64,kubernetes.io/hostname=kind-worker,kubernetes.io/os=linux
kind-worker2        Ready      <none>                 13d    v1.23.4
  beta.kubernetes.io/arch=amd64,beta.kubernetes.io/os=linux,kubernetes.io
  /arch=amd64,kubernetes.io/hostname=kind-worker2,kubernetes.io/os=linux
```

EXAM TIP   On the exam, there may not be a label pre-applied to the node. You can check the labels on a node with the command k get no --show-labels.

Let's apply a new label to the node named kind-worker that will signify that this node has an SSD disk as opposed to HDD. This way, the Pod can be scheduled to the kind-worker node by using a node selector. To apply a label to a node, we use the syntax key=value so we can select that label at a later time. To apply a label with the key disktype and value ssd, we can use the command k label no kind-worker disktype=ssd. Then we can run the show labels command again to see that the label was applied successfully.

```
root@kind-control-plane:/# k label no kind-worker disktype=ssd
node/kind-worker labeled
root@kind-control-plane:/# k get no --show-labels
NAME                STATUS     ROLES                  AGE    VERSION    LABELS
kind-control-plane  Ready      control-plane,master   13d    v1.23.4
  beta.kubernetes.io/arch=amd64,beta.kubernetes.io/os=linux,kubernetes.io
  /arch=amd64,kubernetes.io/hostname=kind-control-
  plane,kubernetes.io/os=linux,node-role.kubernetes.io/control-
  plane=,node-role.kubernetes.io/master=,node.kubernetes.io/exclude-from-
  external-load-balancers=
kind-worker         Ready      <none>                 13d    v1.23.4
  beta.kubernetes.io/arch=amd64,beta.kubernetes.io/os=linux,disktype=ssd,
  kubernetes.io/arch=amd64,kubernetes.io/hostname=kind-
  worker,kubernetes.io/os=linux
kind-worker2        Ready      <none>                 13d    v1.23.4
```

```
beta.kubernetes.io/arch=amd64,beta.kubernetes.io/os=linux,kubernetes.io
/arch=amd64,kubernetes.io/hostname=kind-worker2,kubernetes.io/os=linux
```

Now that the worker node is labeled, we can add the node selector to our Pod YAML to ensure that the Pod gets scheduled to this newly labeled node. Go ahead and open the file `ssd-pod.yaml` in a text editor like Vim (any text editor will do). Once we have it open, we can add the line `nodeSelector:` in line with the word containers, and just below that add `disktype: ssd` indented two spaces. We indent two spaces to indicate that the specified parameters are grouped with the previous block above it (e.g., `disktype` is contained within the block), as shown in figure 4.2.

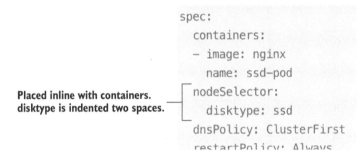

Placed inline with containers. disktype is indented two spaces.

```
spec:
  containers:
  - image: nginx
    name: ssd-pod
  nodeSelector:
    disktype: ssd
  dnsPolicy: ClusterFirst
  restartPolicy: Always
```

Figure 4.2 Selecting the type of node to schedule a Pod to, based on the node label `disk=ssd`

After you've added this, you can save the file. We can use the command `k apply -f ssd-pod.yaml` to create the Pod and schedule it to the node, which we specified in the Pod YAML by using the node selector. Let's now verify that the Pod was scheduled to the intended node by running the command `k get po -o wide`:

```
root@kind-control-plane:/# k get po -o wide
NAME        READY    STATUS     RESTARTS    AGE    IP          NODE
 NOMINATED NODE     READINESS GATES
ssd-pod    1/1      Running    0           25s    10.244.1.2  kind-worker
 <none>             <none>
```

Looks like the Pod was scheduled to the correct node, and the rules for the node selector were applied successfully. Great job!

There are other scenarios in which you would want to change how Pods are scheduled. In most cases, however, you want to limit your alterations to scheduling in Kubernetes. Keep in mind that changing the default rules for scheduling changes the primary functionality of Kubernetes, which is to promote high availability and fault tolerance. You may have a specific need to schedule Pods to certain nodes (as in the previous task), but normally the scheduler is going to distribute workloads properly and efficiently. In figure 4.3, you will see the default labels for both the control plane node and the worker nodes, with the addition of the `disktype` label we applied to `kind-worker` earlier in this chapter.

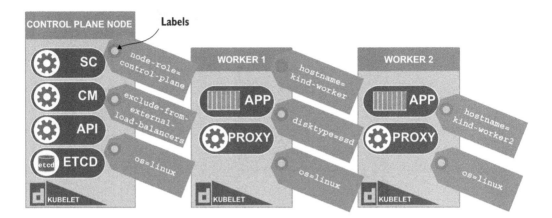

Figure 4.3   All nodes can have different labels that you can select and schedule Pods to by selecting those labels.

4.1.1   Node selectors

As we discussed in the previous section, there may come a time when you'd like to schedule a Pod to a specific node. Perhaps that node has a certain type of CPU or memory that is optimized for your workload. There are many things we can use inside of our Pod YAML (and Deployment YAML) that will help solve this. Let's talk about a couple of them now—the node selector and the node name attribute inside of the manifest. We can add either one (not both) to the YAML manifest and be able to schedule the Pod on a specific node. What's the difference? Well, the node selector is a little bit more flexible, as it identifies a node by its labels. This way, the labels can be applied to many nodes, not just one.

Adding a node name instead of a node selector is just the opposite. You can specify the specific node by name, but as we know, we can't have two nodes with the same name, so that limits our options a bit. What if we have node failure? What if the node runs out of resources? Creating a single point of failure by scheduling a Pod to only a single node is not the best idea. As you'll see in figure 4.4, you can force a Pod to be scheduled to a specific node by label or by name.

A DaemonSet is a type of Kubernetes object that ensures that one Pod replica is always running on every single node in the cluster at all times. Even if you delete the Pod, the DaemonSet will respawn the Pod on any node that's missing that Daemon-Set's Pod. DaemonSets use the node name attribute for all Pods within a DaemonSet to schedule Pods to specific nodes by their name. This ensures that one and only one Pod is assigned to a node, and by using the node name, they ensure that there aren't accidentally two Pods running on a single node, as depicted in figure 4.5 with

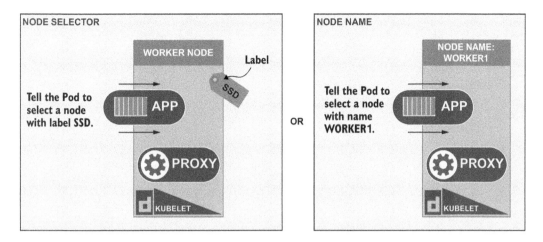

Figure 4.4   When scheduling a Pod, you can force the node to which it is scheduled based on the node's name or label.

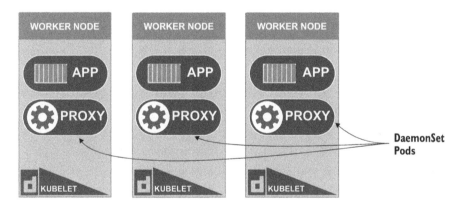

Figure 4.5   The kube-proxy Pods are a part of a DaemonSet and reside on each node in the cluster.

the kube-proxy Pod being an example of one DaemonSet that runs in every Kubernetes cluster.

Let's look at one of the DaemonSet Pods running in our cluster with the command `k -n kube-system get po kindnet-2tlqh -o yaml | grep nodeName -a3`, and you'll see output similar to figure 4.6.

In this command, we are getting the YAML output of the kindnet DaemonSet Pod, which resides in the `kube-system` namespace. Then, we can search through the YAML and find the instance of the node name with the grep tool. As you can see, the node name is added to the Pod YAML for this DaemonSet Pod. Remember, the Pod name will be different for your cluster, so replace the name `kindnet-2tlqh` with the Pod

```
root@kind-control-plane:/# k -n kube-system get po kindnet-2tlqh -o yaml | grep nodeName -a3
  dnsPolicy: ClusterFirst
  enableServiceLinks: true
  hostNetwork: true
  nodeName: kind-control-plane  ◄────────────┐
  preemptionPolicy: PreemptLowerPriority                │
  priority: 0                                           │
  restartPolicy: Always                                 │
                                                        │
```

**This Pod will always be scheduled to
the node named kind-control-plane.**

Figure 4.6 Scheduling a Pod by specifying the node name in the Pod YAML

name in your cluster. The command to retrieve the Pod names is k get po -A. Also, to look at the DaemonSets running in your cluster, type the command k get ds.

Hopefully, you can better understand where the node name is used and why it's used. In most cases, you will use a node selector, and you can probably see the benefits much more clearly. The node selector is used in many more scenarios, as it can apply to many nodes, selecting the node labels. For example, you can label nodes with disk=ssd to indicate that they have solid-state drives, which may make a difference for applications that require high disk I/O.

EXAM TIP You may see a node selector or node name on the exam, where the question might ask you to add the necessary values to an existing Pod YAML. So, become familiar with the placement and proper syntax used here.

The same goes for CPU or memory-intensive applications, as the node's resources have a direct effect on how the applications will run inside of Pods running containers. To take a look at how node selectors are used in our cluster, look no further than the core DNS Pods that are already running in the kube-system namespace. To see the Pod YAML for a CoreDNS Pod, we'll use the same method we did with the DaemonSet Pods with the command k -n kube-system get po coredns-64897985d-4th9h -o yaml | grep nodeSelector -a4, and you'll see output similar to figure 4.7.

NOTE The name of your CoreDNS Pod will be different, so use the command k -n kube-system get po to find your unique name.

In this command, we are getting the Pod YAML output for the CoreDNS Pod, which resides in the kube-system namespace, and searching for the word nodeSelector. Remember, the Pod name will be different for your cluster, so replace the name coredns-64897985d-4th9h with the Pod name in your cluster. The command to retrieve the Pod names is k get po -A. Now that we've taken a look at node names and node selectors in this section, as well as a useful way to edit Kubernetes objects inline, let's move on to another scheduling technique, called *affinity*, to favor certain nodes over others.

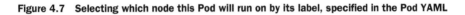

```
root@kind-control-plane:/# k -n kube-system get po coredns-64897985d-4th9h -o yaml | grep nodeSelector -a4
      readOnly: true
  dnsPolicy: Default
  enableServiceLinks: true
  nodeName: kind-control-plane
  nodeSelector:
    kubernetes.io/os: linux  ◄─────
  preemptionPolicy: PreemptLowerPriority
  priority: 2000000000
  priorityClassName: system-cluster-critical
```

**This Pod will be scheduled to nodes with
the label kubernetes.io/os = linux.**

Figure 4.7   Selecting which node this Pod will run on by its label, specified in the Pod YAML

4.1.2   *Node and Pod affinity*

As we know, labels can be applied to both Pods and nodes. We can use these labels to apply affinity. Affinity is a lot like a node selector, but its rules are more expressive. For example, a node selector rule will select a node with a label, whereas an affinity rule will prefer a node with a label but also accept scheduling to another node if that node label is not present.

To better understand affinity, we have to understand the problem it solves. There is an inherent problem in larger Kubernetes clusters where not only Pods come and go but nodes do as well. So, setting hard rules for the Pod to be scheduled to a node based on its name or label doesn't suffice. Instead of alienating a Pod if a node is not present, affinity provides a more flexible ruleset, so applications can be scheduled to a cluster environment that is constantly changing. As you see in figure 4.8, you can set rules that prefer one node, but if that node is unavailable, it will still have the option to be scheduled to a second node.

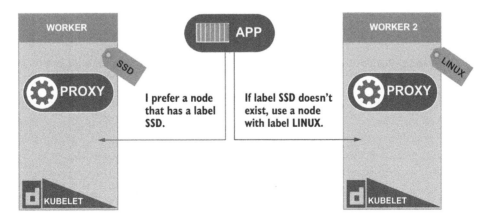

**Figure 4.8   Affinity prefers the Pod be scheduled to a node with the label SSD but will schedule to
node LINUX if none exists.**

Let's go through an example of setting an affinity rule. We'll start with a brand-new Pod, and we'll use the dry run to create a template for our Pod YAML, as we did previously with the command `k run affinity --image nginx --dry-run=client -o yaml > affinity.yaml`. Once we have a file named `affinity.yaml` in our current directory, let's open it up in a text editor and add our node affinity rules. Just below the spec, in line with `containers`, add `affinity:` to the line. Indent two spaces and add `nodeAffinity:`, followed by `requiredDuringSchedulingIgnoredDuringExecution:`. See figure 4.9 for the remaining YAML syntax, as it is quite extensive.

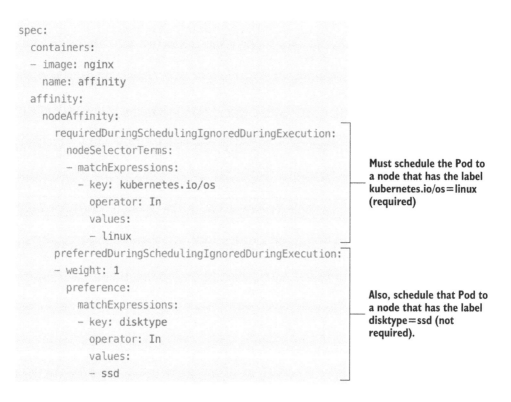

```
spec:
  containers:
  - image: nginx
    name: affinity
  affinity:
    nodeAffinity:
      requiredDuringSchedulingIgnoredDuringExecution:
        nodeSelectorTerms:
        - matchExpressions:
          - key: kubernetes.io/os
            operator: In
            values:
            - linux
      preferredDuringSchedulingIgnoredDuringExecution:
      - weight: 1
        preference:
          matchExpressions:
          - key: disktype
            operator: In
            values:
            - ssd
```

Must schedule the Pod to a node that has the label kubernetes.io/os=linux (required)

Also, schedule that Pod to a node that has the label disktype=ssd (not required).

Figure 4.9   Variations of affinity that prefer to schedule a Pod to a node based on certain expressions

Below node affinity, where we set the required attribute, the scheduler can't schedule the Pod unless this rule is met. This functions like `nodeSelector`, but with a more expressive syntax. The preferred attribute, however, is optional for the scheduler. If there isn't a node that matches this preference, then the Pod will still be scheduled. Also, you can specify a weight between 1 and 100 for each preferred rule, which the scheduler evaluates based on the total weight, based on the score of other priority functions for the node. Nodes with the highest total score will be prioritized. Now that we've added our affinity rules, let's schedule our Pod with the command `k apply -f affinity.yaml`:

```
root@kind-control-plane:/# k apply -f affinity.yaml
pod/affinity created
root@kind-control-plane:/# k get po -o wide
NAME            READY   STATUS    RESTARTS   AGE   IP           NODE
↳               NOMINATED NODE   READINESS GATES
affinity        1/1     Running   0          14s   10.244.1.6   kind-
↳ worker2 <none>                 <none>
pod-tolerate    1/1     Running   0          24h   10.244.2.16  kind-worker
↳       <none>                   <none>
```

From the output of the command k get po -o wide, we see that the Pod was scheduled
to a node that did not have the disktype=ssd label (kind-worker2). That's because
the weight that we set for this preferred rule was too low, and because there was
another Pod already running on kind-worker, the node kind-worker2 had a higher
total weight overall being that it did not already have a Pod running on it (higher
weight equals greater probability that a Pod will be scheduled). If you didn't quite follow, or if you'd like to check your work, apply this YAML to create your Pod with the
command k apply -f https:/ /raw.githubusercontent.com/chadmcrowell/k8s/
main/manifests/pod-node-affinity.yaml.

In the same vein as node affinity is inter-Pod affinity, which is the preference for
a node based on other Pods that are already on that node. To put it in simpler
terms, if a Pod already exists on the node (e.g., nginx), then go ahead and schedule
a new Pod to that same node (the node with the nginx Pod on it), as depicted in figure 4.10. The way Kubernetes checks if the Pod exists is by its label. This works well
with Pods that need to run on the same node because of increased performance or
latency requirements.

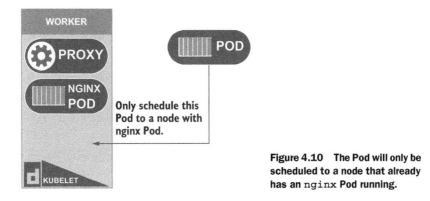

Only schedule this
Pod to a node with
nginx Pod.

**Figure 4.10 The Pod will only be
scheduled to a node that already
has an nginx Pod running.**

To demonstrate inter-Pod affinity, let's first create a Pod that has the label run=nginx
with the command k run nginx --image=nginx. Now, let's go ahead and use the
same YAML file that we were using for node affinity but change only a few lines,
because, as you will see, setting the inter-Pod affinity is very similar to how we set
node affinity. If you don't already have the previous YAML file, you can download it

using curl and the -O flag to save the file with the same name using the command curl -O https://raw.githubusercontent.com/chadmcrowell/k8s/main/manifests/pod-node-affinity.yaml.

Go ahead and open the file in your text editor and change the name of the Pod to pod-affinity to prevent a naming conflict if you still have the Pod running from the previous demonstration. In addition, change nodeAffinity to podAffinity; change the line nodeSelectorTerms: to - labelSelector:; remove the hyphen (-) from match-Expressions; and change the key to run and value to nginx.

Finally, add the topologyKey below the values to be in line with the word label-Selector. The topology key is required for inter-Pod affinity and simply indicates the node label key. In this case, all nodes in our cluster have the kubernetes.io/hostname key, so this will match all nodes. See figure 4.11 for a comparison between node affinity and inter-Pod affinity. You can remove everything below the topology key, as in this example we're just focusing on the inter-Pod affinity required rule.

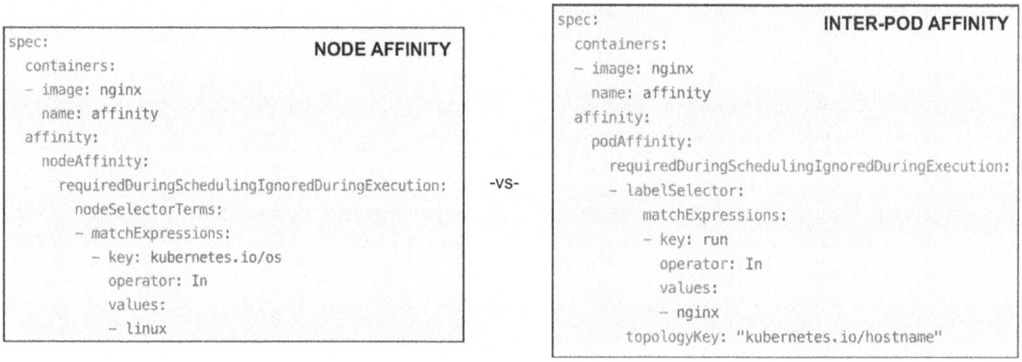

```
spec:                                           NODE AFFINITY
  containers:
  - image: nginx
    name: affinity
  affinity:
    nodeAffinity:
      requiredDuringSchedulingIgnoredDuringExecution:        -vs-
        nodeSelectorTerms:
        - matchExpressions:
          - key: kubernetes.io/os
            operator: In
            values:
            - linux
```

```
spec:                                      INTER-POD AFFINITY
  containers:
  - image: nginx
    name: affinity
  affinity:
    podAffinity:
      requiredDuringSchedulingIgnoredDuringExecution:
      - labelSelector:
          matchExpressions:
          - key: run
            operator: In
            values:
            - nginx
        topologyKey: "kubernetes.io/hostname"
```

Figure 4.11   How inter-Pod affinity is different than node affinity in its structure within the Pod YAML

Now that our nginx Pod is running and we've typed out the YAML for our new Pod with inter-Pod affinity rules, we can go ahead and schedule the Pod with the command k apply -f pod-node-affinity.yaml. Just after you schedule the Pod, you should see that the Pod has been scheduled to the same node as the Pod named nginx by running the command k get po -o wide, and you'll see an output similar to figure 4.12.

You can see how, under normal circumstances, the Pod would have been scheduled to the node named kind-worker, but because we told the scheduler to find all Pods with the run=nginx label and schedule a Pod named pod-affinity to that very same node, it overruled the default scheduler settings. If you are getting different results, or maybe you can't get your Pod to be scheduled at all, please compare what you have to the YAML in this file, which you can download using the command curl -O https://raw.githubusercontent.com/chadmcrowell/k8s/main/manifests/pod-with-pod-affinty.yaml.

```
root@kind-control-plane:/# k run nginx --image=nginx
pod/nginx created
root@kind-control-plane:/# vim pod-node-affinity.yaml
root@kind-control-plane:/# k apply -f pod-node-affinity.yaml
pod/pod-affinity created
root@kind-control-plane:/# k get po -o wide
NAME           READY   STATUS    RESTARTS   AGE     IP           NODE
affinity       1/1     Running   0          5d22h   10.244.1.6   kind-worker2
nginx          1/1     Running   0          50s     10.244.1.7   kind-worker2
pod-affinity   1/1     Running   0          24s     10.244.1.8   kind-worker2
pod-tolerate   1/1     Running   0          6d22h   10.244.2.16  kind-worker
```

Scheduled to the same node

Figure 4.12   The Pods have been scheduled to the same node based on their affinity rules.

Exam exercises

Apply the label `disk=ssd` to a node. Create a Pod named `fast` using the `nginx` image and make sure that it selects a node based on the label `disk=ssd`.

Edit the `fast` Pod using `k edit po fast` and change the node selector to `disk=slow`. Notice that the Pod cannot be changed and the YAML was saved to a temporary location. Take the YAML in `/tmp/` and apply it by force to delete and recreate the Pod using a single imperative command.

Create a new Pod named `ssd-pod` using the `nginx` image, and use node affinity to select nodes based on a weight of 1 to nodes that have a label `disk=ssd`. If the selection criteria don't match, it can also choose nodes that have the label `kubernetes .io/os=linux`.

4.2   Using Helm

With all the different methods to configure applications for Deployment in Kubernetes, therein lies a problem of misconfiguration and also developing redeployable components. For example, when creating Deployments with Services, Ingress, ConfigMaps, Roles, and Role bindings, it can be complex, and it's not always intuitive how the application developer intended for the application to run in order to operate according to best practices. Helm is a package manager for Kubernetes that supports templating to solve this problem.

Testing your knowledge of using Helm will be a part of the exam; therefore, it's important to understand what problem it solves and how to use it. Instead of having to rebuild each YAML file from scratch, they can be packaged up and stored in a repository for others to use and share. In addition to a template engine, much like a package manager in your favorite Linux distro (i.e., `apt` in Ubuntu), Helm allows you to pull down Helm charts from a repository (public or private) and install those Helm charts locally.

To install Helm on macOS, simply perform the command `brew install helm`. To install Helm on Windows, simply perform the command `choco install kubernetes-helm`. To install Helm on Ubuntu or Debian, perform the following commands to add Helm to your package repository and install using `apt`:

```
curl -fsSL -o get_helm.sh
↪ https://raw.githubusercontent.com/helm/helm/main/scripts/get-helm-3
chmod 700 get_helm.sh
./get_helm.sh
```

Once you get Helm installed, you can run the command `helm version --short`, and you'll see output similar to figure 4.13, which will be the version of Helm that is currently installed.

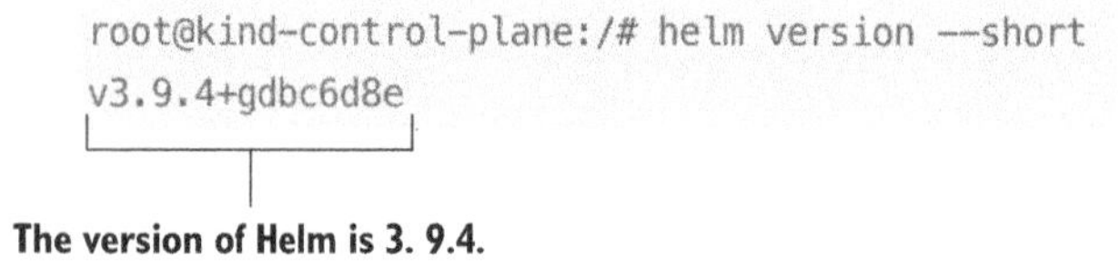

```
root@kind-control-plane:/# helm version --short
v3.9.4+gdbc6d8e
```

The version of Helm is 3. 9.4.

Figure 4.13 Show the version of Helm via the CLI.

Next, we can install a Helm chart, which is nothing more than a group of YAML manifests packaged up into an application that runs in Kubernetes. For Helm to connect to the cluster, it uses the same kubeconfig that `kubectl` uses. Being that Helm is using the same kubeconfig, it can perform the operations, which could be a good thing or a bad thing. For us, it's okay for now, as we'll need admin permissions to create the resources associated with our Helm chart.

We can really use any Helm chart from the public repository located at https://artifacthub.io/. To use a Helm chart, we first must add the repository where the Helm chart exists or else Helm won't know where to pull the chart from. We can run the command `helm repo add hashicorp https://helm.releases.hashicorp.com` to add the repository to Helm, and then run the command `helm repo list` to see that it's been added:

```
root@kind-control-plane:/# helm repo add hashicorp
↪ https://helm.releases.hashicorp.com
"hashicorp" has been added to your repositories
root@kind-control-plane:/# helm repo list
NAME          URL
hashicorp     https://helm.releases.hashicorp.com
```

Now that a repository has been added, we can search that repository for all available charts with the command `helm search repo vault`. You'll see that, within the repo HashiCorp, there's a Helm chart named `hashicorp/vault`, which we can use:

```
root@kind-control-plane:/# helm search repo vault
NAME              CHART VERSION   APP VERSION   DESCRIPTION
hashicorp/vault   0.21.0          1.11.2        Official HashiCorp
↪ Vault Chart
```

Let's add another repo! I thought it would be helpful to install a load balancer in our kind cluster. This will be useful later on when we talk about communication, in chapter 6. A load balancer in Kubernetes allows access to our application from outside the cluster. For example, if we were hosting a web application as a part of a Deployment in Kubernetes, we'd be able to expose it via the LoadBalancer Service. This way, visitors to your application could reach the frontend of the application via its IP address. For now, though, let's focus on adding the repo and installing the Helm chart.

We can add the repository just as we did with the HashiCorp repository using the command `helm repo add metallb https://metallb.github.io/metallb`.

```
root@kind-control-plane:/# helm repo add metallb
➥ https://metallb.github.io/metallb
"metallb" has been added to your repositories
```

Now that we have the repo added, we can search for `metallb` with the command `helm search repo metallb`:

```
root@kind-control-plane:/# helm search repo metallb
NAME                CHART VERSION    APP VERSION     DESCRIPTION
metallb/metallb     0.13.5           v0.13.5         A network load-balancer
➥ implementation for Kube...
```

Sure enough, there it is! Now, before we install it, let's talk about something called the *values file*. Now, we know that Helm is a templating engine. The templating engine takes a file that has values to plug into the template, that changes the configuration of our Helm chart. This values file is written in YAML and will look similar to figure 4.14 for the configuration of a Pod.

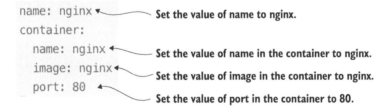

Figure 4.14 How to create a values file and apply values to Helm for a Pod manifest

Then, once we establish these values, the templating in the actual Helm chart looks similar to a regular Pod YAML file that we've created before, but instead of the values filled in, they use the templating syntax {{ .values.name }}, as shown in figure 4.15.

Now that we know what a template file does (it templatizes your YAML files), you may be asking how we apply the values file to our Helm chart. Well, we simply run the command `helm install` and use the `--values` flag. So, to install the MetalLB Helm

```
apiVersion: v1              POD YAML
kind: Pod
metadata:
  name: nginx
spec:
  containers:
  - image: nginx
    name: nginx
    ports:
    - containerPort: 80
```

-vs.-

```
apiVersion: v1              HELM CHART
kind: Pod
metadata:
  name: {{ .values.name }}
spec:
  containers:
  - image: {{ .values.container.image }}
    name: {{ .values.container.name }}
    ports:
    - containerPort: {{ .values.container.port }}
```

Figure 4.15   How a normal Pod YAML would look compared to a Helm chart with templated values

chart, perform the command `helm install metallb metallb/metallb --values values.yaml`. But wait! We haven't created the values file yet. Let's do this now using the following YAML and save it to a file named `values.yaml`:

```
address-pools:
 - name: default
   protocol: layer2
   addresses:
   - 172.18.255.200-172.18.255.250
```

The address range (172.18.255.200-250) is within the address range of your Docker bridge network (the range may be different for you). To find the `kind` Docker bridge CIDR, use the command `docker network inspect -f '{{.IPAM.Config}}' kind` (type `exit` to get out of `kind-control-plane` shell). Once you've created the `values.yaml` file, you can run the command `helm install metallb metallb/metallb --values values.yaml` (type `docker exec -it kind-control-plane bash` to get back into the `kind-control-plane` shell):

```
root@kind-control-plane:/# helm install metallb metallb/metallb --values
↦ values.yaml
NAME: metallb
LAST DEPLOYED: Tue Sep  6 19:06:07 2022
NAMESPACE: default
STATUS: deployed
REVISION: 1
TEST SUITE: None
NOTES:

MetalLB is now running in the cluster. Now you can configure it via its
↦ CRs. Please refer to the MetalLB official docs on how to use the CRs.
```

Now that we've deployed the MetalLB load balancer via Helm, we can see that it was more than just a single resource. It created a Deployment, a DaemonSet, four Secrets, two Service Accounts, and a ConfigMap, as shown in figure 4.16 (obtained by running

```
$ docker exec -it kind-control-plane bash                                    [14:1
root@kind-control-plane:/# alias k=kubectl
root@kind-control-plane:/# k get po,deploy,secret,sa,cm
NAME                                      READY   STATUS                   RESTARTS        AGE
pod/apache-74f79bcc68-57fq9               1/1     Running                  0               3d2h
pod/apache-74f79bcc68-g2qzx               1/1     Running                  0               3d2h
pod/apache-74f79bcc68-gjh2t               1/1     Running                  0               3d2h
pod/apache-74f79bcc68-j99s7               1/1     Running                  0               3d2h
pod/apache-74f79bcc68-n7tt6               1/1     Running                  0               3d2h
pod/metallb-controller-65d5586d7c-jmzcb   0/1     Running                  6 (3m11s ago)   8m21s
pod/metallb-speaker-76fw5                 0/1     CreateContainerConfigError  0            8m21s
pod/metallb-speaker-hx7xm                 0/1     Pending                  0               8m21s

NAME                               READY   UP-TO-DATE   AVAILABLE   AGE
deployment.apps/apache             5/5     5            5           3d2h
deployment.apps/metallb-controller 0/1     1            0           8m21s

NAME                            TYPE                 DATA   AGE
secret/sh.helm.release.v1.metallb.v1   helm.sh/release.v1   1      8m21s
secret/webhook-server-cert      Opaque               0      8m21s

NAME                            SECRETS   AGE
serviceaccount/default          0         20d
serviceaccount/metallb-controller   0     8m21s
serviceaccount/metallb-speaker  0         8m21s

NAME                     DATA   AGE
configmap/kube-root-ca.crt   1   20d
```

All these Kubernetes objects are created by running helm install.

Figure 4.16   Simplifying Kubernetes scheduling and creating multiple Kubernetes objects via a Helm chart

k get po,deploy,ds,secret,sa,cm). All we had to do was run helm install, and it installed all of that! Pretty cool, huh? It reminds me of when I'm at a restaurant and order a delicious meal. I have no idea how it's made or what all of the ingredients are; it just comes out of the kitchen piping hot and tastes so delicious!

To list the Helm charts we have installed, we can run the command helm ls:

```
root@kind-control-plane:/# helm ls
NAME       NAMESPACE     REVISION    UPDATED
              STATUS        CHART                       APP VERSION
metallb    default       1           2022-09-06 19:06:07.164270451 +0000 UTC
           deployed      metallb-0.13.5      v0.13.5
```

We'll come back to using MetalLB in chapter 6. For now, this was good practice using Helm and installing a Helm chart using custom values.

4.3   Pod metadata

After discussing scheduling at great length, let's talk about some of the customizations you can make before scheduling your applications in Kubernetes. There are several options, which we'll cover in this section, but as you can imagine, there's no one size that fits all. Not all Kubernetes objects (Deployments, Pods, Secrets, ConfigMaps, etc.)

are created in the same way. Sometimes you need to consider the underlying hardware, not only in terms of selecting nodes to schedule Pods to, as we discussed in sections 4.1.2 and 4.1.3, but also in terms of resource constraints, additional features, and unique characteristics that each application may need. Let's start with resource requests and limits, which will help us with scheduling a Pod to a node with adequate resources (CPU and RAM).

4.3.1 *Resource requests and limits*

Resource requests are much like labels in that they provide information to the scheduler that determines the node on which a Pod is scheduled to or placed on. The request comes in the form of a CPU and RAM minimum that the Pod requires to run optimally. The limit also comes in the form of a value of CPU or RAM but determines the maximum that the Pod should consume, versus the minimum. These two parameters don't have to be defined at the same time—meaning you can apply requests without limits and vice versa. In the same vein, you can specify a request for only CPU without specifying a request for RAM. So, these fields are not dependent on each other and are totally optional.

On the CKA exam, you will be tested on your knowledge about resource limits and how they can affect how Pods are scheduled. An example of an exam prompt might be "Node 'worker-1' has 500MB of memory and .5 CPU available. Schedule a Pod that would allow for this memory and CPU limitation, and still schedule to the node." Knowing how to modify the Pod YAML to change resource limits will enable you to successfully complete questions like this on exam day.

You can apply resource requests and limits for a Pod by adding it into the container spec via YAML. In line with the name and image of the container, you can add requests and limits as values below the resources. To best accomplish this (without having to know the exact placement within YAML), you can create a dry run of a Pod again by performing the command k run nginx2 --image=nginx --dry-run=client -o yaml > nginx2.yaml.

When you open the file in your favorite text editor, you'll already see a resources section. As we know from the YAML language, we can simply indent two spaces below the word resources and begin defining our requests and limits. The word resources is used to insert resource limits and requests. Resource requests are CPU and memory minimums that you can specify for Pods. Resource limits are the limits you can specify for the same. We'll cover resource limits and requests later in this book. For now, let's delete the curly braces after the word resources, as the curly braces indicate a blank entry, so we're not specifying any resource limits or requests for our Pods. Deleting them will have the same effect. For this container, we'll request 100 milicores of CPU and 128 mebibytes, and we'll limit the container to using no more than 2 CPUs and 1 gigabyte of memory. You can see where to insert the requests and limits in the YAML spec in figure 4.17.

Now, you may be asking why there are different measurements of CPU and memory. In the Kubernetes ecosystem, limits and requests for CPU are measured in CPU

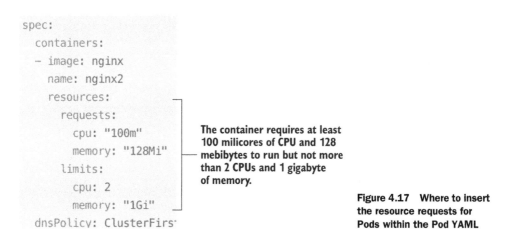

```
spec:
  containers:
  - image: nginx
    name: nginx2
    resources:
      requests:
        cpu: "100m"
        memory: "128Mi"
      limits:
        cpu: 2
        memory: "1Gi"
  dnsPolicy: ClusterFirs
```

The container requires at least 100 milicores of CPU and 128 mebibytes to run but not more than 2 CPUs and 1 gigabyte of memory.

Figure 4.17   Where to insert the resource requests for Pods within the Pod YAML

units. One CPU unit is equivalent to 1 physical CPU core, or 1 virtual core, depending on whether the node is a physical host or a virtual machine running inside a physical machine. You can write the value in milicores, whereas the value 1000m would be the same as 1 CPU. Fractional requests are also allowed, so instead of 1 CPU, we can enter a value of 0.5 CPU (equal to 500m). Memory is measured in mebibytes, which is a measurement based on powers of 2 (a mebibyte equals 2^{20} or 1,048,576 bytes).

The reason we specify the requests and limits is that, if the node where a Pod is running has enough of a resource available, it's possible (and allowed) for a container to use more of a resource than its request for that resource specifies. However, a container is not allowed to use more than its resource limit.

4.3.2   Multicontainer Pods

Sometimes in Kubernetes, it makes sense to have more than one container running inside of the same Pod. This can be useful in some cases because each container inside of a Pod shares the name network namespace and storage, so communication is faster and you don't have to establish additional Services and network policies to communicate between Pods. There are a couple of reasons for creating multiple containers inside of the same Pod. One is for log collection, where all application logs would go to a separate container specifically for logging. Another reason is to ensure the initialization of another container or Service—in other words, running a command from one container would verify that the MySQL Service was up and running, for example. Containers in the same Pod also can share storage. So, you could have a volume attached to both Pods and stream that data to the volume simultaneously. This could be useful if one container were to output the logs to a file, then another container was to read them. In this case, the second container is sometimes referred to as a "sidecar container." This is because it's not acting as the main application; it's just assisting with the collection of logs.

Let's go ahead and see this in action by running the following command to create a sidecar container: `k run sidecar --image=busybox --command "sh" "c" "while` true; do cat /var/log/nginx/error.log; sleep 20; done" --dry-run=client -o yaml > sidecar.yaml. Now, open the file sidecar.yaml in your favorite text editor. Change the c to a -c and add another container that will serve as the main container to the current sidecar container. In addition, to allow the sidecar container to read the log data, we'll go ahead and add a volume mount to an emptyDir volume type, as shown in figure 4.18.

```
spec:
  containers:
  - command:
    - sh                    ─── Change this to -c.
    - -c
    - while true; do cat /var/log/nginx/error.log; sleep 20; done
    image: busybox
    name: sidecar
    resources: {}
    volumeMounts:
      - name: log-vol          ─── Volume mounted to the sidecar
        mountPath: /var/log/nginx     container at /var/log/nginx
  - name: nginx
    image: nginx
    volumeMounts:
      - name: log-vol          ─── Volume mounted to the main
        mountPath: /var/log/nginx     container at /var/log/nginx
  volumes:
    - name: log-vol          ─── The emptyDir volume is ephemeral
      emptyDir: {}                (deleted along with Pod).
  dnsPolicy: ClusterFirst
```

Figure 4.18   Adding an additional container to a Pod, which will serve to read logs from the main application

An emptyDir volume is one of many types of volumes that live and die with the container. This is ephemeral storage, so as soon as the Pod is deleted, the data is also deleted and gone forever.

Another use case for creating multiple containers in the same Pod is to ensure the main application container is initialized. This is called an *init container*, being that its only job is to check on the main container or perform some task, and once it has done its job, the job is complete and doesn't continue to run.

An init container can be added to any Pod manifest, in line with the container's specification. To quickly create our starter YAML, let's run the command k run init

`--image=busybox:1.35 --command "sh" "c" "echo The app is running! && sleep 3600" --dry-run=client -o yaml > init.yaml`. Then, we'll enter `initContainers:` inline with the word `container`. For everything else, we'll mimic the existing container except for the command. We'll run the `until` loop `until nslookup init-svc; do echo waiting for svc; sleep 2; done`. The complete YAML should look similar to what you see in figure 4.19.

```
spec:
  containers:
  - command:
    - sh                   ┌─ Change this to -c.
    - -c  ◄───────────────┘
    - echo The app is running! && sleep 3600
    image: busybox:1.35
    name: init
    resources: {}
  initContainers:
  - name: init-svc
    image: busybox:1.35
    command:
    - sh                                                              ┐  Wait for Service
    - -c                                                             ─┤  named init-svc
    - until nslookup init-svc; do echo waiting for svc; sleep 2; done ┘  before initializing.
  dnsPolicy: ClusterFirst
```

Figure 4.19 Init containers will not allow the main application to start before the Service `init-svc` is created.

Specifying an init container is much like a regular container, but you'll notice the difference more clearly as you begin to create the Pod. Upon creation, you see the Pod go into a pending state. It will stay pending until you create the Service named `init-svc`. When you create the Service with the command `k create svc clusterip init-svc --tcp 80`, the Pod will change from `Init:0/1` to running:

```
root@kind-control-plane:/# k apply -f init.yaml
pod/init created
root@kind-control-plane:/# k get po
NAME    READY    STATUS       RESTARTS    AGE
init    0/1      Init:0/1     0           7s
root@kind-control-plane:/# k create svc clusterip init-svc --tcp 80
service/init-svc created
root@kind-control-plane:/# k get po
NAME    READY    STATUS       RESTARTS    AGE
init    0/1      Init:0/1     0           79s
root@kind-control-plane:/# k get po
NAME    READY    STATUS       RESTARTS    AGE
init    0/1      Init:0/1     0           4m17s
```

```
root@kind-control-plane:/# k get svc
NAME            TYPE        CLUSTER-IP      EXTERNAL-IP    PORT(S)    AGE
init-svc        ClusterIP   10.96.162.73    <none>         80/TCP     6m44s
kubernetes      ClusterIP   10.96.0.1       <none>         443/TCP    10h
root@kind-control-plane:/# k get po
NAME    READY    STATUS      RESTARTS    AGE
init    1/1      Running     0           7m20s
```

Notice, the Pod doesn't start running until approximately 7 minutes later. So if you're getting impatient, just wait a few more minutes for the Pod to come back up.

4.3.3   *ConfigMaps and Secrets*

So now that we've talked about Pods requesting CPU and memory, let's see what else Pods can request by talking about a ConfigMap in Kubernetes. Many times, you'll need to pass configuration data to your application, whether it be to change the log level or to change the background color of your web app. The most common way to do this is by using the ConfigMap object in Kubernetes.

Once you create the ConfigMap object, you can inject it into a Pod using various methods. You can inject it into a Pod via an environment variable or a volume mounted to the container. You can create a ConfigMap from literal values (i.e., username and password), from a file (i.e., `ca.crt`), or from multiple files within a directory.

You can create a ConfigMap by using an imperative command or by creating YAML and checking it into your source code. Because we prefer the latter, let's create the YAML and save it to a file with the command k create `configmap redis-config --from-literal=key1=config1 --from-literal=key2=config2 --dry-run=client -o yaml > redis-config.yaml`. This command will create a ConfigMap named `redis-config`, with literal key `key1` with value `config1`, as well as literal key `key2` with value `config2`.

We'll do a dry run—which means to simulate creating the resource—and finally output that to a file named `redis-config.yaml`. When we open this file in our text editor, we notice that the key and value pairs can be established line by line. Alternatively, we could perform multiline arguments by specifying the key and then a pipe symbol (|), which we have done in previous chapters. Let's replace the existing key-value pairs in our file to store the ConfigMap data in a Redis cache for later use. To do this, delete the lines starting with `key1` and `key2` and add a key named `redis-config` by adding it under `data` for a multiline argument in our YAML file, similar to figure 4.20.

Now that we've created the YAML for our ConfigMap, save and close the file. Create the ConfigMap with the command k apply `-f redis-config.yaml`.

Because the ConfigMap is now available for our application to use, go ahead and create a YAML file for a Redis Pod with the command k run init `--image=redis:7 --port 6379 --command 'redis-server' '/redis-master/redis.conf' --dry-run=client -o yaml > redis.yaml`. Let's add a volume mount to this Pod for the Redis configuration

```
apiVersion: v1
data:
  redis-config: |
    maxmemory 2mb
    maxmemory-policy allkeys-lru
kind: ConfigMap
metadata:
  creationTimestamp: null
  name: redis-config
```

Multiline value for
the key redis-config

**Figure 4.20   Creating a
ConfigMap in Kubernetes
automatically Base64 encodes
the data within.**

data, as well as an `emptyDir`-type volume for any ephemeral data. We can insert the
volumes and mount paths to the YAML spec, as shown in figure 4.21.

```
spec:
  containers:
  - command:
    - redis-server
    - /redis-master/redis.conf
    image: redis:7
    name: redis
    ports:
    - containerPort: 6379
    volumeMounts:
    - mountPath: /redis-master-data
      name: data
    - mountPath: /redis-master
      name: config
    resources: {}
  volumes:
    - name: data
      emptyDir: {}
    - name: config
      configMap:
        name: redis-config
        items:
        - key: redis-config
          path: redis.conf
  dnsPolicy: ClusterFirst
```

Data in the container at /redis-master-data
will reside in an emptyDir volume that gets
deleted along with the Pod.

Attach the config data from ConfigMap
redis-config at key redis-config to
path /redis-master/redis.conf.

**Figure 4.21   Attaching ConfigMap data to the container via an `emptyDir` volume, ensuring
the volume name and the `mountPath` name are the same**

We'll go ahead and create that Pod, and once it's running, we'll put a shell inside of the container with the Redis CLI prompt using the command `k exec -it redis --redis-cli`. Once we've done that, we can issue the Redis-specific commands, which are `CONFIG GET maxmemory` and `CONFIG GET maxmemory-policy`, and you will get an output similar to figure 4.22.

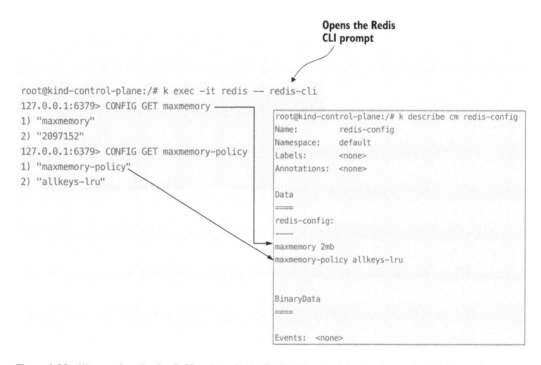

Figure 4.22 **We can view the ConfigMap data via the Redis CLI and relate that to the ConfigMap original data.**

We can match these up directly with our ConfigMap data, and they match! This is a great way to insert configuration data into containers and let that configuration data remain decoupled from the main application.

Secrets are similar to ConfigMaps but different in that they store secret data instead of application configuration data. Whether it be a database password or certificate data, you can store it in Kubernetes with a Base64 encryption. However, don't believe me if I ever say that it's secure, because it's not. Anyone who has access to your cluster can view and read the secret data, so never use this as your only method of security.

You can create a Secret in the familiar way with the command `k create secret generic dev-login --from-literal=username=dev --from-literal=password='S!B\*d$zDsb='  --dry-run=client -o yaml > dev-login.yaml`. Now open the file `dev-login.yaml` in your text editor and you'll notice that both the username and password are Base64 encoded. Secrets values are encoded as Base64 strings and are stored unencrypted by default, as show in figure 4.23.

```
apiVersion: v1
data:
   password: UyFCXCpkJHpEc2I9          The data inside of the secret
   username: ZGV2                       has been Base64 encoded.
kind: Secret
metadata:
  creationTimestamp: null
  name: dev-login
```

Figure 4.23 All of the data inside of our Secret named `dev-login` **is automatically Base64 encoded.**

Now, go ahead and create the Secret with the command `k apply -f dev-login.yaml`. We can take this Secret and make it available to a Pod by mounting it to a directory inside of the container. First, create a Pod YAML with the command `k run secret-pod --image=busybox --command "sh" "c" "echo The app is running! && sleep 3600" --dry-run=client -o yaml > secret-pod.yaml`. Let's open the file `secret-pod.yaml` inside of a text editor and make some modifications. We'll add a volume mount to the container inside of the Pod, and add a volume that's just a type of Secret, which Kubernetes knows how to handle. You can specify this in the Pod YAML, as seen in figure 4.24.

At this point, we can view our secret data from within our Pod by running the command `k exec secret-pod --cat /etc/secret-vol/username && echo` and `k exec secret-pod --cat /etc/secret-vol/password && echo`. You'll see output similar to figure 4.25.

This is not the only way to give secret data to the container; we can also use the Secret inside of the Pod via an environment variable. You can pass the `--env` flag after the `kubectl run` command with `k run secret-env --image=busybox --command "sh" "c" "printenv DEV_USER DEV_PASS; sleep 8200" --env=DEV_PASS=password --dry-run=client -o yaml > secret-env.yaml`. When you open up the `secret-env.yaml` file, you can replace `value:` with `valueFrom:` and remove the value of `password`. Below `valueFrom:`, you can indent two spaces and type `secretKeyRef:`. Below that, you can indent two spaces and type `name:` followed by the name of the Secret that we created earlier, which was `dev-login`. Then, in line with the name, you can type `key:` followed by `username`, as seen in figure 4.26. You can repeat this for however many Secrets or secret values you have in Kubernetes. Also, multiple Pods can reference the same Secret, so we don't have to delete the previous Pod that we created (named `secret-pod`) to use the Secret again inside of a new Pod.

```
apiVersion: v1
kind: Pod
metadata:
  creationTimestamp: null
  labels:
    run: secret-pod
  name: secret-pod
spec:
  containers:
  - command:
    - sh
    - -c
    - echo The app is running! && sleep 3600
    image: busybox
    name: secret-pod
    resources: {}
    volumeMounts:
    - name: secret-vol
      readOnly: true
      mountPath: "/etc/secret-vol"
  volumes:
  - name: secret-vol
    secret:
      secretName: dev-login
  dnsPolicy: ClusterFirst
```

Mount the data to the container, making it accessible from inside the container.

The volume type is secret, which contains the dev-login secret we had previously created.

Figure 4.24   Mount the secret data for the Pod to access, ensuring the data can be reached from `/etc/secret-vol` **inside the container.**

Execute a command inside a single container Pod.   **cat out the file username in the directory /etc/secret-vol.**

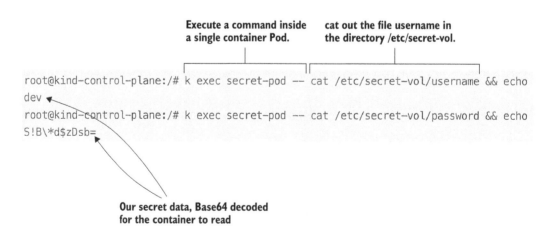

```
root@kind-control-plane:/# k exec secret-pod -- cat /etc/secret-vol/username && echo
dev
root@kind-control-plane:/# k exec secret-pod -- cat /etc/secret-vol/password && echo
S!B\*d$zDsb=
```

Our secret data, Base64 decoded for the container to read

Figure 4.25   Secret data can be obtained by running a command inside of the container.

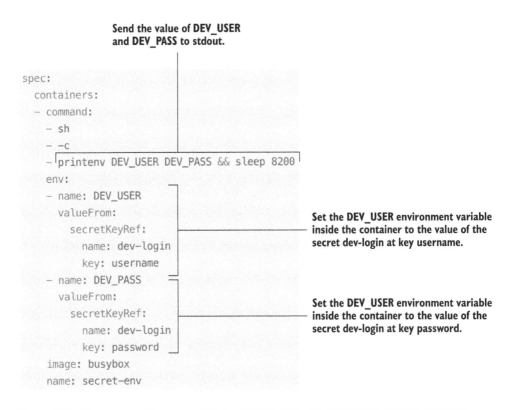

Figure 4.26   You can pass the secret data to a Pod via environment variables. Set the command inside the container to print the environment variables (`printenv`). Don't forget to change the c to -c!

Exam exercises

Create a Pod named `limited` with the image `httpd` and set the resource requests to 1Gi for CPU and 100Mi for memory.

Create a ConfigMap named `ui-data` with the key and value pairs as follows. Apply a ConfigMap to a Pod named `frontend` with the image `busybox:1.28` and pass it to the Pod via the following environment variables:

```
color.good=purple
color.bad=yellow
allow.textmode=true
how.nice.to.look=fairlyNice
```

Summary

- The term *scheduling* refers to creating a Pod and assigning it to a node. You can change which node the Pod is assigned to with a node selector, node name, or affinity rules. Make sure you know the correct YAML syntax for these scheduling changes.

- You can also apply labels to control Pod scheduling. Like a node selector, you can use a label selector to schedule a Pod to a specific node based on its label. For the exam, know how to apply labels to nodes and Pods to affect scheduling.

- Much like a package manager in Linux, Helm is a package manager and templating engine for Kubernetes. Know how to use Helm for the exam and how to use Helm templates to deploy applications to Kubernetes.

- Reserve CPU and memory for Pods using resource requests and limits. This is important for the exam, as the YAML syntax for a Pod or Deployment is slightly harder than most.

- There are specific reasons to create more than one container inside of a Pod. Sharing the same network namespace and storage allows for direct access and communication back and forth.

- Injecting configuration data and sensitive information into Pods is simplified in Kubernetes using ConfigMaps and Secrets. Make sure you know how to use ConfigMaps and Secrets mounted as volumes to a Pod, as well as environment variables.

Running applications in Kubernetes

5

This chapter covers

- Scaling applications for high availability
- Performing rolling updates and rollbacks
- Exposing Deployments to create Services
- Performing maintenance tasks on a Kubernetes cluster

This chapter covers the operations side of Kubernetes as we walk through how to maintain applications that are already running in Kubernetes. The previous chapter covered how to create Deployments (including templating), scheduling attributes, ConfigMaps, and Secrets. This chapter covers common approaches you will take on the exam to complete tasks such as providing additional resources for an application, scaling applications, providing a consistent Endpoint for applications, and rolling out new versions of an application. In continuation of the workloads and scheduling exam curriculum, this chapter, combined with the previous chapter, will cover 15% of the exam and is a part of accomplishing high availability and self-healing for applications running in Kubernetes.

> ### The workloads and scheduling domain
>
> This chapter covers part of the workloads and scheduling domain of the CKA curriculum. This domain addresses how we run applications on Kubernetes. It encompasses the following competencies.
>
> | Competency | Chapter section |
> |---|---|
> | Know how to scale applications. | 5.1 |
> | Understand Deployments and how to perform rolling updates and rollbacks. | 5.1 |
> | Understand the primitives used to create robust, self-healing application Deployments. | 5.2 |

5.1 Orchestrating applications

A Deployment is a core object in Kubernetes by which you achieve high availability, robustness, and self-healing. Stateless applications—as the name implies—do not contain state (data), so the Pods (and containers within) can be replaced and respawned without affecting the overall health of the application. Stateless applications in Kubernetes are commonly managed via Deployments. In contrast, the StatefulSet object in Kubernetes cannot be as easily replaced or respawned, as the data is required for the stateful application to run. Think MySQL where data is being written to a primary database table and replicated to additional read-only database instances. You will not be tested on StatefulSets on the exam, so we will focus solely on Deployments.

5.1.1 Modifying running applications

So far in this book, we've paid special attention to Pods, which is great, but a lot of times just one Pod for your application is not sufficient. In Kubernetes, there's a way to create redundancy and fault tolerance with the creation of a Deployment. The CKA exam will test you on modifying existing Deployments. This includes changing the image and changing the number of Pod replicas. A task on the CKA exam may look something like the following.

> **EXAM TASK**   Create a Deployment named `apache` that uses the image `httpd:2.4.54` and contains three Pod replicas. After the Deployment has been created, scale the Deployment to five replicas and change the image to `httpd:alpine`.

If you don't already have access to an existing Kubernetes cluster, creating a Kubernetes cluster with kind is explained in appendix A. As soon as your kind cluster is built, use the `kubectl` tool preinstalled on the control plane node. You can get a Bash shell to the control plane node by typing the command `docker exec -it kind-control-plane bash` and following along.

In a stateless app in Kubernetes, creating replicas of the same application is not a problem. This is because all microservices data is decoupled from the container itself; therefore, the requests get the same response no matter if they are going to the first replica of the application or the fifteenth. Let's go ahead and create a Deployment named `apache` with the command `k create deploy apache --image httpd:2.4.54 --replicas 3`. Now that we've created the Deployment, we can check on the status with the command `k get deploy`, and we'll see that we have three replicas. Because we want to increase the number of replicas to five, you would "scale the Deployment" by running the command `k scale deploy apache --replicas 5`, which will scale the Deployment from one Pod to two Pods:

```
root@kind-control-plane:/# k create deploy apache --image httpd:2.4.54 -
⮑ replicas 3
deployment.apps/apache created
root@kind-control-plane:/# k get deploy
NAME                    READY    UP-TO-DATE    AVAILABLE    AGE
apache                  3/3      3             3            14s
root@kind-control-plane:/# k scale deploy apache --replicas 5
deployment.apps/apache scaled
root@kind-control-plane:/# k get po
NAME                                    READY    STATUS
⮑ RESTARTS          AGE
apache-74f79bcc68-7lzqz                 1/1      Running
⮑ 0                7s
apache-74f79bcc68-89zwg                 1/1      Running
⮑ 0                33s
apache-74f79bcc68-v6drf                 1/1      Running
⮑ 0                33s
apache-74f79bcc68-x7bfw                 1/1      Running
⮑ 0                33s
apache-74f79bcc68-xdx4b                 1/1      Running
⮑ 0                7s
```

You will notice that the Pods are prefixed with the same name as the Deployment, followed by a suffix that is a hash value, the last five being unique because there cannot be duplicate Pod names in a cluster.

Now that we have a new Deployment running, let's change the image for the Deployment from `httpd:2.4.54` to `httpd:alpine`. We can update the image by running the command `k set image deploy apache httpd=httpd:alpine`; and by performing the command `k get po`, you'll see that a whole new set of Pods have been created for the Deployment:

```
root@kind-control-plane:/# k get po
NAME                                    READY    STATUS
⮑ RESTARTS          AGE
```

```
apache-74f79bcc68-7lzqz                    1/1        Running
⮕ 0                    26m
apache-74f79bcc68-89zwg                    1/1        Running
⮕ 0                    26m
apache-74f79bcc68-v6drf                    1/1        Running
⮕ 0                    26m
apache-74f79bcc68-x7bfw                    1/1        Running
⮕ 0                    26m
apache-74f79bcc68-xdx4b                    1/1        Running
⮕ 0                    26m
root@kind-control-plane:/# k set image deploy apache httpd=httpd:alpine
deployment.apps/apache image updated
root@kind-control-plane:/# k get po
NAME                                       READY      STATUS
⮕ RESTARTS            AGE
apache-698b8cccbd-45nzs                    1/1        Running
⮕ 0                    2s
apache-698b8cccbd-bz4bm                    1/1        Running
⮕ 0                    6s
apache-698b8cccbd-dx4j2                    1/1        Running
⮕ 0                    6s
apache-698b8cccbd-jrz86                    1/1        Running
⮕ 0                    2s
apache-698b8cccbd-z8vnl                    0/1        ContainerCreating
⮕ 0                    6s
apache-74f79bcc68-89zwg                    1/1        Terminating
⮕ 0                    27m
apache-74f79bcc68-v6drf                    1/1        Terminating
⮕ 0                    27m
apache-74f79bcc68-x7bfw                    1/1        Terminating
⮕ 0                    27m
apache-74f79bcc68-xdx4b                    1/1        Terminating
⮕ 0                    26m
```

Modifying the Deployment in this way means that there's no downtime for the application while the new version of the Deployment (with the new image) is rolled out. It also creates flexibility and increased agility to service your end users, accounting for spikes in load and being able to incrementally change the application and add features with little downtime. A Deployment resource is the most common in Kubernetes, as it takes full advantage of the native ecosystem, and we'll focus on it more during the coming sections of this chapter.

5.1.2   *Application maintenance*

Deployments are designed to run multiple instances of the same application, replicated to provide increased availability for the end users. An abstraction of a Deployment that provides additional capabilities is a ReplicaSet. As the name implies, a ReplicaSet's purpose is to maintain a stable set of replica Pods running at any given time. This guarantees the availability of a specified number of identical Pods. List the

ReplicaSets in your cluster with the command `k get rs`. You should get an output similar to the following:

```
root@kind-control-plane:/# k get rs
NAME                DESIRED   CURRENT   READY   AGE
apache-74f79bcc68   1         1         1       28m
```

In figure 5.1, you will see the Deployment and ReplicaSet depicted with three replicated Pods running NGINX, as a part of both the Deployment and ReplicaSet combination of Kubernetes objects.

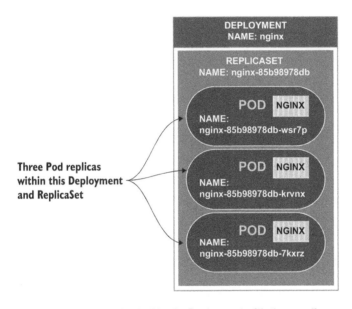

Figure 5.1   A ReplicaSet inside of a Deployment with three replicas, indicating the naming scheme for Kubernetes objects

Speaking of the Deployment configuration YAML, let's take a look at how the Pod YAML is different from a Deployment YAML. It's actually easier than you'd think. You basically take the Pod YAML and put it in the section under `template:`, which is under `spec:` in the Deployment YAML. To prove this, let's perform two different commands— one to create a YAML file for a Pod and one to create a YAML file for a Deployment. The command to create a Pod YAML file is `k run nginx --image nginx --dry-run=client -o yaml > pod.yaml`, and the command to create a Deployment is `k create deploy nginx --image nginx --dry-run=client -o yaml > deploy.yaml`. You can see the similarities between the `pod.yaml` file and the `deploy.yaml` file in figure 5.2.

The Deployment spec, created via YAML, is exactly like the Pod spec, with the additional Deployment spec as a parent resource above it. So there's a spec for the

Figure 5.2   A comparison between the YAML for a Pod and the YAML for a Deployment

Deployment, and within the spec for the Deployment, there's the spec for the Pod. Pretty easy, right?

We can use the Deployment that we created in the exercise at the beginning of this chapter, or we can generate the Deployment from the file we just created with the command k create -f deploy.yaml. We can view the Deployment status with the command k get deploy and the number of replicas in the READY column. We will see five replicas for the Deployment named apache, and because we didn't specify any replicas in the kubectl create command, we only have one for the Deployment named nginx. You can list the ReplicaSets again with the command k get rs:

```
root@kind-control-plane:/# k create deploy nginx --image nginx --dry-
 run=client -o yaml > deploy.yaml
root@kind-control-plane:/# k create -f deploy.yaml
deployment.apps/nginx created
root@kind-control-plane:/# k get deploy
NAME                   READY   UP-TO-DATE   AVAILABLE   AGE
apache                 5/5     5            5           97m
nginx                  1/1     1            1           6s
root@kind-control-plane:/# k get rs
NAME                            DESIRED   CURRENT   READY   AGE
apache-698b8cccbd               5         5         5       74m
```

```
apache-74f79bcc68          0          0          0          101m
nginx-76d6c9b8c            1          1          1          4m38s
```

You will notice from the output that two ReplicaSets start with apache because earlier when we changed the image, the Deployment controller created a new ReplicaSet, as it contains a different configuration. By default, all of the Deployment's rollout history is kept in the system so that you can roll back any time you want. We will review rollouts and rollbacks later in this chapter.

You can scale this Deployment as we did at the beginning of this chapter by modifying the deploy.yaml file, or you can type the command k scale deploy nginx --replicas 2. When modifying the YAML, you can open the file in your text editor and change the line that says replicas: 1 to replicas: 2, as you see in a snapshot of the YAML file in figure 5.3. After you save the file, you can apply the same YAML file with the command k apply -f deploy.yaml. You may get a warning that the resource is missing a "last-applied configuration," but you can safely ignore the warning, as the Deployment is still scaled to two replicas.

The last-applied configuration is added as an annotation to an object upon creation. The annotation contains the contents of the object configuration file that was used to create the object. The warning indicates that this annotation is missing; therefore, the new configuration file will be merged with the current one.

We use apply here, as opposed to create, because a Deployment already exists. The apply command overwrites the existing object, or, if the resource doesn't exist, it will create it. The create command will only create the object if one doesn't already exist but will return an error if the object exists.

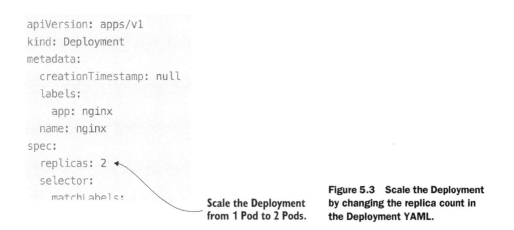

Figure 5.3 Scale the Deployment by changing the replica count in the Deployment YAML.

Scale the Deployment from 1 Pod to 2 Pods.

The Deployment was scaled from one Pod to two Pods, and you can view the replica change with the command k get deploy nginx -o yaml. Behind the scenes, the ReplicaSet that's associated with that Deployment was also modified. We can see this in action by looking at the events inside of the replica set by running the command k describe rs; you'll see an output similar to figure 5.4.

**Get more details about
the ReplicaSet object.**

```
root@kind-control-plane:/# k describe rs
Name:             nginx-85b98978db
Namespace:        default
Selector:         app=nginx,pod-template-hash=85b98978db
Labels:           app=nginx
                  pod-template-hash=85b98978db
Annotations:      deployment.kubernetes.io/desired-replicas: 2
                  deployment.kubernetes.io/max-replicas: 3
                  deployment.kubernetes.io/revision: 1
Controlled By:    Deployment/nginx
Replicas:         2 current / 2 desired
Pods Status:      2 Running / 0 Waiting / 0 Succeeded / 0 Failed
Pod Template:
  Labels:  app=nginx
           pod-template-hash=85b98978db
  Containers:
   nginx:
    Image:        nginx
    Port:         <none>
    Host Port:    <none>
    Environment:  <none>
    Mounts:       <none>
  Volumes:        <none>
Events:
  Type    Reason           Age    From               Message
  ----    ------           ----   ----               -------
  Normal  SuccessfulCreate 22s    replicaset-controller  Created pod: nginx-85b98978db-mbqj6
  Normal  SuccessfulCreate 4s     replicaset-controller  Created pod: nginx-85b98978db-vpt5?
```

**The ReplicaSet was
changed when scaling
the Deployment.**

Figure 5.4   Describe the ReplicaSet to get more information about the changes in its configuration.

The ReplicaSet is created along with the Deployment. If we delete the Deployment, we can see that the ReplicaSet is deleted as well. Delete the Deployment with the command k delete deploy nginx:

```
root@kind-control-plane:/# k delete deploy nginx
deployment.apps "nginx" deleted
root@kind-control-plane:/# k get deploy
No resources found in default namespace.
root@kind-control-plane:/# k get rs
No resources found in default namespace.
```

EXAM TIP   If you want to describe everything (i.e., all ReplicaSets) all at once, instead of listing the names one by one in the command line, you can just type the name of the resource (e.g., k describe rs), and the output will include all resources that currently exist.

So, we've seen what happens to a ReplicaSet if we modify the Deployment replica count. If we modify the Deployment image, it creates a brand-new ReplicaSet, as we saw earlier. The ReplicaSet contained a new set of Pods, with new names and a new configuration, as depicted in figure 5.5.

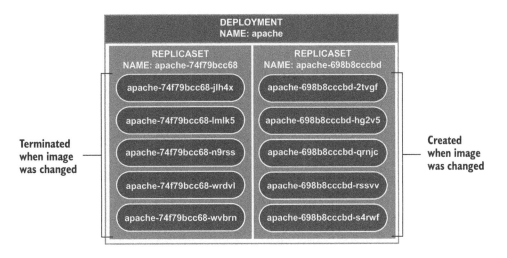

Figure 5.5 When the Deployment image is changed, a new ReplicaSet is created with a new set of Pod replicas.

If you're fast enough, you can see the old Pods being terminated and the new Pods being created. You can run the command k get po no later than 3 seconds after running the set image command. After you do so, you'll see an output similar to figure 5.6. You can also run the command k get po -w to watch the Pods change status in real time.

You'll find that there's a lot of interesting information in the output of the kubectl get po command, including that the name of the Pod actually comes from the name of the ReplicaSet. Also, the Pods from the old ReplicaSet won't terminate until the new ReplicaSet Pods are all up and running. This is called a *rollout strategy*, which ensures that the application can still operate, even in an upgrade scenario. This prevents downtime of the app and ensures that no connections are severed if someone is trying to access the application from outside of the cluster, as shown in figure 5.7.

This is the benefit of stateless apps that contain multiple replicas of the same application. A rollout strategy is defined in the Deployment spec, which you can locate by running the command k edit deploy apache. You'll see an output similar to figure 5.8. If no strategy is defined when the Deployment is created, the default will be applied, which is called a *rolling update*. A rolling update is what we just described, where the Pods from an old ReplicaSet don't terminate until the new ReplicaSet Pods are ready.

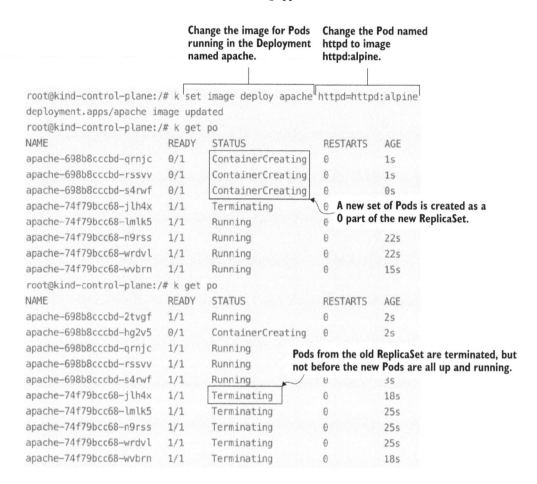

Figure 5.6   Changing the image for Pods in the Deployment results in a new ReplicaSet.

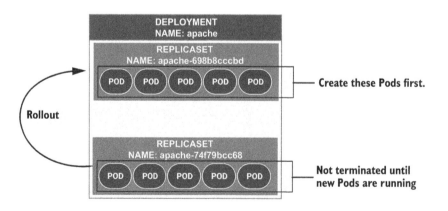

Figure 5.7   Rollout strategy in Kubernetes that states only a certain number of replicated Pods can be unavailable when rolling out a new version

```
apiVersion: apps/v1
kind: Deployment
metadata:
  annotations:
    deployment.kubernetes.io/revision: "2"
  creationTimestamp: "2023-05-31T16:54:32Z"
  generation: 3
  labels:
    app: apache
  name: apache
  namespace: default
  resourceVersion: "858"
  uid: e46c0aa7-5fc9-4326-b7ec-966c41217ed2
spec:
  progressDeadlineSeconds: 600
  replicas: 5
  revisionHistoryLimit: 10
  selector:
    matchLabels:
      app: apache
  strategy:
    rollingUpdate:
      maxSurge: 25%
      maxUnavailable: 25%
    type: RollingUpdate
```

RollingUpdate rollout strategy for new rollouts or rollbacks. At most, 25% of Pods will be added. At most, 25% of Pods can be unavailable

Figure 5.8 The rollout strategy is set to `rollingUpdate` with a max surge of 25% and a max unavailable of 25%.

The other type of strategy is called a *recreate* strategy. A recreate strategy will terminate the old ReplicaSet Pods before the new ReplicaSet Pods are running. This strategy requires a period of downtime for the application.

If you wanted to change the strategy to recreate, you would change the type from `rollingUpdate` to `Recreate` and delete the lines that start with `rolling-Update`, `maxSurge`, and `maxUnavailable`. A recreate strategy is good for many Deployments because it offers the fastest rollout strategy, but as we discussed, there will be downtime.

EXAM TIP If you find yourself wondering what values go where in a YAML file during the exam, you can use `k explain`. For example, the command `k explain deploy.spec.strategy` will list values that are available for input in the `spec` field. Try it out!

In a rolling update rollout strategy, the max surge and max unavailable fields are optional and can be a percentage or a whole number. The max surge specifies the maximum number of Pods that can be created over the amount set by the replicas in the Deployment. For example, in figure 5.8, because the replica count is three, and the maxSurge is 25%, the Pods cannot surge above four Pods (percentages round up for a surge). The max unavailable is just as it sounds—the number of Pods that can be unavailable for the Deployment. In our example, since maxUnavailable is set to 25%, no more than one Pod can ever be unavailable at once.

Wait, there's more! In addition to a ReplicaSet, there's a tracking capability for Deployments called *rollouts*.

5.1.3   *Application rollouts*

Application rollouts are a way for a Kubernetes administrator or developer to roll back to a previous version, or record the number of revisions that the Deployment has, as depicted in figure 5.9.

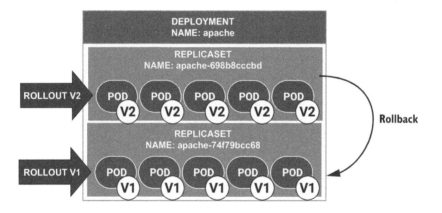

Figure 5.9   Two rollout revisions remain, in case you need to roll back to a previous version of the application.

Every time Pods are changed within a Deployment, a new revision is created. We can see the rollout history by typing the command k rollout history deploy apache:

```
root@kind-control-plane:/# k rollout history deploy apache
deployment.apps/apache
REVISION  CHANGE-CAUSE
1         <none>
2         <none>
```

In this case, there are two revisions, one for the initial Deployment (when we created the Deployment with the k create deploy command), and a second when we changed the image tag from alpine to 2.

If you take a look at the CHANGE-CAUSE column, you can see it says none. The change-cause column is an opportunity to record a note along with your Deployment change. So, let's say you wanted to add a note in the change-cause column that says "updated image tag from alpine to 2." You can apply this to revision 2 by typing the command k annotate deploy apache kubernetes.io/change-cause="updated image tag from alpine to 2":

```
root@kind-control-plane:/# k annotate deploy apache kubernetes.io/change-
➥ cause="updated image tag from alpine to 2"
deployment.apps/apache annotated
root@kind-control-plane:/# k rollout history deploy apache
deployment.apps/apache
REVISION   CHANGE-CAUSE
1          <none>
2          updated image tag from alpine to 2
```

As you can see, the change-cause column for revision 2 has been changed. Now you can tell why the Deployment was revised and what changes occurred from revision 1 to revision 2.

Having a revision history like this allows you to revert to a previous revision, which is called a *rollback*. Let's say when you deployed the new version of your application and changed the image tag for your Deployment, you introduced a bug in your application. You must quickly revert to prevent users of your application from experiencing that bug. You can roll back to the previous revision with the command k rollout undo deploy apache:

```
root@kind-control-plane:/# k rollout undo deploy apache
deployment.apps/apache rolled back
root@kind-control-plane:/# k rollout history deploy apache
deployment.apps/apache
REVISION   CHANGE-CAUSE
2          updated image tag from alpine to 2
3          <none>
```

You've reverted to the previous revision, which in turn creates a new revision. The revision number will never go backward; it will always go forward. You can now enter a message into the change-cause column for revision 3 with the command k annotate deploy apache kubernetes.io/change-cause="reverted back to the original":

```
root@kind-control-plane:/# k annotate deploy apache kubernetes.io/change-
➥ cause="reverted back to the original"
deployment.apps/apache annotated
root@kind-control-plane:/# k rollout history deploy apache
deployment.apps/apache
REVISION   CHANGE-CAUSE
2          updated image tag from alpine to 2
3          reverted back to the original
```

Both of the revisions are recorded with notes. You can't see revision 1 any longer because reverting to revision 1 would be the same as reverting to revision 3, so to save duplication, revision 1 is removed.

Let's say that you wanted to check the status of the rollout. Maybe the rollout didn't go well. This can happen if the image tag is not available. Maybe you typed it incorrectly, or the image tag is no longer available from your image registry. You can check the status of your rollout based on the revision with the command k rollout status deploy apache --revision 3:

```
root@kind-control-plane:/# k rollout status deploy apache --revision 3
deployment "apache" successfully rolled out
```

Our Deployment was successfully rolled out when we reverted to revision 1, so that's good. No misspellings or unavailable images for us. Phew!

Lastly, I wanted to show you how to pause the rollout, so that only some of the Pods in the Deployment are on revision 3, and half of the Pods are on revision 4. We can see this in action with the commands k set image deploy apache httpd=httpd:2.4 and k rollout pause deploy apache (note: you have to perform these two commands within one second of each other). When you get the status of the rollout, you'll see a message that says "Waiting for Deployment 'apache' rollout to finish: 2 out of 3 new replicas have been updated . . . ," which means that the rollout is paused.

```
root@kind-control-plane:/# k set image deploy apache httpd=httpd:2.4
deployment.apps/apache image updated
root@kind-control-plane:/# k rollout pause deploy apache
deployment.apps/apache paused
root@kind-control-plane:/# k rollout status deploy apache
Waiting for deployment "apache" rollout to finish: 2 out of 3 new replicas
➡ have been updated...
```

There are now two out of three new replicas running as a part of the new revision. Let's go ahead and resume (unpause) the Deployment, so that the revision can finish, with the command k rollout resume deploy apache:

```
root@kind-control-plane:/# k rollout resume deploy apache
deployment.apps/apache resumed
root@kind-control-plane:/# k rollout status deploy apache
deployment "apache" successfully rolled out
```

Now we have successfully rolled out to revision 4, where the new image for the Pods in the Deployment is set to httpd:2.4.

EXAM TIP If you're unsure of the order of the command or need examples of common ones, utilize the help menu in the terminal with the command k rollout --help and k rollout status -help, and you can easily obtain the correct command syntax.

5.1.4 Exposing Deployments

Exposing a Deployment means that the Deployment can be accessed from the end user, potentially from outside the cluster (depending on the type of Service you create). We are going to go into depth about Services in chapter 6, but I wanted to mention that there's an easy way to create a Service that is connected to a Deployment. Instead of creating a Service from scratch, you can use the command k expose deploy nginx --name nginx-svc --port 80 --type ClusterIP --dry-run=client -o yaml > nginx-svc.yaml. You'll see a snapshot of the YAML that this command creates in figure 5.10. Of course, because we like to do things declaratively in Kubernetes, we'll do a dry run and create a file named nginx-svc.yaml.

```
apiVersion: v1
kind: Service
metadata:
  creationTimestamp: null
  labels:
    app: nginx
  name: nginx-svc
spec:
  ports:
  - port: 80
    protocol: TCP
    targetPort: 80
  selector:
    app: nginx
  type: ClusterIP
status:
  loadBalancer: {}
```

Use the selector field to attach to Deployments with the label app=nginx.

Figure 5.10 Selecting a Deployment via a Service in Kubernetes

The important part to notice about the Deployment is the selector. If you remember, we talked about node selectors and label selectors in the last chapter, and here we're talking about *Service selectors* to associate a Service to the Pods within a Deployment. This particular Service will associate itself with any Deployment that has the label app=nginx. This is useful information to know as we proceed through this book and will come in handy as foundational knowledge for the next chapter, where we talk about Services in depth.

Exam exercises

Using `kubectl`, create a Deployment named `apache` using the image `httpd:latest` with one replica. After the Deployment is running, scale the replicas up to five.

Update the image for the Deployment `apache` from `httpd:latest` to `httpd:2.4.54`. Do not create a new YAML file or edit the existing resource (only use `kubectl`).

Using `kubectl`, view the events of the ReplicaSet that was created as a result of the image change from the previous exercise.

Using `kubectl`, roll back to the previous version of the Deployment named `apache`.

For the existing Deployment named `apache`, change the rollout strategy for a Deployment to `Recreate`.

5.2   *Application maintenance*

In the life cycle of your application running in Kubernetes, there may come a time when the underlying nodes require maintenance, or the application requires additional resources to optimize performance. This highlights the robustness of Deployments, as they can move Pods around the cluster from node to node, facing no downtime. With redundancy and high availability built into the Kubernetes ecosystem, we'll learn how to safely perform maintenance to create robust application Deployments.

For the exam, you will need to know how to move a Pod to a different node. An exam task will look something like the following.

EXAM TASK   The node named `kind-worker` on the cluster `b8s` is experiencing problems with leaking memory. You must take down the node for maintenance by first disabling the scheduling of new Pods to the node `kind-worker`. Then, evict all Pods that are currently running on `kind-worker`. Finally, once you've verified that no Pods are running on `kind-worker`, enable scheduling once again.

For this exam task, you'll have to use a two-node kind cluster, and you'll need to off-load a Pod to a secondary node, so you'll need at least one running Pod in the cluster as well. If you do not have access to a two-node cluster, I recommend you create one as explained in appendix A. Once you've opened a shell to the control plane node using the command `docker exec -it kind-control-plane bash`, you can run the command `k create deploy nginx -image nginx` to get a Pod running in the cluster. Now you can begin the exam task by disabling scheduling for the `kind-worker` node.

To disable scheduling to a node, you can use the command `k cordon no kind-worker`. You will get output similar to this:

```
root@kind-control-plane:/# k cordon kind-worker
node/kind-worker cordoned
```

```
root@kind-control-plane:/# k get no
NAME                     STATUS                       ROLES            AGE
➥ VERSION
kind-control-plane       Ready                        control-plane    7m
➥ v1.25.0-beta.0
kind-worker              Ready,SchedulingDisabled     <none>           6m38s
➥ v1.25.0-beta.0
```

If you run the command `k get no` right after, you'll notice that the status changes from `Ready` to `Ready,SchedulingDisabled`. So if you try to create a second Pod, the Pod will remain pending, because the scheduler has marked the node as unavailable. We can see this in action with the command `k create deploy nginx2 -image nginx`, followed by the `k get po` command to see the status. The output should look like this:

```
root@kind-control-plane:/# k create deploy nginx2 --image nginx
deployment.apps/nginx2 created
root@kind-control-plane:/# k get po
NAME                     READY   STATUS    RESTARTS   AGE
nginx-76d6c9b8c-hr9z6    1/1     Running   0          111s
nginx2-b648d744f-n6xb9   0/1     Pending   0          3s
```

We need to move all running Pods on that node to take it down for maintenance. This process is called *draining the node,* as in evicting the Pods and moving them to another node. To do this in our two-node kind cluster, we must first remove the taint applied to the control plane node that prevents Pods from being scheduled to it, for the Pods to move from the worker node (when we drain it) to the control plane node. We talked about taints in chapter 2, so this should be a familiar concept. Perform the command `k taint no kind-control-plane node-role.kubernetes.io/control-plane:NoSchedule-` to untaint the control plane node. The output will look like this:

```
root@kind-control-plane:/# k taint no kind-control-plane node-
➥ role.kubernetes.io/control-plane:NoSchedule-
node/kind-control-plane untainted
```

Now that the control plane node is untainted, we can drain the node `kind-worker` with the command `k drain kind-worker --ignore-daemonsets`. The output will look similar to this:

```
root@kind-control-plane:/# k drain kind-worker --ignore-daemonsets
node/kind-worker already cordoned
Warning: ignoring DaemonSet-managed Pods: kube-system/kindnet-h7695, kube-
➥ system/kube-proxy-j8wbc
evicting pod default/nginx-76d6c9b8c-hr9z6
pod/nginx-76d6c9b8c-hr9z6 evicted
node/kind-worker drained
root@kind-control-plane:/# k get po -o wide
NAME                     READY   STATUS    RESTARTS   AGE    IP
➥ NODE
nginx-76d6c9b8c-4494r    1/1     Running   0          52s    10.244.0.7
➥ kind-control-plane
```

```
nginx2-b648d744f-n6xb9    1/1      Running   0         3m6s   10.244.0.6
  kind-control-plane
```

You'll see that by running the command k get po -o wide again, the Pods are running on the control plane node. To complete our exam task, let's enable scheduling for the node once again by running the command k uncordon kind-worker. The output will look like this:

```
root@kind-control-plane:/# k uncordon kind-worker
node/kind-worker uncordoned
```

This completes the exam task. You should now be familiar with how to move Pods from one node to another using the cordon, drain, and uncordon options with kubectl.

5.2.1 *Cordoning and draining nodes*

Cordon is an interesting word, isn't it? The official meaning is to form a barrier around, meaning a protective barrier. In the context of Kubernetes, the act of cordoning takes place on a node and is marking the node unschedulable. If you cordon a node, this puts the node out of service and routinely ready for maintenance, as shown in figure 5.11. You might be wondering what kind of maintenance. Well, you might need to upgrade the RAM on a node, patch a security vulnerability, or replace it entirely.

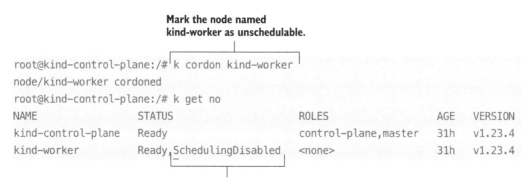

Figure 5.11 Cordon a node to disable scheduling.

As you see, when you perform the command k cordon kind-worker, you disable scheduling to the node; therefore, any Pods that would normally tolerate this node for scheduling can't until the cordon is released.

> **EXAM TIP** After you cordon a node, make sure you uncordon it. If the node has scheduling disabled, you may get points deducted from your final score.

So, that begs the question, what about existing Pods running on that node? You have marked the node as unschedulable, but that only applies to scheduling from that point onward. It does not take into account Pods that are currently running on that node, as shown in figure 5.12. You may have guessed from the title of this section that the act of moving the Pods off of the node and scheduling them elsewhere is called *draining*.

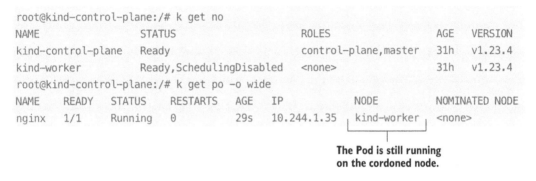

Figure 5.12 Cordoning the node doesn't mean it will evict a Pod from a node.

The act of draining is just how it sounds—draining the node of all Pods that are currently running on it. If the Pod(s) are managed by a ReplicaSet, the same rules of scheduling still apply, and for that matter, the Pod doesn't move. It actually is deleted and recreated on another node; it just happens in a way that ensures the old Pod is not removed before the new Pod is running, much like a rollout. If you don't already have a Deployment running, you can start one with the command k create deploy nginx --image nginx, and you too can follow along in the fun.

In the spirit of fun, let's see what happens to all the Pods that are currently running on that node when it's drained. To drain the node and ignore the kube-proxy and kubenet DaemonSets that are running on every node in the cluster, perform the command k drain kind-worker --ignore-daemonsets --force. Force is necessary in this case, because one of the Pods is not managed by a ReplicaSet. You will see an output similar to figure 5.13.

As you can see, a couple of actions occur. First, the node is drained, and the Pods are moved off, but one of the Pods is deleted and does not return. This is because it wasn't managed by a ReplicaSet, so there's no mechanism to reschedule that Pod. Second, the Pod that was a part of a ReplicaSet is in a pending state.

As we learned in the previous chapter, the control plane nodes have a taint applied to them that requires a toleration to successfully schedule Pods to them. In this case, because the Pod doesn't have a toleration for that taint, it will remain in the pending state until either a taint is applied, a toleration is added to the Pod, or a new node

```
root@kind-control-plane:/# k get po -o wide
NAME                      READY   STATUS    RESTARTS   AGE   IP           NODE          NOMINATED NODE   READINESS GATES
nginx                     1/1     Running   0          35s   10.244.1.2   kind-worker   <none>           <none>
nginx-85b98978db-kxxfc    1/1     Running   0          28s   10.244.1.3   kind-worker   <none>           <none>
root@kind-control-plane:/# k drain kind-worker --ignore-daemonsets --force                    Ignore kube-system Pods.
node/kind-worker cordoned Drain node kind-worker.
WARNING: deleting Pods not managed by ReplicationController, ReplicaSet, Job, DaemonSet or StatefulSet: default/nginx; ignor
ing DaemonSet-managed Pods: kube-system/kindnet-dfxxp, kube-system/kube-proxy-nq72h
evicting pod default/nginx-85b98978db-kxxfc
evicting pod default/nginx
pod/nginx-85b98978db-kxxfc evicted
pod/nginx evicted  ◄─────── The Pod was deleted, as it wasn't managed by a ReplicaSet.
node/kind-worker drained
root@kind-control-plane:/# k get po -o wide
NAME                      READY   STATUS    RESTARTS   AGE   IP        NODE      NOMINATED NODE   READINESS GATES
nginx-85b98978db-fnnb6    0/1     Pending   0          4s    <none>    <none>    <none>           <none>
```

Figure 5.13 Draining the node removes all Pods running on the specified node, where some are deleted permanently.

without a taint is added. For simplicity's sake, let's go ahead and remove the taint with the command k taint no kind-control-plane node-role.kubernetes.io/master-:

```
root@kind-control-plane:/# k taint no kind-control-plane node-
➥ role.kubernetes.io/master-
node/kind-control-plane untainted
root@kind-control-plane:/# k get po -o wide
NAME                      READY   STATUS    RESTARTS   AGE   IP
➥ NODE
nginx-85b98978db-fnnb6    1/1     Running   0          20m   10.244.0.5
➥ kind-control-plane
```

By running the command k get po -o wide, the container is now running on the kind-control-plane node. Later in this chapter we'll try joining a node to a cluster, where we can simulate another scenario in which the Pod may move out of a pending state without potentially putting the control plane node at risk (by limited resources). For now, you can uncordon the kind-worker node with the command k uncordon kind-worker. Additionally, you could also reapply the taint to the control plane node with the command k taint no kind-control-plane node-role.kubernetes.io/master :NoSchedule.

5.2.2   *Adding application resources (nodes)*

Cases may occur within the lifetime of your Kubernetes cluster in which you need to insert additional nodes—whether you need more resources for your application, or you've lost a node due to failure or planned downtime. No matter the reason, adding a node to an existing kubeadm cluster is simplified by enabling bootstrap token authentication in the Kubernetes API. An exam question might read something like the following.

> **EXAM TASK** There's a third node in the cluster named ik8s, but it is not appear-
> ing when you perform the kubectl get nodes command. The name of the node
> is node02. Allow node02 to join the cluster by recreating the join command and
> ensuring that the node is in a Ready state when you list all the nodes in the cluster.

When you first create a Kubernetes cluster, kubeadm creates an initial bootstrap token
with a 24-hour TTL, but you can create additional tokens on demand. You can see the
bootstrap token mechanism enabled in our kind Kubernetes cluster by opening the
file /etc/kubernetes/manifests/kube-apiserver.yaml and looking under command.
You'll see an ouput similar to figure 5.14.

```
root@kind-control-plane:/# cd /etc/kubernetes/manifests/
root@kind-control-plane:/etc/kubernetes/manifests# ls | grep apiserver
kube-apiserver.yaml
```

```
apiVersion: v1
kind: Pod                    /etc/kubernetes/manifests/kube-apiserver.yaml
metadata:
  annotations:
    kubeadm.kubernetes.io/kube-apiserver.advertise-ad
  creationTimestamp: null
  labels:
    component: kube-apiserver
    tier: control-plane
  name: kube-apiserver
  namespace: kube-system
spec:
  containers:
  - command:
    - kube-apiserver
    - --advertise-address=172.18.0.2
    - --allow-privileged=true
    - --authorization-mode=Node,RBAC
    - --client-ca-file=/etc/kubernetes/pki/ca.crt
    - --enable-admission-plugins=NodeRestriction
    - --enable-bootstrap-token-auth=true
    - --etcd-cafile=/etc/kubernetes/pki/etcd/ca.crt
```

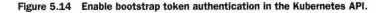

This setting allows you to add a
node via an authentication token.

Figure 5.14   Enable bootstrap token authentication in the Kubernetes API.

Bootstrap tokens are essentially bearer tokens used when creating new clusters or join-ing new nodes to an existing cluster. These tokens were primarily built for kubeadm but can also be used in other scenarios without kubeadm, such as with third-party applications. A bootstrap token works much like a Service Account token in that the token allows the third-party app to authenticate with the Kubernetes API and commu-nicate with objects inside of the cluster.

In the context of joining a node to the cluster, bootstrap tokens establish bidirec-tional trust between the node that's joining the cluster and a control plane node. We can generate a new token in our kind Kubernetes cluster with the command `kubeadm token create --print-join-command`:

```
root@kind-control-plane:/# kubeadm token create --print-join-command
kubeadm join kind-control-plane:6443 --token l5kotg.hiivo73eu000bbfu -
    discovery-token-ca-cert-hash
    sha256:13b3aac808908114d45b6ad91640babd8613d8136b21d405711a1204c68fa8a4
```

> **EXAM TIP** On exam day, don't be afraid to use the help menu (`kubeadm -help`). The help menu will contain examples, in some cases, that you can copy and paste right into the command line.

Let's proceed with adding a new node to our kind Kubernetes cluster. To create a new node, we must first create a secondary cluster, and then orphan the node from the new cluster, adding it to our original cluster. We do this because the orphaned node will have all the necessary prerequisites (containerd, kubelet, and kubeadm) to run this node as a Kubernetes node. On the CKA exam, you may come across a node that needs to be added to a cluster after being orphaned, but you most likely will not have to install the prerequisites. We can create the new kind cluster with the command `kind create cluster --config config2.yaml --name cka` using the `config.yaml` file that we used in chapter 2, but modified slightly. You will get an output similar to fig-ure 5.15.

```
kind: Cluster
apiVersion: kind.x-k8s.io/v1alpha4
nodes:
- role: control-plane
- role: worker
```

Now that we have created a new cluster named `cka`, our context has already been switched to the new cluster. We can simply run the command `k delete no cka-worker` to remove the node from that cluster, as we see in figure 5.16.

Even though we deleted `cka-worker`, the node is still running and can be accessed from outside of Kubernetes. You can get a shell to it with the command `docker exec -it`

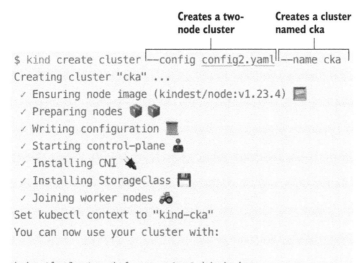

Creates a two-node cluster   **Creates a cluster named cka**

```
$ kind create cluster --config config2.yaml --name cka
Creating cluster "cka" ...
 ✓ Ensuring node image (kindest/node:v1.23.4) 🖼
 ✓ Preparing nodes 📦 📦
 ✓ Writing configuration 📜
 ✓ Starting control-plane 🕹
 ✓ Installing CNI 🔌
 ✓ Installing StorageClass 💾
 ✓ Joining worker nodes 🚜
Set kubectl context to "kind-cka"
You can now use your cluster with:

kubectl cluster-info --context kind-cka

Thanks for using kind! 😊
```

Figure 5.15 Create a new cluster named `cka` with a two-node configuration.

```
$ k get no
NAME                STATUS   ROLES                   AGE   VERSION
cka-control-plane   Ready    control-plane,master    9h    v1.23.4
cka-worker          Ready    <none>                  9h    v1.23.4


$ k delete no cka-worker  ←——  Delete the node named
node "cka-worker" deleted        cka-worker from the cluster.

                          Kubernetes is no longer
                          aware that the node exists.
$ k get no  ←——————————
NAME                STATUS   ROLES                   AGE   VERSION
cka-control-plane   Ready    control-plane,master    9h    v1.23.4
```

Figure 5.16 Deleting the node removes it from context, but it still lives as a Docker container.

cka-worker bash. Now let's run the command kubeadm reset to revert to a fresh state for this node and clear its affiliation with the cka cluster:

```
$ docker exec -it cka-worker bash
root@cka-worker:/# kubeadm reset
[reset] WARNING: Changes made to this host by 'kubeadm init' or 'kubeadm
➥ join' will be reverted.
[reset] Are you sure you want to proceed? [y/N]: y
[preflight] Running pre-flight checks
W0527 01:56:05.673626    3614 removeetcdmember.go:80] [reset] No kubeadm
➥ config, using etcd pod spec to get data directory
[reset] No etcd config found. Assuming external etcd
[reset] Please, manually reset etcd to prevent further issues
[reset] Stopping the kubelet service
[reset] Unmounting mounted directories in "/var/lib/kubelet"
[reset] Deleting contents of config directories: [/etc/kubernetes/manifests
➥ /etc/kubernetes/pki]
[reset] Deleting files: [/etc/kubernetes/admin.conf
➥ /etc/kubernetes/kubelet.conf /etc/kubernetes/bootstrap-kubelet.conf
➥ /etc/kubernetes/controller-manager.conf /etc/kubernetes/scheduler.conf]

➥ [reset] Deleting contents of stateful directories: [/var/lib/kubelet
➥ /var/lib/dockershim /var/run/kubernetes /var/lib/cni]

The reset process does not clean CNI configuration. To do so, you must
➥ remove /etc/cni/net.d

The reset process does not reset or clean up iptables rules or IPVS tables.
If you wish to reset iptables, you must do so manually by using the
➥ "iptables" command.

If your cluster was setup to utilize IPVS, run ipvsadm --clear (or similar)
to reset your system's IPVS tables.

The reset process does not clean your kubeconfig files and you must remove
➥ them manually.
Please, check the contents of the $HOME/.kube/config file.
```

We can go ahead and apply the join command that we generated earlier. This command will use kubeadm to join the node to our cluster named kind, pass the token for authentication, and also pass --discovery-token-ca-cert-hash to validate the public key of the root certificate authority(CA) presented by the control plane. You'll see an output similar to figure 5.17.

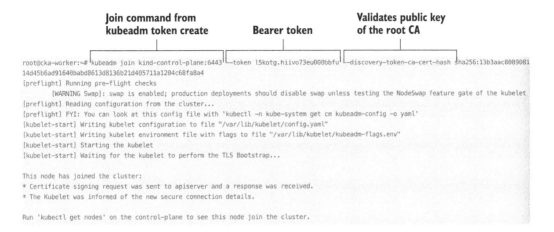

Figure 5.17 Use the `join` **command to join a node to an existing cluster.**

We can go back over to the kind cluster and look at our nodes from that context:

```
root@cka-worker:~# exit
exit
$ docker exec -it kind-control-plane bash
                                              root@kind-control-
      plane:/# alias k=kubectl
root@kind-control-plane:/# k get no
NAME                   STATUS    ROLES           AGE      VERSION
cka-worker             Ready     <none>          15m      v1.23.4
kind-control-plane     Ready     control-plane   2d1h     v1.24.0
kind-worker            Ready     <none>          2d1h     v1.24.0
```

Congratulations! You've successfully added a node to an existing cluster, making it a three-node cluster. Now you can continue to schedule Pods to it and use it just as you would any other worker node in the Kubernetes cluster.

Exam exercises

From a three-node cluster, cordon one of the worker nodes. Schedule a Pod without a `nodeSelector`. Uncordon the worker node and edit the Pod, applying a new node name to the YAML (set it to the node that was just uncordoned). After replacing the YAML, see if the Pod is scheduled to the recently uncordoned node.

Start a basic nginx Deployment; remove the taint from the control plane node so that Pods don't need a toleration to be scheduled to it. Add a `nodeSelector` to the Pod spec within the Deployment, and see if the Pod is now running on the control plane node.

Summary

- Deployments are a common resource in Kubernetes, and the ReplicaSets within are important for keeping the desired number of replicas running.
- Rollouts are versioned, and you can optionally leave notes for other Kubernetes administrators or developers.
- You can expose a Deployment, which creates a Service for users to access the application from outside the cluster.
- Maintenance is inevitable and will mean that at some point, you must know how to cordon and drain to perform OS upgrades or add resources to a node.
- Use kubeadm to upgrade control plane components so that the cluster can stay updated with the latest patches to prevent CVEs.
- You can easily add a node to an existing cluster to provide additional resources to applications running on Kubernetes.

Communication
in a Kubernetes cluster

This chapter covers

- How nodes communicate via CNI and the different CNIs available
- How Pod-to-Pod communication happens
- Types of Services in Kubernetes and when they are used
- Assigning IP addresses to Pods
- Communication via DNS and how to use CoreDNS
- Using Ingress and Ingress controllers

Many find that networking in Kubernetes is complex, but we will break it down fully in this chapter, especially since it's 20% of the CKA exam. There are a few important concepts that will clear up a lot of confusion, and because we've covered how bridge networking works within containers, I think it will all start to come together. By the end of this chapter, you'll know how Pods talk to each other within a cluster, which is the essence of the Services and networking section of the exam.

The Services and networking domain

This chapter covers the Services and networking domain of the CKA curriculum. This domain includes the way nodes and Pods communicate with each other in the cluster. It encompasses the following competencies.

Competency	Chapter section
Understand host networking configuration on the cluster nodes.	6.5
Understand connectivity between Pods.	6.2
Understand ClusterIP, NodePort, and LoadBalancer Service types and Endpoints.	6.4
Know how to use Ingress controllers and Ingress resources.	6.3
Know how to configure and use CoreDNS.	6.1, 6.2
Choose an appropriate container network interface plugin.	6.5

6.1   *Configuring DNS*

Inside a Kubernetes cluster, CoreDNS is responsible for resolving hostnames to IP addresses. As of version 1.12 of Kubernetes, CoreDNS has been the default DNS server and will be present on the exam. CoreDNS is also used in our kind Kubernetes cluster.

The CKA exam asks you to configure and use CoreDNS, which includes resolving hostnames to IP addresses, making changes to how DNS works, and knowing where the CoreDNS configuration is located and how to change it. For example, the exam question will say something like the following.

EXAM TASK In cluster `k8s`, change the IP addresses given to new Services to a CIDR range of 100.96.0.0/16. Change the IP address associated with the cluster DNS Service to match this new Service range. Proceed to change the kubelet configuration so that new Pods can receive the new DNS Service IP address, and so they can resolve domain names. Edit the kubelet ConfigMap so that kubelet is updated in place and immediately reflected. Upgrade the node to receive the new kubelet configuration. Finally, test this by creating a new Pod and verifying that the Pod has the new IP address of the DNS Service.

If you don't already have access to an existing Kubernetes cluster, creating a Kubernetes cluster with kind as explained in appendix A. A single-node cluster will suffice for this type of task. As soon as you have access to your kind cluster, get a shell to the control plane node with the command `docker exec -it kind-control-plane bash`. Once you have a shell, set your alias k to equal `kubectl` with the command `alias k=kubectl`. On the exam, they will already have this alias set for you, so it's good to get used to using k as opposed to typing `kubectl` over and over again.

Let's change the Service CIDR block that is given to each Service that's created in the cluster. This is a feature that's controlled by the API server. We can locate the API server configuration in the directory `/etc/kubernetes/manifests`, and the name of the file is `kube-apiserver.yaml`. Let's open this file to edit it with the command `vim /etc/kubernetes/manifests/kube-apiserver.yaml`; it will open in the Vim text editor. Under the command section of YAML, we'll place our cursor at the line that begins with `- --service-cluster-ip-range` and change the CIDR range from 10.96.0.0/16 to 100.96.0.0/16 (just add a 0 after the 10). The result should be exactly like the YAML in figure 6.1.

```
- --service-account-key-file=/etc/kubernetes/pki/sa.pub
- --service-account-signing-key-file=/etc/kubernetes/pki/sa.key
- --service-cluster-ip-range=100.96.0.0/16
- --tls-cert-file=/etc/kubernetes/pki/apiserver.crt
- --tls-private-key-file=/etc/kubernetes/pki/apiserver.key
image: registry.k8s.io/kube-apiserver:v1.25.0-beta.0
```

Figure 6.1 **Change the Service CIDR range that gives each new Service a new IP address.**

After you've changed the cluster IP range to 100.96.0.0/16, save and close the file. This will automatically restart the API server, so you will have to wait up to 2 minutes for the API server to reboot and run any additional `kubectl` commands.

Next, let's change the IP address associated with the cluster DNS Service. We examine Services in depth later in this chapter. For now, just know that it's a cluster-wide communication mechanism for DNS. The DNS Service is in the `kube-system` namespace, and we can view the Service with the command `k -n kube-system get svc`. You will see the Service named `kube-dns`. The output looks like this:

```
root@kind-control-plane:/# alias k=kubectl
root@kind-control-plane:/# k -n kube-system get svc
NAME        TYPE         CLUSTER-IP    EXTERNAL-IP    PORT(S)
⇒ AGE
kube-dns    ClusterIP    10.96.0.10    <none>         53/UDP,53/TCP,9153/TCP
⇒ 73s
```

EXAM TIP Type the namespace just after the k to autocomplete the Kubernetes resources (press the Tab key to autocomplete the name of the resource). On the exam, they will have longer and more complicated names, which are prone to typos. Always copy and paste where you can, and use autocomplete to prevent typos!

To edit this Service, we can type the command `k -n kube-system edit svc kube-dns`, and it will bring up the YAML in a Vi text editor (you may have to install Vim first with the command `apt update; apt install -y vim`). The Vi text editor will look similar to figure 6.2. Bring your cursor down to the line that starts with `clusterIP`, press the I key (insert mode) on the keyboard, and replace the value 10.96.0.10 with 100.96.0.10 (add a zero after the first 10). Do the same for the line under `clusterIPs`, so this will also have the new value of 100.96.0.10.

```
apiVersion: v1
kind: Service
metadata:
  annotations:
    prometheus.io/port: "9153"
    prometheus.io/scrape: "true"
  creationTimestamp: "2022-09-14T15:28:58Z"
  labels:
    k8s-app: kube-dns
    kubernetes.io/cluster-service: "true"
    kubernetes.io/name: CoreDNS
  name: kube-dns
  namespace: kube-system
  resourceVersion: "238"
  uid: 01da05fb-8ba2-4626-90ae-3542b8281599
spec:
  clusterIP: 10.96.0.10 100.96.0.10
  clusterIPs:
  - 10.96.0.10 100.96.0.10
  internalTrafficPolicy: Cluster
  ipFamilies:
  - IPv4
```

Delete 10.96.0.10 and replace with 100.96.0.10.

Figure 6.2   Edit the `kube-dns` Service in place, replacing the values for `clusterIP` and `clusterIPs`.

Once you've replaced the values, press the Esc key on the keyboard to get out of insert mode, followed by `:wq` to save and quit. You will receive the following message: "services 'kube-dns' was not valid: spec.clusterIPs[0]: Invalid value: []string{"100.96.0.10"}: may not change once set." The message in figure 6.3 will appear at the top of the page.

This is expected here because only certain types of parameters can be changed for Kubernetes objects that are in a running state, so proceed to type `:wq` once again and

```
# Please edit the object below. Lines beginning with a '#' will be ignored,
# and an empty file will abort the edit. If an error occurs while saving this file will be
# reopened with the relevant failures.
#
# services "kube-dns" was not valid:
# * spec.clusterIPs[0]: Invalid value: []string{"100.96.0.10"}: may not change once set
#
apiVersion: v1
kind: Service
metadata:
  annotations:
    prometheus.io/port: "9153"
```

Figure 6.3   After editing the `kube-dns` Service, you will receive a message that the `clusterIP` value may not be changed.

return to the command prompt, ignoring the error message. When you return to the command prompt, you will get a message that says the following:

```
error: services "kube-dns" is invalid
A copy of your changes has been stored to "/tmp/kubectl-edit-3485293250.yaml"
error: Edit cancelled, no valid changes were saved.
```

Disregard the error; this is also what we expected. The location in which the YAML was stored may be different for you, but we will use that YAML to replace the Service with force. To do this, we'll type the command k `replace -f /tmp/kubectl-edit-3485293250.yaml --force`. The output will be similar to this:

```
root@kind-control-plane:/# k replace -f /tmp/kubectl-edit-3485293250.yaml -
↩ -force
service/kube-dns replaced
```

Now that we've changed the `kube-dns` Service, the new IP address is given with the command k `-n kube-system get svc`, as you see in the output here:

```
root@kind-control-plane:/# k -n kube-system get svc
NAME        TYPE        CLUSTER-IP      EXTERNAL-IP    PORT(S)
↩ AGE
kube-dns    ClusterIP   100.96.0.10     <none>         53/UDP,53/TCP,9153/TCP
↩ 2m13s
```

For newly created Pods to receive the new DNS information, we need to modify the kubelet configuration. There are two places where we can adjust the kubelet configuration. The first place is the YAML file, which is the configuration YAML manifest for the kubelet. Let's perform the command `vim /var/lib/kubelet/config.yaml` to open the kubelet YAML manifest. When you have it open, you'll notice that there's a section called `clusterDNS:`. Change the value from 10.96.0.10 to 100.96.0.10 (press the I key for insert mode), which is the new Service IP address for the Service named `kube-dns`. The result should be what you see in figure 6.4.

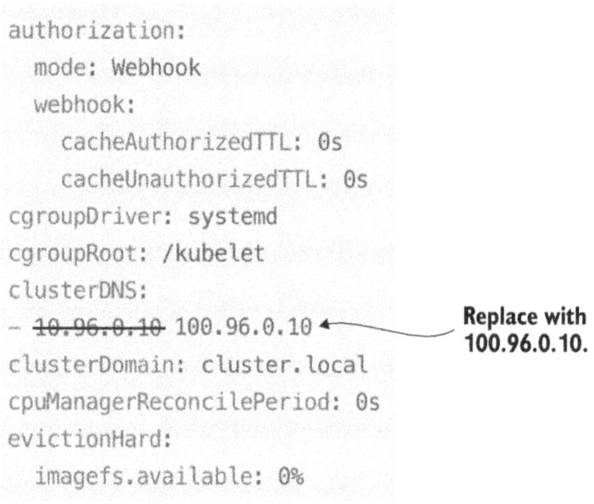

```
authorization:
  mode: Webhook
  webhook:
    cacheAuthorizedTTL: 0s
    cacheUnauthorizedTTL: 0s
cgroupDriver: systemd
cgroupRoot: /kubelet
clusterDNS:
  - 10.96.0.10 100.96.0.10 ◀──────  Replace with
clusterDomain: cluster.local                100.96.0.10.
cpuManagerReconcilePeriod: 0s
evictionHard:
  imagefs.available: 0%
```

Figure 6.4   The file `/var/lib/` `kubelet/config.yaml` **replaces the** `clusterDNS` **with the new IP address of DNS.**

Once you've made the change, you can press the Esc key on your keyboard to get out of insert mode, followed by `:wq` to save the file and quit Vim. As you may have noticed, this didn't do much; it just changed a file that didn't affect the cluster. To affect the cluster and have our changes implemented immediately, you need to edit the Config-Map associated with the kubelet configuration. To do this, perform the command `k -n kube-system edit cm kubelet-config`. You'll see the same type of YAML structure as you saw in the `config.yaml` file. Again go to the line that starts with clusterDNS, and change the value from 10.96.0.10 to 100.96.0.10 (don't forget insert mode!). Once you've done this, press the Esc key and type `:wq` to save the file and quit to save the ConfigMap. The output will look similar to this:

```
root@kind-control-plane:/# k -n kube-system edit cm kubelet-config
configmap/kubelet-config edited
```

Because the kubelet is a daemon that's currently running on the node, we must update the node of this configuration, as well as reload the daemon and restart the kubelet Service on the node. First, to update the kubelet configuration on the node, perform the command `kubeadm upgrade node phase kubelet-config`. The output will look like this:

```
root@kind-control-plane:/# kubeadm upgrade node phase kubelet-config
[upgrade] Reading configuration from the cluster...
```

```
[upgrade] FYI: You can look at this config file with 'kubectl -n kube-
⮡ system get cm kubeadm-config -o yaml'
W0914 17:44:33.203828    3618 utils.go:69] The recommended value for
⮡ "clusterDNS" in "KubeletConfiguration" is: [10.96.0.10]; the provided
⮡ value is: [100.96.0.10]
[kubelet-start] Writing kubelet configuration to file
⮡ "/var/lib/kubelet/config.yaml"
[upgrade] The configuration for this node was successfully updated!
[upgrade] Now you should go ahead and upgrade the kubelet package using
⮡ your package manager.
```

Now that we've upgraded the kubelet configuration for the node, we can reload the daemon with the command `systemctl daemon-reload` and restart the Service with the command `systemctl restart kubelet`. You will not get an output; you will just return to the command prompt, so as long as there are no error messages, you have successfully restarted the kubelet Service.

> **EXAM TIP**   You may be presented with tasks on the exam that require you to start, restart, or reload the kubelet daemon. The commands `systemctl stop kubelet systemctl start kubelet`, `systmectl restart kubelet`, and `systemctl daemon-reload` are good to memorize.

Finally, to test all the changes we made so far, we can create a new Pod and check that the DNS IP address is correct and that DNS is able to resolve example.com. Let's perform the command `kubectl run netshoot --image=nicolaka/netshoot --command sleep --command "3600"` to create a new Pod in the default namespace. I like to use this image because it comes preinstalled with DNS utilities, which are handy for testing the network. If you'd like to know more details about this image, visit the Docker-Hub page here: https://hub.docker.com/r/nicolaka/netshoot.

We run the two commands `sleep` and `3600` so that the Pod will stay in a running state (for 3600 seconds, or 60 minutes). We can check if the Pod is in a running state with the command `k get po`. The output should look similar to this:

```
root@kind-control-plane:/# kubectl run netshoot --image=nicolaka/netshoot -
⮡ -command sleep --command "3600"
pod/netshoot created
root@kind-control-plane:/# k get po
NAME        READY    STATUS     RESTARTS    AGE
netshoot    1/1      Running    0           40s
```

The Pod is running, so now you can get a Bash shell to the container. To do this, perform the command `k exec -it netshoot --bash`. You will notice that your prompt changes, which means you have successfully entered the container within the Pod. The output should look like this:

```
root@kind-control-plane:/# k exec -it netshoot --bash
bash-5.1#
```

Now that you have a Bash shell open in the container, you can run the command `cat /etc/resolv.conf` to check that the correct DNS IP address is listed. The output should be similar to this:

```
root@kind-control-plane:/# k exec -it netshoot --bash
bash-5.1# cat /etc/resolv.conf
search default.svc.cluster.local svc.cluster.local cluster.local
nameserver 100.96.0.10
options ndots:5
```

The DNS is correctly configured; therefore, Pods can resolve DNS names using CoreDNS in the cluster. You can check that this Pod can resolve a DNS query to example.com with the command `nslookup example.com`. `nslookup` is a DNS utility that allows you to query name servers. The output should look like this:

```
bash-5.1# nslookup example.com
Server:     100.96.0.10
Address:    100.96.0.10#53

Non-authoritative answer:
Name:    example.com
Address: 93.184.216.34
Name:    example.com
Address: 2606:2800:220:1:248:1893:25c8:1946
```

Because the container is using the correct DNS server (100.96.0.10), it was able to resolve example.com to 93.184.216.34; therefore, our configuration of CoreDNS was successful, and all the preceding steps were effective in customizing CoreDNS to correctly address the needs of this exam task.

In summary, to complete this task, we modified the API configuration in `/etc/kubernetes/manifests/kube-apiserver.yaml`; we edited the Service named `kube-dns` in the `kube-system` namespace; we modified the `kubeclet` configuration at `/var/lib/kubelet/config.yaml`; we changed the kubelet ConfigMap named `kubelet-config` in the kube-system namespace; and then we upgraded the node and reloaded the kubelet daemon.

6.2 CoreDNS

The magic behind CoreDNS is the ability to resolve domain names quickly so that Services can talk to each other, and more importantly, so applications (running in Pods) can talk to each other and communicate as requests arise. To solve this locally, you can add values to our `/etc/hosts` file for each Pod, but that's not scalable. Instead, we have a central location (central to the cluster) where Pods can query a cumulative list of hostnames and IP addresses, as in figure 6.5.

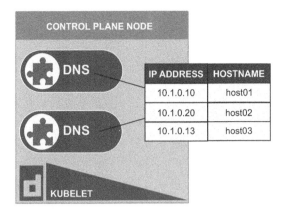

Figure 6.5 CoreDNS provides a central place for the mapping of hostnames to IP addresses in the Kubernetes cluster.

6.2.1 Config files

The kubelet plays a special role in the Kubernetes DNS configuration. Kubelet is a Service that exists directly on each node. As we saw in section 6.1, we can start, stop, and restart that Service via `systemctl`. Kubelet is responsible for creating the CoreDNS Pod and injecting the configuration into that Pod. That configuration file is in the `/var/lib/kubelet/config.yaml` directory. This is a special kind of configuration file, just for the kubelet, and will include the authentication for the kubelet, the health Endpoints, and, most importantly, the cluster DNS. Fun fact: `kube-dns` built with SkyDNS used to be the primary DNS resolution in Kubernetes. The name of the Service remained even after CoreDNS replaced it. CoreDNS became a much more efficient and well-rounded option and replaced `kube-dns` in Kubernetes version 1.11.

> **EXAM TIP** There's a special directory in the Kubernetes cluster for static Pods. This location is `/etc/kubernetes/manifests/`, and anything in this directory will autoprovision without the scheduler's awareness.

There are two ConfigMaps—one for the kubelet and one for the CoreDNS—and each contains their respective applied configurations because the kubelet is responsible for creating new Pods in a Kubernetes cluster, and CoreDNS will be the DNS server. You can view these ConfigMaps with the command `k -n kube-system get cm`.

6.2.2 Replicating DNS

As you may have noticed in our cluster, there are two instances of CoreDNS running as Pods in the `kube-system` namespace. You can view them with the command `k -n kube-system get po`. The output will look something like this:

```
root@kind-control-plane:/# k -n kube-system get po
NAME                                         READY     STATUS
⇒ RESTARTS        AGE
coredns-565d847f94-4pnf4                     1/1       Running
⇒ 0               143m
```

```
coredns-565d847f94-xstnx                          1/1      Running
➥ 0                143m
etcd-kind-control-plane                           1/1      Running
➥ 0                143m
kindnet-75z9k                                     1/1      Running
➥ 3 (46m ago)     143m
kube-apiserver-kind-control-plane                 1/1      Running
➥ 0                94m
kube-controller-manager-kind-control-plane        1/1      Running
➥ 1 (95m ago)     143m
kube-proxy-s5vps                                  1/1      Running
➥ 0                143m
kube-scheduler-kind-control-plane                 1/1      Running
➥ 1 (95m ago)     143m
```

As you see, there are two replicas of the CoreDNS Pods running. This is the benefit of a Deployment, as you can easily scale them up and down to get faster DNS resolution. Nobody likes to wait a long time for DNS queries. You can view the CoreDNS Deployment with the command k -n kube-system get deploy. The output will look similar to this:

```
root@kind-control-plane:/# k -n kube-system get deploy
NAME      READY   UP-TO-DATE   AVAILABLE    AGE
coredns   2/2     2            2            147m
```

This Deployment is called *CoreDNS*, and it is similar to any other Deployment in Kubernetes. Let's say that DNS queries are taking a long time and causing delays for our application, we can scale the CoreDNS Deployment with the command k -n kube-system scale deploy coredns --replicas 3 and see that there are now three Pod replicas. The output will be similar to this:

```
root@kind-control-plane:/# k -n kube-system scale deploy coredns --replicas 3
deployment.apps/coredns scaled
root@kind-control-plane:/# k -n kube-system get po
NAME                                         READY    STATUS     RESTARTS
➥            AGE
coredns-565d847f94-4pnf4                     1/1      Running    0
coredns-565d847f94-lqkbd                     1/1      Running    0
coredns-565d847f94-xstnx                     1/1      Running    0
etcd-kind-control-plane                      1/1      Running    0
kindnet-75z9k                                1/1      Running    3
kube-apiserver-kind-control-plane            1/1      Running    0
kube-controller-manager-kind-control-plane   1/1      Running    1
kube-proxy-s5vps                             1/1      Running    0
kube-scheduler-kind-control-plane            1/1      Running    1
```

Scaling the DNS server replicas simply allows for greater performance when making DNS queries, which makes managing your DNS servers much easier.

If this solution didn't exist, we would have to apply the hostname to the IP address manually for every Pod. Let's simulate this by scaling the CoreDNS Deployment down to zero and then trying to communicate with a Service in the cluster. To scale the

Deployment down, we would run the command `k -n kube-system scale deploy` `Coredns --replicas 0`. This would terminate all of the CoreDNS Pods currently running in the cluster, which would look like the following:

```
root@kind-control-plane:/# k -n kube-system scale deploy coredns -
 replicas 0
deployment.apps/coredns scaled
root@kind-control-plane:/# k get po -A
NAMESPACE           NAME                                          READY
 STATUS
default             netshoot                                      1/1
 Running
kube-system         coredns-565d847f94-ctlpt                      1/1
 Terminating
kube-system         coredns-565d847f94-z65fz                      1/1
 Terminating
kube-system         coredns-565d847f94-zv28n                      1/1
 Terminating
kube-system         etcd-kind-control-plane                       1/1
 Running
kube-system         kindnet-75z9k                                 1/1
 Running
kube-system         kube-apiserver-kind-control-plane             1/1
 Running
kube-system         kube-controller-manager-kind-control-plane    1/1
 Running
kube-system         kube-proxy-s5vps                              1/1
 Running
kube-system         kube-scheduler-kind-control-plane             1/1
 Running
local-path-storage  local-path-provisioner-684f458cdd-qgncs       1/1
 Running
```

DNS is not available in the cluster, so we won't be able to resolve hostnames. Let's create a Deployment along with a Service. We'll talk about Services later in this chapter, but for now, we'll use this Service to communicate with the underlying Pods in the Deployment. Create a Deployment and Service with the command `k create deploy` `apache --image httpd; k expose deploy apache --name apache-svc --port 80`. The output will look similar to this:

```
root@kind-control-plane:/# k create deploy apache --image httpd; k expose
 deploy apache --name apache-svc --port 80
deployment.apps/apache created
service/apache-svc exposed
```

Grab the IP address of the Service by running the command `k get svc`. The output will look like this, where the cluster IP address is 100.96.102.73 for me:

```
root@kind-control-plane:/# k get svc
NAME         TYPE        CLUSTER-IP      EXTERNAL-IP   PORT(S)    AGE
apache-svc   ClusterIP   100.96.102.73   <none>        80/TCP     25m
kubernetes   ClusterIP   10.96.0.1       <none>        443/TCP    6h36m
```

If you still have the `netshoot` container running from the exercise earlier, let's get a Bash shell to it. If you've deleted the `netshoot` container, you can restart it with the command `kubectl run netshoot --image=nicolaka/netshoot --command sleep --command "3600"`. Let's get a Bash shell to it by running the command `k exec --it netshoot --bash`. You should now have a new prompt that looks something like this:

```
root@kind-control-plane:/# k exec -it netshoot --bash
bash-5.1#
```

To verify that DNS is not working, let's try to communicate with the Service that we just created, called `apache-svc`. We can do this with the command `wget -O- apache-svc`. You should get the following output:

```
bash-5.1# wget -O- apache-svc
wget: bad address 'apache-svc'
```

To fix this, we'll add the hostname-to-IP mapping to the `/etc/hosts` file within the Pod. We can do this with a single command: `echo "100.96.102.73   apache-svc" >> /etc/hosts`. Now let's run the `wget` command again, and you should get the standard Apache homepage, which looks something like this:

```
bash-5.1# wget -O- apache-svc
Connecting to apache-svc (100.96.102.73:80)
writing to stdout
<html><body><h1>It works!</h1></body></html>
-                        100%
|**************************************************************************
**********************|    45  0:00:00 ETA
written to stdout
```

This worked because we wrote our own DNS locally to the Pod. As you can see, it would be hard to do on every Pod if you have hundreds of Pods, and as we know, Pods are ephemeral, so doing this for every Pod would be a hassle. I hope this exercise proved the importance of CoreDNS and also gave you a few tools to test communication to Services.

6.2.3 *Pod-to-Pod connectivity*

Let's look at how Pods communicate across namespaces so we can become more familiar with how DNS works inside a Kubernetes cluster. Create a similar Deployment and Service, but create it inside of a new namespace called `c01383`.

> **EXAM TIP** These complex names for namespaces will appear a lot on the exam, so it's good to practice using autocomplete as much as possible. To install autocomplete in kind, see appendix B.

First, let's create a namespace with the command `k create ns c01383`. We can view the namespaces in our cluster with the command `k get ns`. You will see an output similar to this:

```
root@kind-control-plane:/# k create ns c01383
namespace/c01383 created
root@kind-control-plane:/# k get ns
NAME                STATUS    AGE
c01383              Active    2s
default             Active    8h
kube-node-lease     Active    8h
kube-public         Active    8h
kube-system         Active    8h
local-path-storage  Active    8h
```

Once we've created the namespace `c01383`, we can create a Deployment and Service inside of that namespace with the command `k -n c01383 create deploy nginx --image nginx; k -n c01383 expose deploy nginx --name nginx-svc --port 80`. You can see the Deployment and the Service in the `c01383` namespace by typing `k -n c01383 get deploy,svc`. The output will be similar to this:

```
root@kind-control-plane:~# k -n c01383 create deploy nginx --image nginx; k
➥ -n c01383 expose deploy nginx --name nginx-svc --port 80
deployment.apps/nginx created
service/nginx-svc exposed
root@kind-control-plane:/# k -n c01383 get deploy,svc
NAME                     READY    UP-TO-DATE    AVAILABLE    AGE
deployment.apps/nginx    1/1      1             1            57s

NAME                TYPE        CLUSTER-IP       EXTERNAL-IP    PORT(S)    AGE
service/nginx-svc   ClusterIP   100.96.138.162   <none>         80/TCP     57s
```

Do you think if we connect to one of the Pods from the Deployment, we'll be able to reach the Service named `apache-svc` in the default namespace? Let's try! Type the command `k -n c01383 get po` to retrieve the Pod name. It will start with `nginx`, followed by a dash, then a unique value that represents the ReplicaSet, another dash, and then another unique value that represents the Deployment. This is best demonstrated by the output shown in figure 6.6.

Now that we have the name of the Pod, we can open a Bash shell to it with the command `k -n c01383 exec -it nginx-76d6c9b8c-8lqgg --bash`. You will see your prompt change, which means you are now looking at the filesystem of the container inside the Pod. From inside the container, run the command `curl apache-svc`. You should get the result "Could not resolve host," and it will look like this:

```
root@kind-control-plane:/# k -n c01383 exec -it nginx-76d6c9b8c-8lqgg --
➥ bash
root@nginx-76d6c9b8c-8lqgg:/# curl apache-svc
curl: (6) Could not resolve host: apache-svc
```

Let's try to run the command `curl apache-svc.default`. It worked! You should see the following:

```
root@nginx-76d6c9b8c-8lqgg:/# curl apache-svc.default
<html><body><h1>It works!</h1></body></html>
```

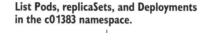

List Pods, replicaSets, and Deployments
in the c01383 namespace.

```
root@kind-control-plane:/# k -n c01383 get po,rs,deploy
NAME                        READY   STATUS    RESTARTS   AGE
pod/nginx-76d6c9b8c-8lqgg   1/1     Running   0          92m

NAME                              DESIRED   CURRENT   READY   AGE
replicaset.apps/nginx-76d6c9b8c   1         1         1       92m

NAME                      READY   UP-TO-DATE   AVAILABLE   AGE
deployment.apps/nginx     1/1     1            1           92m
```

Same unique
identifier

Figure 6.6   The Pod name comes from an auto-assigned unique identifier that prevents conflicting Pod names.

This is because each Service is given its own unique domain name in Kubernetes, which is different between namespaces. The *fully qualified domain name (FQDN)* for Services in a Kubernetes cluster is `<service-name>.<namespace-name>.svc.cluster.local`, as depicted in figure 6.7.

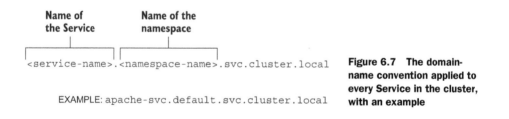

Name of
the Service

Name of the
namespace

```
<service-name>.<namespace-name>.svc.cluster.local
```

EXAMPLE: `apache-svc.default.svc.cluster.local`

Figure 6.7   The domain-name convention applied to every Service in the cluster, with an example

We saw this previously when we looked at the `resolv.conf` within the Pod back in section 6.1 of this chapter. Let's look at it again from the shell that we're already in with the command `cat /etc/resolv.conf`. The output should look similar to this:

```
root@nginx-76d6c9b8c-8lqgg:/# cat /etc/resolv.conf
search c01383.svc.cluster.local svc.cluster.local cluster.local
nameserver 100.96.0.10
options ndots:5
```

The line that begins with `search` will indicate the DNS names that are associated with the Services in that namespace. You don't see `default.svc.cluster.local` in this list, which is why when we tried the name `apache-svc`, the name would not resolve.

Pods also have an FQDN, which is the IP address, but CoreDNS converts the dots into dashes, so it looks like this: `10-244-0-14.default.pod.cluster.local`, where

10.244.0.14 is the IP address of the Pod within the default namespace. We can perform the same curl command but use the Pod FQDN like so:

```
root@kind-control-plane:/# k get po apache-855464645-npcf5 -o wide
NAME                        READY    STATUS     RESTARTS    AGE    IP
⇨ NODE                      NOMINATED NODE    READINESS GATES
apache-855464645-npcf5      1/1      Running    0           21h    10.244.0.14
⇨ kind-control-plane        <none>            <none>
root@kind-control-plane:/# k -n c01383 exec -it nginx-76dc9b8c-8lqgg --
⇨ bash
root@nginx-76dc9b8c-8lqgg:/# curl 10-244-0-14.default.pod.cluster.local
<html><body><h1>It works!</h1></body></html>
```

We could have also performed the command `10-244-0-14.default.pod`, and DNS would have resolved it due to `cluster.local` being in the `resolv.conf` search criteria.

Exam exercises

`exec` into a Pod and `cat` out the DNS resolver file to see the IP address of the DNS server that the Pod uses to resolve domain names.

Open the file that contains the configuration for the kubelet and change the value for `clusterDNS` to `100.96.0.10`. Save and quit the file.

Stop and reload the kubelet daemon. Verify that the Service is active and running.

Locate the `kube-dns` Service. Try to edit the Service in place by changing the value of both `clusterIP` and `ClusterIPs` to `100.96.0.10`. When the values cannot be updated, force a replacement of the Service with the correct `kubectl` command-line argument.

Edit the ConfigMap that contains the kubelet configuration. Change the IP address value that is set for `clusterDNS` to `100.96.0.10`. Make sure to edit the resource without writing a new YAML file.

Scale the CoreDNS Deployment to three replicas. Verify that the Pods have been created as a part of that Deployment.

Test access from a Pod to a Service by first creating a Deployment with the `apache` image, followed by exposing that Deployment. Create a Pod from the `netshoot` image, and verify that you can reach the Service that you just created.

Using the `netshoot` Pod created in the previous exercise, locate the Service in the default namespace by its DNS name. Use as few letters as possible for DNS search functionality.

6.3 Ingress and Ingress controllers

When it comes to performing application layer (layer-7) routing to your application running in Kubernetes, the term that's used is *Ingress*. Let's cover Ingress first, before Services, as it is a preferred approach to exposing your app along with a Service, and the exam objective states that you must know how to use Ingress and Ingress controllers. The reason it's a preferred method is that Ingress provides a single gateway (only one entry) into the cluster and can route traffic to multiple Services using simple path-based routes. Along with an Ingress controller, you can set these routes in the Ingress resource, and it will be directed to each Service, as is depicted in figure 6.8.

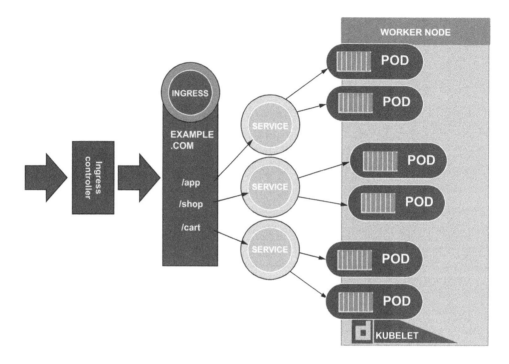

Figure 6.8   Ingress flow of traffic and the redirection to multiple Services based on the path rules

You will be tested on creating Ingress and an Ingress controller, so let's review what an exam task might look like.

EXAM TASK   In cluster `ik8s`, install an Ingress controller to proxy communication into the cluster via an Ingress resource. Then, create a Deployment named `hello` using the image `nginxdemos/hello:plain-text`. The container is exposed on port 80. Create a Service named `hello-svc` that targets the `hello` Deployment on port 80. Then, create an Ingress resource that will allow you to resolve the DNS name `hello.com` to the ClusterIP Service named `hello-svc` in Kubernetes.

To complete these exam tasks, we'll have to create a new kind cluster. See appendix A, section A.3, for instructions on how to build a single-node kind cluster with additional ports exposed and labels applied on the nodes. As soon as you have access to your kind cluster, get a shell to the control plane node with the command `docker exec -it ingress-control-plane bash`. Once you have a shell, set your alias `k` to equal `kubectl` with the command `alias k=kubectl`. On the exam, they will already have this alias set for you, so it's good practice to use `k` as opposed to having to type `kubectl` over and over again.

Now that we've built the cluster and have a shell to the control plane node, let's begin the process of installing the Ingress controller, which will be a similar process on the exam. The Ingress controller YAML creates several resources. You can apply all of these resources at once with the command `k apply -f https://raw.githubusercontent` `.com/chadmcrowell/acing-the-cka-exam/main/ch_06/nginx-ingress-controller.yaml`. In the output of this command, the resources that have been created in the cluster will look similar to this:

```
root@ingress-control-plane:/# k apply -f
⮡ https://raw.githubusercontent.com/chadmcrowell/acing-the-cka-
⮡ exam/main/ch_06/nginx-ingress-controller.yaml
namespace/ingress-nginx created
serviceaccount/ingress-nginx created
serviceaccount/ingress-nginx-admission created
role.rbac.authorization.k8s.io/ingress-nginx created
role.rbac.authorization.k8s.io/ingress-nginx-admission created
clusterrole.rbac.authorization.k8s.io/ingress-nginx created
clusterrole.rbac.authorization.k8s.io/ingress-nginx-admission created
rolebinding.rbac.authorization.k8s.io/ingress-nginx created
rolebinding.rbac.authorization.k8s.io/ingress-nginx-admission created
clusterrolebinding.rbac.authorization.k8s.io/ingress-nginx created
clusterrolebinding.rbac.authorization.k8s.io/ingress-nginx-admission created
configmap/ingress-nginx-controller created
service/ingress-nginx-controller created
service/ingress-nginx-controller-admission created
deployment.apps/ingress-nginx-controller created
job.batch/ingress-nginx-admission-create created
job.batch/ingress-nginx-admission-patch created
ingressclass.networking.k8s.io/nginx created
validatingwebhookconfiguration.admissionregistration.k8s.io/ingress-nginx-
⮡ admission created
```

The Kubernetes objects have been created in their own namespace, called `ingress-nginx`, and you can view these resources all at once using the command `k -n ingress-nginx get all`. The output will look similar to this:

```
root@ingress-control-plane:/# k get all -n ingress-nginx
NAME                                            READY   STATUS
⮡ RESTARTS    AGE
pod/ingress-nginx-admission-create-lccjf        0/1     Completed
⮡ 0           27s
pod/ingress-nginx-admission-patch-bzjfm         0/1     Completed
⮡ 0           27s
pod/ingress-nginx-controller-6c695f6cc7-ntjbt   1/1     Running
⮡ 0           27s
```

```
NAME                                            TYPE        CLUSTER-IP
➦ EXTERNAL-IP    PORT(S)                         AGE
service/ingress-nginx-controller                NodePort    10.96.134.48
➦ <none>          80:32745/TCP,443:31396/TCP    27s
service/ingress-nginx-controller-admission      ClusterIP   10.96.130.242
➦ <none>          443/TCP                        27s

NAME                                        READY   UP-TO-DATE   AVAILABLE
➦ AGE
deployment.apps/ingress-nginx-controller   1/1     1            1
➦ 27s

NAME                                                    DESIRED   CURRENT
➦ READY     AGE
replicaset.apps/ingress-nginx-controller-6c695f6cc7     1         1
➦ 1         27s

NAME                                        COMPLETIONS   DURATION   AGE
job.batch/ingress-nginx-admission-create    1/1           5s         27s
job.batch/ingress-nginx-admission-patch     1/1           5s         27s
```

Verify that the Pod with the name that starts with `ingress-nginx-controller` is running. This means that you are ready to proceed and create a Deployment, a Service, and an Ingress.

We'll start with the deployment, which you can create with the command `k`
➦ `create deploy hello --image nginxdemos/hello:plain-text --port 80`. The
    output will look like this:
```
root@ingress-control-plane:/# k create deploy hello -image
➦ nginxdemos/hello:plain-text -port 80
deployment.apps/hello created
```

Now we can create a Service by exposing the Deployment with the command `k expose deploy hello -name hello-svc -port 80`. The output will look like the following:

```
root@ingress-control-plane:/# k expose deploy hello -name hello-svc -port 80
service/hello-svc exposed
```

You will now see the following when you type `k get deploy,svc`:

```
root@ingress-control-plane:/# k get deploy,svc
NAME                        READY   UP-TO-DATE   AVAILABLE   AGE
deployment.apps/hello       1/1     1            1           5m32s

NAME                     TYPE        CLUSTER-IP      EXTERNAL-IP   PORT(S)   AGE
service/hello-svc        ClusterIP   10.96.255.66    <none>        80/TCP    20s
service/kubernetes       ClusterIP   10.96.0.1       <none>        443/TCP   28m
```

Let's finish the exam task by creating an Ingress resource. Type the command `k apply -f https://raw.githubusercontent.com/chadmcrowell/acing-the-cka-exam/main/ch_06/hello-ingress.yaml` to create the Ingress resource. You will see the following output after you perform this command:

```
root@ingress-control-plane:/# k apply -f
➥ https://raw.githubusercontent.com/chadmcrowell/acing-the-cka-
➥ exam/main/ch_06/hello-ingress.yaml
ingress.networking.k8s.io/hello created
```

After about 20 seconds, you will see the Ingress resource by typing the command `k get ing`, like so:

```
root@ingress-control-plane:/# k get ing
NAME    CLASS     HOSTS        ADDRESS      PORTS    AGE
hello   <none>    hello.com                 80       9s
hello   <none>    hello.com    localhost    80       15s
```

Finally, let's test our setup by adding `hello.com` to our `/etc/hosts` file. Open the hosts file by typing `vim /etc/hosts` (you may need to run `apt update; apt install -y vim` first to install Vim). Type the IP address of the control plane node, which you can see next to the word `localhost` in the `hosts` file, followed by `hello.com`. The file will look similar to the `hosts` file contents in figure 6.9.

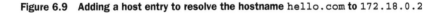

```
                   127.0.0.1           localhost
                   ::1        localhost ip6-localhost ip6-loopback
                   fe00::0 ip6-localnet
                   ff00::0 ip6-mcastprefix
                   ff02::1 ip6-allnodes
Use the same IP    ff02::2 ip6-allrouters
address as on this line
(different for you).  →  172.18.0.2          ingress-control-plane
                   fc00:f853:ccd:e793::2    ingress-control-plane
Add this line. ──── 172.18.0.2          hello.com
```

Figure 6.9 Adding a host entry to resolve the hostname `hello.com` to `172.18.0.2`

Once you have saved this file, perform the command `curl hello.com`. You will get the following output, which will be the output of the hello application that we deployed earlier:

```
root@ingress-control-plane:/# curl hello.com
Server address: 10.244.0.8:80
Server name: hello-665cb98d5f-cfmll
Date: 30/Sep/2022:20:38:01 +0000
URI: /
Request ID: fbba7de007d520e7f3e6ea9e0b4a69ad
```

The output is the response that you get from the Pod, so the server address will match the IP address of the Pod. You can see that if you type the command `k get po -o wide`.

That completes our exam task of installing an Ingress controller and creating a Deployment named `hello`, a Service named `hello-svc`, and an Ingress resource that resolves `hello.com` to the `hello-svc` Service.

You'll see from the exam task that we simply typed `curl hello.com`, and it magically routed us to the correct Service and, in turn, the correct Pod. This magic is performed by the admission controller. An Ingress controller is software that intercepts requests to the Kubernetes API. In our case, it's a Pod running in the `ingress-nginx` namespace. This Pod intercepted the request that we made to `hello.com` and rerouted the request to the hello app with assistance from the Ingress resource. This was just a simple example, but we could have also added a path to the URL (e.g., `hello.com/app`) and directed the request to a different Service. This Service will be a ClusterIP Service, because the Ingress controller is already exposed to the outside, helping the traffic into the cluster.

Let's go through the Ingress YAML and modify the Ingress resource. You can edit the Ingress resource with the command `k edit ingress hello`. The YAML will now appear in the Vim editor. Starting from the top, as you can see in figure 6.10, the host is the domain where clients will be accessing your application (hello.com). This could be a domain name that you've purchased from a domain registrar, or this could be something local to the cluster, as we have chosen. The HTTP section and the following text define the rules for resolving HTTP (port 80) traffic. The rule states that any request made to the host hello.com will be directed to the `hello-svc` Service on port 80. This is the default route because an explicit path is not specified (e.g., `hello.com/path`). To add another rule—let's say, to take requests from `hello.com/app` to a different Service named `nginx` over port 8080—we'd add another block under `path:` to specify that rule. The result will look similar to figure 6.10.

In figure 6.10, the Ingress rules show routes to two different Services. Those Services are defined as *backends*, meaning once the traffic enters the Ingress, it will enter the backend (what happens behind the scenes). In this case, two backend routes define the specifics of the individual Services to which they route. The first goes to a Service named `hello-svc` and uses port 80. This requires us to have a ClusterIP Service in our cluster that is exposed on port 80. The second route is backend to a Service named `nginx`. The client would have to type `http://hello.com/app` to route to this Service. You will also see a `pathType`, as each Ingress path is required to have.

There are three supported path types—`Exact`, `Prefix`, and `Implementation-Specific`. The `Exact` path type has to match the path exactly (case-sensitive) for the path to be valid (e.g., `hello.com/app`). The `Prefix` path type matches the URL path split by a forward slash (`/`), where the characters between the slash are the element's prefix. The `ImplementationSpecific` path type leaves it up to the `Ingress` class to decide a prefix or an exact path type.

In the YAML for an Ingress resource, you don't have to only choose path-based routing (`hello.com/app`); you can also choose subdomain-type routing. For example, you can choose a different backend when the client types `http://app.hello.com`,

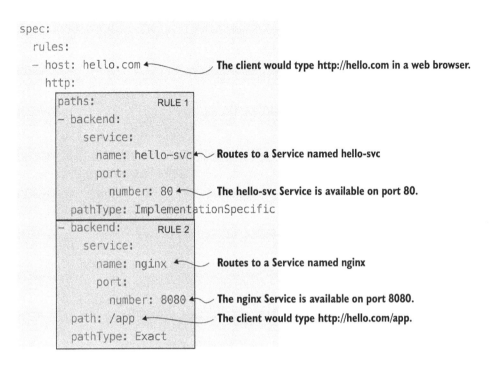

Figure 6.10   Adding a rule to Ingress, routing to a different Service named `nginx`

which may be more flexible depending on the type of application you have. The
YAML would then change to something like this:

```
apiVersion: networking.k8s.io/v1
kind: Ingress
metadata:
  name: hello
spec:
  rules:
  - host: hello.com
    http:
      paths:
      - pathType: ImplementationSpecific
        path: "/"
        backend:
          service:
            name: hello-svc
            port:
              number: 80
  - host: app.hello.com
    http:
      paths:
      - pathType: Exact
        path: "/"
        backend:
```

```
service:
  name: nginx
  port:
    number: 8080
```

6.4   *Services*

Pods are ephemeral by nature and are meant to be killed and respawned at a moment's notice. As a result, their IP addresses are constantly changing. Services are a way for the traffic to always reach the correct Pod, whether that Pod has been moved to a new node, killed, or scaled. Services provide a distributed load balancer for the Pods, and they evenly distribute the load between multiple Pods within the same Deployment and also help with detecting exactly where those Pods are in the cluster, as depicted in figure 6.11.

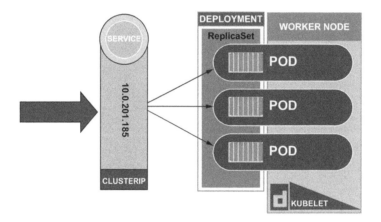

Figure 6.11   A Service accepts incoming traffic on behalf of each Pod, load balancing the traffic.

Services contain a consistent IP address and DNS name for the Pod or set of Pods. This consistent address helps maintain existing connections and manage the routing of traffic as Pods come and go. Pods can communicate with each other via Services, all within the cluster, so no matter what node the Pod is running on, it will be able to locate that Pod as a part of that cluster-wide Service. Endpoints are the exposed ports on Pods that associate with the Pods and represent a target where the Pods can be reached. We can see a list of Endpoints, which take on the same name of the Service, by typing the command k get ep. The output will look similar to this:

```
root@kind-control-plane:/# k get ep
NAME         ENDPOINTS          AGE
apache-svc   10.244.0.14:80     129m
kubernetes   172.18.0.2:6443    8h
```

The types of Services are ClusterIP, NodePort, and LoadBalancer. ClusterIP Services are designed to make Pods internally available within the cluster only, whereas NodePort- and LoadBalancer-type Services are designed to expose a port and create outside access to the cluster. NodePort exposes a port on the node's IP address, but Load-Balancer allows an external load balancer (outside the cluster) to control the traffic into each node port. This allows you to use more common ports (80,443) instead of the NodePort restriction of ports 30,000–32,768. You'll notice when you create a NodePort Service that you are extending a ClusterIP-type Service at the same time, as depicted in figure 6.12.

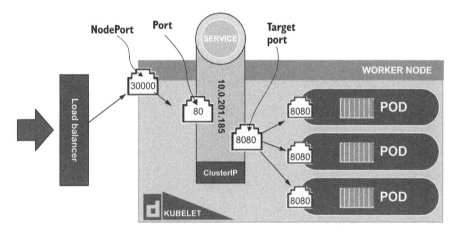

Figure 6.12   A LoadBalancer-type Service, which is a superset of the NodePort- and ClusterIP-type Services, provides a single entry point into the cluster and the underlying Pods.

6.4.1   ClusterIP Service

The ClusterIP Service is for internal cluster communication only. You would usually create a Service like this to communicate from the frontend of your application, in one Pod in the cluster, to the backend, which is in a different Pod. You can specify the ports to use when you create the Service initially, or you can modify it later. Like a lot of other resources in Kubernetes, you can run an imperative command to create a Service like `k create svc clusterip internal-svc --tcp 8080:80`, or you can create a YAML spec file with the command `k create svc clusterip internal-svc --tcp 8080:80 -dry-run=client -o yaml > svc.yaml`. Go ahead and run the latter command and take a look at the YAML spec by opening in it Vim with the command `vim svc.yaml`. You'll see, as in figure 6.13, in the ports section, that there's a port and a target port. The target port is the port that's exposed on the container itself. Not all containers have exposed ports, but in the case of the `nginx` image, for example, port 80 is exposed.

The exposed port is defined in the Dockerfile (how the image is built), so if you're ever wondering what ports the container is exposed on, look at the Dockerfile for that

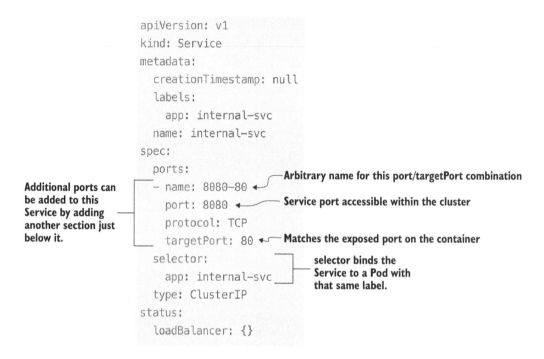

Figure 6.13   YAML spec for a Service

image. Going back to the Service YAML, the port is exposed within the cluster, as in figure 6.12 where the port is 80. You can have multiple Services with the same port exposed because each Service has its own IP address and DNS name, which allows an incoming request to differentiate between Services. As long as the Service name is different, you can have as many Services as you want with port 80 exposed. Notice in the YAML spec that this Service has a selector, as in figure 6.13. This is how the Service can *bind* itself to Pods. Any Pod with the label `app=internal-svc`, in this case, will be associated with that Service. This works similarly to `nodeSelectors`, which we touched on in section 4.1.

Let's say that we want to expose another port within this Service; we could do that as well. Copy everything just below the word `ports` in the YAML file, and paste it just below the word `targetPort`. We can now change the name to `search`; the port and the target port can be 9200. The result should be similar to this:

```
spec:
  ports:
  - name: 8080-80
    port: 8080
    protocol: TCP
    targetPort: 80
  - name: search
    port: 9200
```

```
      protocol: TCP
      targetPort: 9200
    selector:
      app: internal-svc
    type: ClusterIP
status:
    loadBalancer: {}
```

This resembles an elastic search Pod that may be running in your cluster. If a client reaches out to this Service, both Pods that have port 80 exposed—as well as the Pods that have port 9200 exposed—can be reached by accessing just one Service.

It is possible to bypass the Service altogether and go directly to the Pod. This is called a *headless Service.* To demonstrate this, let's add a line to our YAML spec. Just below the spec, let's insert the line `clusterIP: none`. The result should look like the following:

```
spec:
  clusterIP: "None"
  ports:
  - name: 8080-80
    port: 8080
    protocol: TCP
    targetPort: 80
  - name: search
    port: 9200
    protocol: TCP
    targetPort: 9200
```

This will not only remove the IP address from the Service, but when DNS is used to look up the Pod via its Service, the communication will go directly to the Pod. This is needed in the case of a database cluster, where only one of the database copies is responsible for writing to the database, and all others are only allowed to read. The client can easily look up the Pods that are associated with the headless Service and determine which Pod is responsible for writing to the database.

Let's create this headless multiport Service with the command `k create -f svc.yaml`. The Service named `internal-svc` does not have a cluster IP like the others do. Also, there are two groups of ports—8080 and 9200. The output will look similar to this:

```
root@kind-control-plane:/# k create -f svc.yaml
service/internal-svc created
root@kind-control-plane:/# k get svc
NAME            TYPE        CLUSTER-IP      EXTERNAL-IP
⇒ PORT(S)                  AGE
apache-svc      ClusterIP   100.96.102.73   <none>
⇒ 80/TCP                   22h
internal-svc    ClusterIP   None            <none>
⇒ 8080/TCP,9200/TCP   29s
kubernetes      ClusterIP   10.96.0.1       <none>
⇒ 443/TCP                  28h
```

6.4.2 NodePort Service

A NodePort Service is not only able to communicate internally to all other cluster components but can also expose a static port on the node that can be used for external traffic. This is useful for testing the communication to a Pod but comes with a certain number of limitations. You will have to know the IP address of the node, and you will also have to know which port is exposed because the available port range for a NodePort Service is 30000–32768.

As with the ClusterIP Service type and many other resources in Kubernetes, you can create a Service by performing the imperative command `k create svc nodeport no --node-port 30000 --tcp 443:80`, or you can create a declarative YAML file with the command `k create svc nodeport no --node-port 30000 --tcp 443:80 --dry-run=client -o yaml > nodeport.yaml`. Let's open the YAML in Vim and look at how this is different than the ClusterIP Service. To open the file `nodeport.yaml`, type `vim nodeport.yaml`. You'll see that it's very similar, but instead of the type being `ClusterIP`, it's `NodePort`, and it has a line added to the port name section. The line `nodePort: 30000` has been added, which is the static port number that will be exposed on each node in the cluster, as in the YAML displayed in figure 6.14.

Just like in ClusterIP Services, we can have multiple ports and target ports assigned to this Service, but there is no option for headless Service. This is good because if the

```
apiVersion: v1
kind: Service
metadata:
  creationTimestamp: null
  labels:
    app: "no"
  name: "no"
spec:
  ports:
  - name: 443-80
    nodePort: 30000◄──────────  Port exposed on each node in the cluster
    port: 443
    protocol: TCP
    targetPort: 80
  selector:
    app: "no"
  type: NodePort ◄──────────  Signals this is a NodePort Service
status:
  loadBalancer: {}
```

Figure 6.14 YAML that creates a NodePort Service

node is exposed, another user can gain an entryway directly into your Pod. Let's create a NodePort Service by typing the command `k apply -f nodeport.yaml`, which will have an output similar to the following:

```
root@kind-control-plane:/# k apply -f nodeport.yaml
service/no created
root@kind-control-plane:/# k get svc
NAME            TYPE        CLUSTER-IP      EXTERNAL-IP
➥ PORT(S)             AGE
apache-svc      ClusterIP   100.96.102.73   <none>
➥ 80/TCP              23h
internal-svc    ClusterIP   None            <none>
➥ 8080/TCP,9200/TCP  21m
kubernetes      ClusterIP   10.96.0.1       <none>
➥ 443/TCP             29h
no              NodePort    100.96.95.252   <none>
➥ 443:30000/TCP       3s
```

The NodePort Service has an additional parameter under ports that signifies the specific node port used out of 30,000. The Pods will be available at `100.96.95.252:30000` on the node through the Service named `no`.

6.4.3 *LoadBalancer Service*

A LoadBalancer Service is just as it sounds—a load-balancing device that is either provisioned in the cloud or a bare metal device. For the CKA exam, you will not have to worry about the actual load balancer device; you will just have to know how to create a LoadBalancer Service and the associated YAML. Let's do just that! Type the command `k create svc loadbalancer lb-svc --tcp 8080:8080 --dry-run=client -o yaml > lb-svc.yaml`. Open the file by typing the command `vim lb-svc.yaml`. Look at the differences between this LoadBalancer Service and the NodePort and ClusterIP Services displayed in figure 6.15.

You'll notice that there's not much difference between the YAML for a LoadBalancer Service and a ClusterIP Service. The only difference is that the type is set to `LoadBalancer`. This means that the node port doesn't have to be used to access the application, which therefore makes it slightly easier with which to communicate. There is an option to add a NodePort to the YAML here, which means that the port is still exposed, but the node port will not be exposed as a method to access the application.

Before we create a LoadBalancer Service, let's create a load balancer in our kind cluster. One load balancer that works well with kind is MetalLB. You may remember installing the MetalLB load balancer with Helm in chapter 4. Let's deploy it again, but this time we'll install it via a YAML manifest. Run the command `k apply -f https://raw.githubusercontent.com/chadmcrowell/acing-the-cka-exam/main/ch_06/metallb-native.yaml` to install the MetalLB load balancer. Next, we need to configure the load balancer for your cluster. To do this, type `k get no -o wide` to find the IP

```
apiVersion: v1
kind: Service
metadata:
  creationTimestamp: null
  labels:
    app: lb-svc
  name: lb-svc
spec:
  ports:
  - name: 8080-8080
    port: 8080
    protocol: TCP
    targetPort: 8080
  selector:
    app: lb-svc
  type: LoadBalancer  ◄──────── This is a LoadBalancer Service type.
status:
  loadBalancer: {}
```

Figure 6.15   YAML that creates a LoadBalancer Service

address of your nodes. The output will look similar to the following (but with different IP addresses):

```
root@kind-control-plane:/# k get no -o wide
NAME                   STATUS    ROLES           AGE    VERSION
⇒  INTERNAL-IP
kind-control-plane     Ready     control-plane   32h    v1.25.0-beta.0
⇒  172.18.0.2
```

Under the `Internal-IP` column, copy the first two octets (`172.18` for me), because you will change the values for the next file, which you can download with the command `curl -O https://raw.githubusercontent.com/chadmcrowell/acing-the-cka-exam/main/ch_06/metallb-layer2-config.yaml`. Once you've downloaded the file, open it with the command `vim metallb-layer2-config.yaml`. Change the value just below the addresses to match what you found your node IP addresses to be. The output should be as follows:

```
---
apiVersion: metallb.io/v1beta1
kind: IPAddressPool
metadata:
  name: first-pool
```

```
    namespace: metallb-system
spec:
  addresses:
  - 172.18.255.1-172.18.255.50
---
apiVersion: metallb.io/v1beta1
kind: L2Advertisement
metadata:
  name: example
  namespace: metallb-system
```

In the file `metallb-layer2-config.yaml`, I changed the addresses to `172.18.255.1-`
`172.18.255.50` to match the same first two octets from my node IP addresses. Now we
can apply the YAML with the command `k create -f metallb-layer2-config.yaml`.
You should see the following output:

```
root@kind-control-plane:/# k create -f metallb-layer2-config.yaml
ipaddresspool.metallb.io/first-pool created
l2advertisement.metallb.io/example created
```

Now we can create our LoadBalancer Service. Instead of creating a new one, let's
modify the existing Service named `apache-svc` and change it from a ClusterIP Service
to a LoadBalancer Service. To do this, type the command `k edit svc apache-svc`,
which will open the YAML spec in Vim. Scroll down to the line starting with the word
`type` and change `ClusterIP` to `LoadBalancer` (case-sensitive). Don't forget to press
the I key on the keyboard to enter insert mode!

Once you've made that change, press the Esc key on the keyboard to get out of
insert mode and type `:wq` to save the file and quit. This will apply the changes. You can
now perform the command `k get svc` and see the following:

```
root@kind-control-plane:/# k get svc
NAME            TYPE          CLUSTER-IP      EXTERNAL-IP
⇒ PORT(S)       AGE
apache-svc      LoadBalancer  100.96.25.132   172.18.255.1
⇒ 80:30499/TCP           30s
internal-svc    ClusterIP     None            <none>
⇒ 8080/TCP,9200/TCP   3h43m
kubernetes      ClusterIP     10.96.0.1       <none>
⇒ 443/TCP               32h
no              NodePort      100.96.95.252   <none>
⇒ 443:30000/TCP      3h22m
```

The type changed to `LoadBalancer`, and now there's an IP address in the `External-IP`
column. This is the IP address of the MetalLB load balancer, which we can use to
access our application (running in a Pod). Type `curl 172.18.255.1` and you should
get the following result:

```
root@kind-control-plane:/# curl 172.18.255.1
<html><body><h1>It works!</h1></body></html>
```

6.5   *Cluster node networking configuration*

When trying to communicate within a Kubernetes cluster, it's not much different than communicating from one server to another, with some added capabilities. These capabilities are generally called *network overlays,* and they are essentially network abstractions on top of the network you already have. Why is this? Because every Pod in the Kubernetes cluster requires its own IP address, you may not have enough IP addresses reserved for every Pod, especially as the cluster scales up to dozens of nodes and potentially hundreds of Pods. This overlay is sometimes referred to as a *VXLAN.*

A VXLAN sits on top of the existing physical network and uses an encapsulation protocol to tunnel layer-2 connections over a layer-3 network. As the communication goes back and forth from node to node, as in figure 6.16, when trying to reach a Pod, the encapsulation helps with routing to the correct destination by placing a header on the packet.

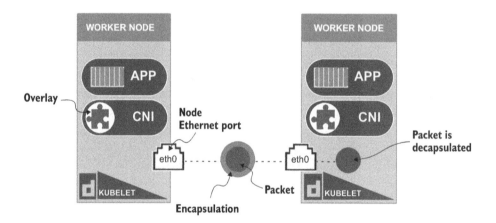

Figure 6.16   Encapsulated packet moving from node to node via CNI

The overlay follows a set of specifications and libraries for writing plugins to configure network interfaces in Linux containers. The term for this overlay is the *container network interface (CNI).* CNI is a Cloud Native Computing Foundation (CNCF) project that is not exclusive to Kubernetes, as it is a general framework for creating networks between containers. However, when used with Kubernetes, it is a DaemonSet that runs in the cluster, creating a virtual network interface in the root namespace, which is an intermediary between packets flowing in and out of a node.

Popular CNI plugins for Kubernetes are Flannel, Calico, Weavenet, Cilium, and more. On the CKA exam, only Flannel and Calico are used, so we'll focus on them. The kindnet DaemonSet is running in our cluster and is the CNI used for a kind cluster. You can see this by typing the command k get ds -n kube-system. The output will look like this:

```
root@ingress-control-plane:/# k get ds -n kube-system
NAME           DESIRED    CURRENT    READY    UP-TO-DATE    AVAILABLE    NODE
⇒ SELECTOR                AGE
kindnet        1          1          1        1             1
⇒ <none>                  47h
kube-proxy     1          1          1        1             1
⇒ kubernetes.io/os=linux  47h
```

This serves as a VXLAN. For the exam, you'll need to know how to choose an appropriate CNI plugin. We can install the flannel CNI by first creating a new kind cluster without a CNI, using the steps defined in appendix C. Once you've created a new kind cluster, get a shell to both of the node containers—one at a time–with the commands docker exec -it kind-control-plane bash and docker exec -it kind-worker bash. When you have a Bash shell to the container, go ahead and run the command apt update; apt install wget on both kind-control-plane and kind-worker. This will install wget, a command-line tool that we can use to download files from the web, which is what we're going to do with the command wget https://github.com/containernetworking/plugins/releases/download/v1.1.1/cni-plugins-linux-amd64-v1.1.1.tgz. Because this file is a tarball, you'll have to untar it with the command tar -xvf cni-plugins-linux-amd64-v1.1.1.tgz. The output will look similar to this:

```
root@kind-control-plane:/# tar -xvf cni-plugins-linux-amd64-v1.1.1.tgz
./
./macvlan
./static
./vlan
./portmap
./host-local
./vrf
./bridge
./tuning
./firewall
./host-device
./sbr
./loopback
./dhcp
./ptp
./ipvlan
./bandwidth
```

The bridge file is the most important for our case, as it will provide the necessary plugin for Kubernetes to use Flannel as a CNI. It also needs to be in a specific directory—/opt/cni/bin/—to be picked up for the cluster. We'll move the file bridge to that directory with the command mv bridge /opt/cni/bin/.

Now that we've installed the bridge plugin on both `kind-control-plane` and `kind-worker`, we can install Flannel CNI by creating the `flannel` Kubernetes objects inside our cluster—while inside of a shell on the control plane node—with the command `kubectl apply -f https:/ /raw.githubusercontent.com/flannel-io/flannel/master/ Documentation/kube-flannel.yml`. You can verify that the nodes are in a ready state with the command `kubectl get no`. The output will look similar to this:

```
root@kind-control-plane:/# kubectl get no
NAME                 STATUS    ROLES           AGE    VERSION
kind-control-plane   Ready     control-plane   16m    v1.25.0-beta.0
kind-worker          Ready     <none>          16m    v1.25.0-beta.0
```

We can also verify that the CoreDNS Pods are running—and that the `flannel` Pods are created and running—with the command `kubectl get po -A`. The output will look similar to this:

```
root@kind-control-plane:/# k get po -A
NAMESPACE           NAME                                         READY
↳     STATUS
kube-flannel        kube-flannel-ds-d6v6t                        1/1
↳     Running
kube-flannel        kube-flannel-ds-h7b5v                        1/1
↳     Running
kube-system         coredns-565d847f94-txdvw                     1/1
↳     Running
kube-system         coredns-565d847f94-vb4kg                     1/1
↳     Running
kube-system         etcd-kind-control-plane                      1/1
↳     Running
kube-system         kube-apiserver-kind-control-plane            1/1
↳     Running
kube-system         kube-controller-manager-kind-control-plane   1/1
↳     Running
kube-system         kube-proxy-9hsvk                             1/1
↳     Running
kube-system         kube-proxy-gkvrz                             1/1
↳     Running
kube-system         kube-scheduler-kind-control-plane            1/1
↳     Running
local-path-storage  local-path-provisioner-684f458cdd-8bwkh      1/1
↳     Running
```

You now have the Flannel CNI installed in your kind cluster and are ready to communicate across nodes using the CNI, as well as to provide encapsulation to packets flowing back and forth.

Exam exercises

Create a Deployment named `hello` using the image `nginxdemos/hello:plain-text` with the `kubectl` command line. Expose the Deployment to create a ClusterIP Service named `hello-svc` that can communicate over port 80 using the `kubectl` command line. Use the correct `kubectl` command to verify that it's a ClusterIP Service with the correct port exposed.

Change the `hello-svc` Service created in the previous exercise to a NodePort Service, where the NodePort should be 30000. Be sure to edit the Service in place, without creating a new YAML or issuing a new imperative command. Communicate with the Pods within the hello Deployment via the NodePort Service using curl.

Install an Ingress controller in the cluster using the command `k apply -f https://raw.githubusercontent.com/chadmcrowell/acing-the-cka-exam/main/ch_06/nginx-ingress-controller.yaml`. Change the `hello-svc` Service back to a ClusterIP Service and create an Ingress resource that will route to the `hello-svc` Service when a client requests hello.com.

Create a new kind cluster without a CNI. Install the bridge CNI, followed by the Calico CNI. After installing the CNI, verify that the CoreDNS Pods are up and running and the nodes are in a ready state.

Summary

- For Service discovery, DNS resolution happens via CoreDNS in a Kubernetes cluster. We explored how to discover both Pods and Services via DNS queries. For the exam, you will be expected to know how to configure and use CoreDNS.
- CoreDNS is running in a Deployment in the `kube-system` namespace. We can replicate the Pods in the CoreDNS Deployment to get faster domain-name resolution.
- The kubelet is responsible for populating each Pod with the proper CoreDNS IP address to allow for the Pod's DNS resolution. For the exam, remember that there's the `/etc/kubernetes/manifests` directory on the control plane node where the kubelet will automatically start Pods (called static Pods).
- The DNS resolver file in a Pod is `/etc/resolv.conf`, which will have certain search criteria according to the Services in the cluster. The `resolv.conf` file also contains the DNS IP address. When resolving hostnames on the exam, don't forget to use the Pod's FQDN if it's in a different namespace.
- Ingress and Ingress controllers allow layer-7 routing to the cluster to communicate to a Pod via a Service. Ingress can handle routing to multiple Services in the same Ingress resource, and you'll need to know how to configure this routing for the exam. Also, you'll need to know how to use Ingress controllers and Ingress resources.

- There are three different types of Services in Kubernetes, all of which allow communication from Pod to Pod in the cluster. You will need to understand the connectivity between Pods for the exam.
- The kubelet is a Service running on the node itself. You can reload the daemon and restart the Service, as you change the configuration for creating Pods. For the exam, you will be expected to know how to stop, start, and reload the kubelet daemon.
- The cluster networking interface (CNI) in Kubernetes assists with communication from node to node by encapsulating the packet and adding a header for the source and destination route. For the exam, you'll need to understand host networking configuration on cluster nodes.

Storage in Kubernetes

This chapter covers

- Creating a volume in Kubernetes
- Persistent volume claims and storage classes
- Using storage with applications in Kubernetes

As we've seen from previous exercises, the life of a Pod is short, and so is the life of the data that resides in that Pod. To solve this problem and retain the data that a Pod uses, we create persistent volumes (PVs). On the exam, you'll be tested on your ability to create a PV, as well as a persistent volume claim (PVC) and a storage class. We'll discuss each of these topics in this chapter.

The storage domain

This chapter covers the storage domain of the CKA curriculum, which consists of 10% of the questions on the exam. This domain covers the methods by which application data is used in Kubernetes, including mounting storage to Pods for use with containers. It encompasses the following competencies.

(continued)

Competency	Chapter section
Understand storage classes and PVCs.	7.1, 7.3
Understand volume mode, access modes, and reclaim policies for volumes.	7.1.1, 7.1.2, 7.1.3
Understand PVC primitives.	7.2
Know how to configure applications with persistent storage.	7.1, 7.2, 7.3, 7.4

7.1 Persistent volumes

To prevent data loss in Kubernetes, data is decoupled from the Pod itself by creating an entirely separate Kubernetes object called a *persistent volume*, which is available to all Pods in the cluster, as PVs are not namespaced. As Pods come and go, the data is not tied to the Pod itself, so it lives beyond the life of the Pod inside of its own managed resource. You can continue to add data objects to the volume, and the persistent volume will not change if another Pod is planning to mount that same volume, as is depicted in figure 7.1. The actual storage is backed by the host, a

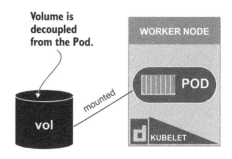

Figure 7.1 A persistent volume (PV) that is mounted to a Pod, which can act as an independent entity

network file system (NFS) server, a Simple Storage Solution (S3) bucket in Amazon, or any other storage provider.

The CKA exam will test you on three types of storage: (1) the `emptyDir` volume, (2) the `hostPath` volume, and (3) the `nfs` volume, so these are the types we'll focus on in this chapter (as opposed to many other types). For example, the exam question may say something like the following.

EXAM TASK In cluster `ek8s`, configure a `hostPath` PV named `vol02833` with a size of 10 MB of local storage from the worker node host `node01`. The directory on the host should be `/mnt/data`. Create a PVC named `claim-02833` that will reserve 90 MB of storage from the volume `vol02833`. Mount it to a Pod within a Deployment named `frontend0113`; the mount path within the container should be `/usr/share/nginx/html`. The name of the YAML file should be `deploy.yaml`.

If you don't already have access to an existing Kubernetes cluster, creating a Kubernetes cluster with kind is explained in appendix A. Be sure to create a two-node cluster, as we'll use the worker node's local storage to create the PV resource. As soon as you have access to your two-node cluster, get a shell to the control plane node by running the command `docker exec -it kind-control-plane bash`. Once you have a shell, set your alias `k` to equal `kubectl` with the command `alias k=kubectl`. On the exam, they will already have this alias set for you, so it's good to get used to using `k`, as opposed to having to type `kubectl` repeatedly.

To create this PV resource, we'll use the Kubernetes documentation to copy some YAML, which you'll also be able to do during the exam. Not only is this good practice for exam day, but we're also doing it this way because, by design, we're not able to create the YAML template like we were with Deployments using `--dry-run=client`. Accessing the YAML using the documentation will allow you to become familiar with Kubernetes docs and how to navigate them.

> **EXAM TIP** In the new exam environment, use the keyboard shortcut CTRL-SHIFT-C to copy and CTRL-SHIFT-V to paste. This, along with knowing how to search Kubernetes documentation, will save you time on the exam when you cannot easily create persistent storage with `kubectl`.

Go to https://kubernetes.io/docs and use the search bar on the left side of the screen to search for the phrase `use a persistent volume`. Click on the link that says "Configure a Pod to Use a PersistentVolume for Storage | Kubernetes" and scroll down to the section "Create a Persistent Volume." The full URL of the page is http://mng.bz/rW0y. Copy and paste the YAML from this page into a new file named `pv.yaml`. The result should look similar to figure 7.2.

```yaml
pv.yaml
1 apiVersion: v1
2 kind: PersistentVolume
3 metadata:
4   name: task-pv-volume
5   labels:
6     type: local
7 spec:
8   storageClassName: manual
9   capacity:
10    storage: 10Gi
11  accessModes:
12    - ReadWriteOnce
13  hostPath:
14    path: "/mnt/data"
```

Figure 7.2 The YAML copied and pasted from Kubernetes documentation into a file named `pv.yaml`

We'll change the name of the PV from `task-pv-volume` to `vol02883` (figure 7.2, line 4) and change the storage from `10Gi` to `100Mi` (figure 7.2, line 10). Save the file `pv.yaml` and create the PV with the command `k create -f pv.yaml`. If you perform the command `k get pv`, you will see an output similar to the following:

```
root@kind-control-plane:/# k get pv
NAME          CAPACITY   ACCESS MODES   RECLAIM POLICY   STATUS      CLAIM
➥  STORAGECLASS
vol02833   100Mi      RWO            Retain           Available
➥  manual
```

You will see from the output that the status is available, which means it's ready to be claimed. Let's create our claim by scrolling down on that same page in the Kubernetes documentation. That page, again, is http://mng.bz/Bm92. Paste the YAML into a file named `pvc.yaml`. The file contents should be similar to figure 7.3.

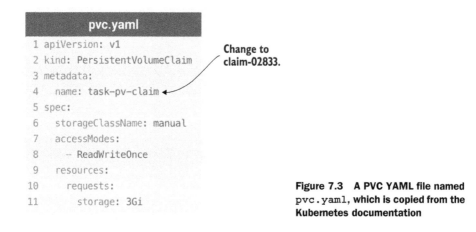

Figure 7.3   **A PVC YAML file named** `pvc.yaml`, **which is copied from the Kubernetes documentation**

Change the name of the PVC from `task-pv-claim` to `claim-02833` and change storage from `3Gi` to `90Mi` (figure 7.3, line 11). Create the PVC with the command `k apply -f pvc.yaml`. Once the resource is created, you can view the PVC with the command `k get pvc`, and you can also view the PV with the command `k get pv`. The output of that command will look like this:

```
root@kind-control-plane:/# k get pvc
NAME             STATUS   VOLUME     CAPACITY   ACCESS MODES   STORAGECLASS
➥  AGE
claim-02833   Bound    vol02833   100Mi      RWO            manual
➥  4m
root@kind-control-plane:/# k get pv
NAME          CAPACITY   ACCESS MODES   RECLAIM POLICY   STATUS
➥  CLAIM                  STORAGECLASS
vol02833   100Mi      RWO            Retain           Bound
➥  default/claim-02833    manual
```

EXAM TIP You can list multiple Kubernetes resources at once by just placing a comma in between the resource names. For example, perform the command k get pv,pvc to list both PVs and PVCs in the default namespace.

If you notice from the output, even though we specified 90Mi in the PVC YAML, the capacity is 100Mi. This is because the PVC will try to find the closest fit to the nearest PV that can fulfill that claim but cannot reserve only a portion of the PV. If we had requested 110Mi, the PVC would not be satisfied, as there is no matching PV with the requested amount of storage.

Let's proceed to create a Deployment, so we can use our volume mounted to the container in the Pod. We can create a Deployment YAML with the command k create deploy frontend0113 --image nginx --dry-run=client -o yaml > deploy.yaml. Once our file is created, we'll open it in Vim with the command vim deploy.yaml. The contents of the file should look similar to figure 7.4.

Under the spec, we'll add the YAML for our volume inline with containers by typing volumes: on line 24 (you can delete status: {} as it is not required). Under volumes:, type - name: vol-33. Below that, inline with name, type persistentVolumeClaim:. Under

```
                    deploy.yaml
 1 apiVersion: apps/v1
 2 kind: Deployment
 3 metadata:
 4   creationTimestamp: null
 5   labels:
 6     app: frontend0113
 7   name: frontend0113
 8 spec:
 9   replicas: 1
10   selector:
11     matchLabels:
12       app: frontend0113
13   strategy: {}
14   template:
15     metadata:
16       creationTimestamp: null
17       labels:
18         app: frontend0113          Add volumes
19       spec:                        here under spec.
20         containers:
21         - image: nginx
22           name: nginx
23           resources: {}
24 status: {}
                    Delete this line.
```

Figure 7.4 YAML for a Deployment that was created using the kubectl command

persistentVolumeClaim:, indent two spaces and type `claimName: claim-02833`. Finally, delete the line `creationTimestamp: null`. The result will look like figure 7.5.

```
19    spec:
20      containers:
21      - image: nginx
22        name: nginx
23        resources: {}
24      volumes:
25      - name: vol-33
26        persistentVolumeClaim:
27          claimName: claim-02833
```

Figure 7.5   Adding the `volumes` **syntax to a Deployment spec in the YAML file** `deploy.yaml`

Before we create the Deployment, we'll have to specify the mount path for the volume within the container. We'll do that by adding a line below line 23. Inline with resources, type `volumeMounts:`. Below that, type `- name: vol-33` (has to be the same as the volume name). Just below `name: vol-33`, inline with name, type `mountPath: "/usr/share/nginx/html"`. The contents of the final Deployment YAML will look like figure 7.6.

```
1 apiVersion: apps/v1
2 kind: Deployment
3 metadata:
4   creationTimestamp: null
5   labels:
6     app: frontend0113
7   name: frontend0113
8 spec:
9   replicas: 1
10  selector:
11    matchLabels:
12      app: frontend0113
13  strategy: {}
14  template:
15    metadata:
16      creationTimestamp: null
17      labels:
18        app: frontend0113
19    spec:
20      containers:
21      - image: nginx
22        name: nginx
23        resources: {}
24        volumeMounts:
25        - name: vol-33
26          mountPath: "/usr/share/nginx/html"
27      volumes:
28      - name: vol-33
29        persistentVolumeClaim:
30          claimName: claim-02833
```

Figure 7.6   The complete YAML for a Deployment with a volume named `vol-33` **attached**

Now we can save our YAML file and create the Deployment with the command k apply -f deploy.yaml. You can list the Deployment with the command k get deploy and list the Pods within the Deployment with the command k get po. The output will look similar to this:

```
root@kind-control-plane:/# k get deploy
NAME            READY   UP-TO-DATE   AVAILABLE   AGE
frontend0113    1/1     1            1           8s
root@kind-control-plane:/# k get po
NAME                           READY   STATUS    RESTARTS   AGE
frontend0113-6d6c77b9b6-62qbh  1/1     Running   0          11s
```

You will see that the container is running. This means that our volume was successfully mounted. To prove this, type the command k describe po, followed by the name of the Pod (the name of the Pod will be different for you). My command is k describe po frontend0113-6d6c77b9b6-62qbh. In the volume section of the output, you will see the volume named vol-33 and the PVC that we created earlier. The abbreviated output will look similar to figure 7.7.

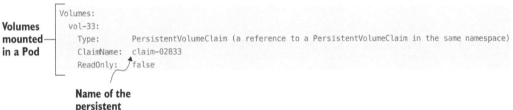

Figure 7.7 Abbreviated output from the k describe po command, which shows the volume mounted to the Pod

Now that we've successfully created a PV, a PVC, and a Deployment that mounts that volume to a Pod, we have successfully completed this exam task.

7.1.1 The problem with hostPath

The problem with using the hostPath-type volume is that, in multiple node clusters, the data is written to all of the nodes in the cluster, with the expectation that the storage configuration on all nodes is the same. If not, the data will only be written to one node. This means that if the Pod is scheduled to a node, there is a probability that the data will not reside on that node.

> **EXAM TIP** If you get a question on the exam that indicates that the storage must persist beyond the life of the Pod, hostPath is going to be the volume type you need to provision unless stated otherwise. If you get a question that requires the data to exist on something besides local storage, the exam will state what the volume type should be (e.g., nfs).

To get around this problem, you can use the `nfs` volume type. An `nfs` volume allows you to store the data mounted to a Pod in an `nfs` share on the network. The `nfs` type also supports multiple writers; therefore, many Pods can use the volume simultaneously. Because we don't have an `nfs` server running in our lab, I'll show a simple example of a Pod that uses an `nfs` PV here:

```
apiVersion: v1
kind: PersistentVolume
metadata:
  name: nfs-pv
spec:
  capacity:
    storage: 1Mi
  accessModes:
    - ReadWriteMany
  nfs:
    server: nfs-server.default.svc.cluster.local
    path: "/"
  mountOptions:
    - nfsvers=4.2
```

The PV looks a little different than the previous one, as we have added the `nfs` field with the server and path. The path is where the mount is located on the `nfs` server. The mount options are based on the version of `nfs` that your server is using. Once we create this PV, we can create a PVC like this:

```
apiVersion: v1
kind: PersistentVolumeClaim
metadata:
  name: nfs-pvc
spec:
  accessModes:
    - ReadWriteMany
  storageClassName: ""
  resources:
    requests:
      storage: 1Mi
  volumeName: nfs-pv
```

As you can see, the structure of the claim is very much the same as the previous claim, except for the access mode. This is because you can write `nfs` volumes to multiple sources (Pods). Within a PVC, we can also specify which PV we want the claim to be bound to by specifying the `volumeName`, as on the very last line. Once we have both a PV and a PVC, we can create the YAML for our Pod as follows:

```
apiVersion: v1
kind: Pod
metadata:
  creationTimestamp: null
  labels:
    run: nfs-pod
```

```
    name: nfs-pod
spec:
  containers:
  - image: nginx
    name: nfs-pod
    volumeMounts:
      - name: nfs-vol
        mountPath: "/usr/share/nginx/html"
    resources: {}
  dnsPolicy: ClusterFirst
  restartPolicy: Always
  volumes:
  - name: nfs-vol
    persistentVolumeClaim:
      claimName: nfs-pvc
```

Again, if you run this in your lab, it will fail because you do not have a running NFS server on your network; however, on the exam, it will be different. If there is a question that indicates you must use an `nfs` volume, you will most certainly be provided a running `nfs` server, in the form of a server address and path.

7.1.2 *Volume modes*

The *volume mode* is the type of volume being accessed in Kubernetes. By default, if you don't include a specific mode, a PV will assume the volume mode `FileSystem`, as opposed to `Block`. We didn't have to specify it in the YAML initially, but you can see what mode it defaults to by running the command `k describe pv vol02833`. The output of that command will look like this:

```
root@kind-control-plane:/# k describe pv vol02833
Name:            vol02833
Labels:          type=local
Annotations:     pv.kubernetes.io/bound-by-controller: yes
Finalizers:      [kubernetes.io/pv-protection]
StorageClass:    manual
Status:          Bound
Claim:           default/claim-02833
Reclaim Policy:  Retain
Access Modes:    RWO
VolumeMode:      FileSystem
Capacity:        100Mi
Node Affinity:   <none>
Message:
Source:
    Type:        HostPath (bare host directory volume)
    Path:        /mnt/data
    HostPathType:
Events:          <none>
```

As you see, between `Access Modes:` and `Capacity:` is `VolumeMode: FileSystem`. The filesystem mode is intended to be mounted into Pods as a directory. The block mode is backed by a block device, where the device is empty (unformatted). Some examples of block devices are Amazon Elastic Block Store (EBS), Azure Disk, iSCSI disks, FC (Fibre Channel) disks, CephFS, or even local disks (like we used in the exam task). For the CKA exam, you won't have to create the block storage itself, you will only need to know how to change the volumeMode in the YAML spec. Because we still have the file pv.yaml from section 7.8, we'll open this up and add one line to it. Just below storageClassName, inline, add volumeMode: Block. Also change the name of the PV, as you can't have two volumes with the same name. The final YAML for our new block storage volume will look like figure 7.8.

```
 1 apiVersion: v1
 2 kind: PersistentVolume
 3 metadata:
 4   name: vol028333
 5   labels:
 6     type: local
 7 spec:
 8   storageClassName: manual
 9   volumeMode: Block
10   capacity:
11     storage: 100Mi
12   accessModes:
13     - ReadWriteOnce
14   hostPath:
15     path: "/mnt/data"
```

I added a 3 to the end to make the volume name unique. → (line 4)

Create a volume in block storage mode. → (line 9)

Figure 7.8 Adding line 9 to create a PV in Block mode

You can create this new PV with the command k apply -f pv.yaml, and you will see the PV right beside the existing PV. The output will look similar to this:

```
root@kind-control-plane:/# k apply -f pv.yaml
persistentvolume/vol028333 created
root@kind-control-plane:/# k get pv
NAME            CAPACITY   ACCESS MODES   RECLAIM POLICY   STATUS
⮡  CLAIM                   STORAGECLASS
vol02833        100Mi      RWO            Retain           Bound
⮡  default/claim-02833     manual
vol028333       100Mi      RWO            Retain           Available
⮡                          manual
```

You'll notice that these look exactly the same in terms of their composition, but one is in FileSystem mode and one is in Block mode.

7.1.3 Access modes

Access mode determines how the volume is to be accessed, by what permissions, and from which applications running in Kubernetes. You may have noticed, both in our `pv.yaml` file and our `pvc.yaml` file, we had specified an access mode of `ReadWrite-Once`. What does this mean? Think of it from the node's perspective, as the node is the one accessing the volume. `ReadWriteOnce` means that only one node can mount the volume and read and write to it. The three other modes are `ReadOnlyMany`, which means multiple nodes can mount the volume for reading only; `ReadWriteMany`, which means multiple nodes can mount the volume for writing and reading; and `ReadWriteOncePod`, which means that only one Pod on that one node can mount that volume for reading and writing.

A PV can have more than one access mode, whereas a PVC can only have one. Even if there are many modes specified in the PV YAML, the node can only utilize one access mode at a time, so you must choose one out of the four modes. For example, if we had added an access mode to our PV YAML, as in figure 7.9, you would have to choose either `ReadWriteOnce` or `ReadOnlyMany` in the PVC.

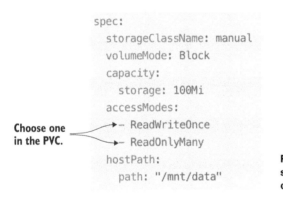

Choose one in the PVC.

```
spec:
    storageClassName: manual
    volumeMode: Block
    capacity:
        storage: 100Mi
    accessModes:
    - ReadWriteOnce
    - ReadOnlyMany
    hostPath:
        path: "/mnt/data"
```

Figure 7.9 Multiple access modes specified in the YAML for a PV, of which only one can be used in the PVC

Also, most importantly, certain volumes only support certain access modes. For example, the type that we have here, `hostPath`, is not able to support `ReadOnlyMany`, `ReadWriteMany`, or `ReadWriteOncePod`. This is important to remember, as this may come up as a trick question on the exam.

> **EXAM TIP** The exam may not explicitly state whether the access mode is `ReadOnlyMany` or `ReadWriteOnce`, as it assumes you know that `hostPath`-type volumes only support `ReadWriteOnce`. Alternatively, `nfs` volumes support `ReadWriteOnce`, `ReadOnlyMany`, and `ReadWriteMany`. The exam will only cover `emptyDir`, `hostPath`, and `nfs` volume types; `emptyDir` is not a PV type, so access modes are not available.

The short form of each access mode can be found in table 7.1; however, you only see these modes in short form when you describe either a PV or PVC.

Table 7.1   Access modes and their short form, used in the YAML for a PV or PVC

Access mode	Short form	Description
ReadWriteOnce	RWO	Only one node can mount the volume and read and write to it.
ReadOnlyMany	ROX	Multiple nodes can mount the volume for reading only.
ReadWriteMany	RWX	Multiple nodes can mount the volume for writing and reading.
ReadWriteOncePod	RWOP	Only one Pod on that one node can mount that volume for reading and writing.

7.1.4   *Reclaim policies*

Another default value that was applied to our PV in the exam task was the *reclaim policy*. A reclaim policy is for deciding what to do with the volume once the PVC bound to it is deleted. If you perform the command k describe pv vol02833, you will see the reclaim policy is set to Retain by default. The output from the describe command will look something like this:

```
root@kind-control-plane:/# k describe pv vol02833
Name:              vol02833
Labels:            type=local
Annotations:       pv.kubernetes.io/bound-by-controller: yes
Finalizers:        [kubernetes.io/pv-protection]
StorageClass:      manual
Status:            Bound
Claim:             default/claim-02833
Reclaim Policy:    Retain
Access Modes:      RWO
VolumeMode:        FileSystem
Capacity:          100Mi
Node Affinity:     <none>
Message:
Source:
    Type:          HostPath (bare host directory volume)
    Path:          /mnt/data
    HostPathType:
Events:            <none>
```

Between the Claim and Access Modes is the Reclaim Policy. This reclaim policy can also be set to Recycle or Delete. Retain means the volume can be used again, as it retains the data on the volume. It can then be used by another claim. Recycle means that the volume has been scrubbed (i.e., rm -f), but this policy has been deprecated, so use Retain or Delete instead. Delete indicates that the backed storage (i.e., Amazon EBS, Azure Disk) has been deleted as well as the PV object in Kubernetes. Only Amazon EBS, GCE PD, Azure Disk, and Cinder volumes support the delete policy.

7.2   Persistent volume claim

As we experienced in the exam task in section 7.1, the PVC consumed the entire PV, even though the claim was for 10Mi less than the requested amount. To fulfill the request for storage, instead of waiting for an exact match, the PVC will choose the vol-ume that is closest to match the request of that claim (figure 7.10).

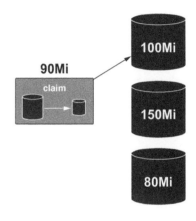

The job of the PVC is to reserve this storage on behalf of the container (within a Pod), so once this claim is in a `Bound` status, the claim will not release the volume, even if an administrator tries to delete the volume with force. For example, let's try to delete the PV `vol02833` that we created as part of the exam task. Perform the command `k delete pv vol02833 -force`, and you will see an output similar to the following (use CTRL-C to get back to your prompt after running this command):

Figure 7.10   A PVC will choose the closest available volume size to fulfill the claim.

```
root@kind-control-plane:/# k delete pv vol02833 --force
Warning: Immediate deletion does not wait for confirmation that the running
⮑  resource has been terminated. The resource may continue to run on the
    cluster indefinitely.
persistentvolume "vol02833" force deleted
^Croot@kind-control-plane:/# k get pv
NAME          CAPACITY    ACCESS MODES    RECLAIM POLICY    STATUS
⮑  CLAIM                  STORAGECLASS
vol02833      100Mi       RWO             Retain            Terminating
⮑  default/claim-02833    manual
vol028333     100Mi       RWO             Retain
⮑  Available              manual
```

The PV will remain in a `Terminating` state, until the PVC is deleted. The PVC is not able to be deleted until the Pod is deleted. This prevents Kubernetes administrators from accidentally removing the underlying storage from a running Pod, which is a feature and not a bug. Try deleting the PVC with the command `k delete pvc claim-02833 -force`, and you'll see the same output (use CTRL-C again to get your prompt back). The output will look similar to this:

```
root@kind-control-plane:/# k delete pvc claim-02833 --force
Warning: Immediate deletion does not wait for confirmation that the running
  resource has been terminated. The resource may continue to run on the
  cluster indefinitely.
persistentvolumeclaim "claim-02833" force deleted
^Croot@kind-control-plane:/# k get pvc
NAME            STATUS         VOLUME      CAPACITY    ACCESS MODES
  STORAGECLASS
claim-02833    Terminating    vol02833    100Mi       RWO           manual
```

The PVC will continue to be in a `Terminating` state until the Deployment is deleted (and subsequently the Pod). In the meantime, the volume will continue to stay mounted to the Pod and usable—just as it did before the delete command was run—and will not affect the applications that are currently accessing the Pod and its storage. The *phase* of the Pod determines its state and can be obtained from the command `k get po`. A volume can be in one of the following phases:

- Available
- Bound
- Released
- Failed

We saw this when the PV was first created in section 7.1. This is a requirement for the PVC: to claim the volume, it must be available to claim. *Bound* is the phase of the PV that indicates that it's already claimed, which deems it unavailable to a new PVC. The *released* phase is significant because, if the PV is set to `retain` in the reclaim policy, it's released and waiting for a new PVC to reclaim it. The *failed* phase means that during the reclaim process, the failed volume was not effective in bounding to a new PVC.

7.3   *Storage class*

While following the exam task from section 7.1, you may have noticed that we included a storage class in the YAML. A storage class is nothing more than a "storage profile" for a grouping of similar types of storage. It's a lot like a label in that it doesn't affect the underlying storage capability; it simplifies the process of creating persistent storage in Kubernetes. You can see existing storage classes in your cluster with the command `k get sc`. The output will look similar to this:

```
root@kind-control-plane:/# k get sc
NAME                 PROVISIONER           RECLAIMPOLICY
  VOLUMEBINDINGMODE      ALLOWVOLUMEEXPANSION
standard (default)   rancher.io/local-path    Delete
  WaitForFirstConsumer    false
```

In this kind Kubernetes cluster, a local path-type volume is precreated. This was created as part of the cluster creation process, not something I created manually. You'll experience this in a lot of other cluster bootstrapping tools (as with kind), such as on the CKA exam with kubeadm, which will have preprovisioned storage classes that you will be asked to use with a PVC. An example of an exam question follows.

EXAM TASK In cluster `ek8s`, create a PVC named `claim-03833` based on an existing storage class named `standard`. Claim 1 GB of storage space. Mount it to a Pod, within a Deployment named `backend0113`; the mount path within the container should be `/var/lib/mysql`. The name of the YAML file should be `backend.yaml`.

Using the same cluster that you used in section 7.1, copy the previous `pvc.yaml` file and rename it `newpvc.yaml` with the command `cp pvc.yaml newpvc.yaml`. Open the file `newpvc.yaml` in Vim with the command `vim newpvc.yaml`. Change the name from `claim-02833` to `claim-03833` and change the `storageClassName` from `manual` to `standard`. Finally, change the `storage` from `90Mi` to `1Gi`. The final contents of the file will look like figure 7.11.

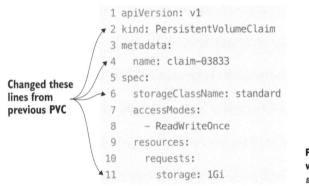

Changed these lines from previous PVC

```
 1 apiVersion: v1
 2 kind: PersistentVolumeClaim
 3 metadata:
 4   name: claim-03833
 5 spec:
 6   storageClassName: standard
 7   accessModes:
 8     - ReadWriteOnce
 9   resources:
10     requests:
11       storage: 1Gi
```

Figure 7.11 The PVC used with the storage class named `standard`

To create the PVC, subsequently dynamically provisioning a PV, save and quit Vim, then type the command `k apply -f newpvc.yaml`. This is where things get interesting, and I must remind you NOT to panic if you experience this during the exam. When you list the PVC, you should get the following (which is a good thing):

```
root@kind-control-plane:/# k get pvc
NAME          STATUS    VOLUME      CAPACITY    ACCESS MODES    STORAGECLASS
claim-02833   Bound     vol028333   100Mi       RWO             manual
claim-03833   Pending                                           standard
```

The PVC is pending because the storage is only provisioned when a Pod—in other words, a "consumer"—is created to use (consume) that PVC, which is intelligent, as you don't want to preprovision a bunch of volumes if they are not in use. This is the major difference between static provisioning—what we did in section 7.1—and the dynamic provisioning that occurs with storage classes. You will see this echoed if you run the command `k describe pvc claim-03833`. The output should look like this (abbreviated):

```
Access Modes:
VolumeMode:      FileSystem
Used By:         <none>
Events:
  Type    Reason             Age                       From
                       Message
  ----    ------   ------            ----                      ----
                       -------
  Normal  WaitForFirstConsumer  50s (x26 over 6m51s)  persistentvolume-
  controller  waiting for first consumer to be created before binding
```

Now that we know our PVC is waiting for a consumer, let's create one! Again, let's copy the previous YAML file `deploy.yaml` to a new file named `backend.yaml` with the command `cp deploy.yaml backend.yaml`. Open the file `backend.yaml` with the command `vim backend.yaml`. Change the name and labels to `backend0113`, the image to `mysql:8.0`, the name of the container to `mysql`, the name of the `volumeMounts` to `mysqldata`, the `mountPath` to `"/var/lib/mysql"`, and most importantly the PV name to `claim-03833`. We'll add the environment variable for the MySQL password and expose port 3306 on the container. The final YAML will look like figure 7.12.

Let's save the file and exit Vim. If you didn't quite catch all of those changes and additions, you can download the file with the command `curl -O https://raw.git-hubusercontent.com/chadmcrowell/acing-the-cka-exam/main/ch_07/backend.yaml`. We can create the Deployment with the command `k apply -f backend.yaml`. Almost immediately, we'll see that our PVC is bound, and there's a new PV that was automatically provisioned. To list both the PVC and PV, run the command `k get pvc,pv`. The output of that command will look similar to this:

```
root@kind-control-plane:/# k get pvc,pv
NAME                                STATUS   VOLUME
            CAPACITY   ACCESS MODES   STORAGECLASS   AGE
persistentvolumeclaim/claim-02833   Bound    vol028333
            100Mi      RWO            manual         55m
persistentvolumeclaim/claim-03833   Bound    pvc-5cc8fff1-e8a2-4934-ae17-
  fa4e3ecbcb40   1Gi        RWO            standard       54m

NAME                                                       CAPACITY
  ACCESS MODES   RECLAIM POLICY   STATUS   CLAIM
      STORAGECLASS
persistentvolume/pvc-5cc8fff1-e8a2-4934-ae17-fa4e3ecbcb40   1Gi         RWO
            Delete          Bound    default/claim-03833   standard
persistentvolume/vol028333                                 100Mi       RWO
            Retain          Bound    default/claim-02833   manual
```

```
                backend.yaml
 1 apiVersion: apps/v1
 2 kind: Deployment
 3 metadata:
 4   creationTimestamp: null
 5   labels:
 6     app: backend0113
 7   name: backend0113
 8 spec:
 9   replicas: 1
10   selector:
11     matchLabels:
12       app: backend0113
13   strategy: {}
14   template:
15     metadata:
16       creationTimestamp: null
17       labels:
18         app: backend0113
19     spec:
20       containers:
21       - image: mysql:8.0
22         name: mysql
23         env:
24         - name: MYSQL_ROOT_PASSWORD
25           value: password
26         ports:
27         - containerPort: 3306
28         resources: {}
29         volumeMounts:
30         - name: mysqldata
31           mountPath: "/var/lib/mysql"
32       volumes:
33       - name: mysqldata
34         persistentVolumeClaim:
35           claimName: claim-03833
```

Figure 7.12   A Deployment that uses the PVC named `claim-03833` **mounted in the container at** `/var/lib/mysql`

You have created a PVC that utilizes the standard storage class, created a Deployment that mounted the volume to a Pod, and completed the exam task.

7.3.1   *Inheriting from the storage class*

As you may have noticed, the PV inherited certain properties of the storage class. One was the reclaim policy, which was set to delete. Others were the volume type (`hostPath` in our case) and volume binding mode. We can look at the YAML from a storage class with the command `k get sc standard -o yaml`. The output should look as follows (the annotations are shortened to make it easier to read):

```
root@kind-control-plane:/# k get sc standard -o yaml
apiVersion: storage.k8s.io/v1
kind: StorageClass
metadata:
  annotations:
    storageclass.kubernetes.io/is-default-class: "true"
  creationTimestamp: "2022-10-06T21:10:24Z"
  name: standard
  resourceVersion: "264"
  uid: 6caa1035-1584-4356-a060-90c923293a3b
provisioner: rancher.io/local-path
reclaimPolicy: Delete
volumeBindingMode: WaitForFirstConsumer
```

These settings are applied automatically to each PV that is automatically provisioned with the storage class.

Exam exercises

Create a storage class named `node-local` that uses the provisioner `kubernetes .io/no-provisioner`. The volume binding mode should be `WaitForFirstConsumer`.

Create a PVC named `claim-sc` that will claim 39 MB of volume from the previously created class. The access mode should be `ReadWriteOnce`.

Create a Pod named `pod-sc` with the image `nginx` that will use the PVC from the previous step, and mount the volume inside the container at `/usr/nginx/www/html`.

7.4   *Nonpersistent volumes*

To fully realize the benefits of PVs, you must gain some exposure working with volumes that do not persist—by this, I mean the `emptyDir` volume type. This volume type uses storage from the container itself. This will most likely turn up on the exam, so let's go through another exam scenario.

EXAM TASK   In cluster `ek8s`, create a Pod named `log-collector` that uses a volume with type `emptyDir` named `logvol`. Mount the volume in the container at `/var/log`. The name of the YAML file should be `log-collector.yaml`.

We can continue to use the same cluster that we've been using since the beginning of the chapter. Go ahead and create the Pod YAML file with the command `k run log-collector --image busybox --command sleep --command "3600" --dry-run=client -o yaml > log-collector.yaml`. Open the file `log-collector.yaml` with the command `vim log-collector.yaml`. Just below the `restartPolicy`, we'll insert `volumes:`. Just below that, on the next line, we'll insert `- name: logvol`, and on the next line, inline with `name`, we'll add `emptyDir: {}` (figure 7.13).

```
19  dnsPolicy: ClusterFirst
20  restartPolicy: Always
21  volumes:
22  - name: logvol
23    emptyDir: {}
```

Figure 7.13   The end of a Pod YAML spec, where the volume is set to a type emptyDir

Much like we did with our Deployment YAML in section 7.1, we'll add the volume-Mounts to the container as well, which must be the same name as the volume that we added in figure 7.13. Just below resources in the Pod YAML, insert volumeMounts: followed by - mountPath: /var/log just below. Finally, inline with mountPath, type name: logvol. The result should be similar to the following:

```
 1 apiVersion: v1
 2 kind: Pod
 3 metadata:
 4   creationTimestamp: null
 5   labels:
 6     run: log-collector
 7   name: log-collector
 8 spec:
 9   containers:
10   - command:
11     - sleep
12     - "3600"
13     image: busybox
14     name: log-collector
15     resources: {}
16     volumeMounts:
17     - mountPath: /var/log
18       name: logvol
19   dnsPolicy: ClusterFirst
20   restartPolicy: Always
21   volumes:
22   - name: logvol
23     emptyDir: {}
```

As you see, it is very similar to how we mounted the volume to the Deployment in section 7.1, except we changed the volume type, the names, and the mount path. Let's create the Pod with the command k create -f log-collector.yaml. The output of the command k get po should look like this:

```
root@kind-control-plane:/# k get po
NAME                            READY  STATUS   RESTARTS   AGE
backend0113-7dbcbc574f-s45mx    1/1    Running  . 0        67m
frontend0113-6d6c77b9b6-h9hrj   1/1    Running   0         107m
log-collector                   1/1    Running   0         11m
```

Also, if you run the command `k describe po log-collector`, you should see in the `Volumes:` section that the volume is in fact mounted as type `EmptyDir`. Here's an abbreviation of the output, which you should see as well:

```
Volumes:
  logvol:
    Type:        EmptyDir (a temporary directory that shares a pod's
⮡ lifetime)
    Medium:
    SizeLimit:   <unset>
```

You have successfully created a Pod that mounts a volume of type `EmptyDir` and completed the task. When using this volume, you should understand that the data will not persist beyond the life of the Pod. If the Pod is killed, then the data will be deleted as well.

Exam exercises

Create a Pod named `two-web` with two containers. The first container will be named `httpd` and will use the image `httpd:alpine3.17`. The second container will be named `nginx` and will use the image `nginx:1.23.3-alpine`.

Both containers should access the same volume that is shared from local storage on the container itself.

`Container1` will mount the volume to `/var/www/html/` and `Container2` will mount the volume to `/usr/share/nginx/html/`.

Start up the Pod and ensure everything is mounted and shared correctly.

Summary

- To have data persist beyond the life of a Pod, we use PVs. For the exam, if you are asked to retain data after deleting a Pod, make sure to create a PV.
- A volume is reserved or claimed for the Pod by a resource in Kubernetes called persistent volume claim, or PVC, which chooses the volume with the size nearest to the requested capacity. You will need to know how to mount a volume in a Deployment or Pod for the exam.
- There are two volume modes to choose from when creating a PV—`FileSystem` and `Block`. If none is specified in the YAML, `FileSystem` mode is chosen. For the exam, look for an indication that the volume should be a directory; in this case, you would use the `FileSystem` volume type. If there's mention of a raw file system, you would use the `Block` volume mode.
- There are three reclaim policies available to a PV—`Retain`, `Recycle`, and `Delete`. The reclaim policy tells the PV what to do after it's unmounted from the Pod. Watch out for words like *retain* or *delete* for exam questions like these.

- There are four different access modes: ReadWriteOnce, ReadOnlyMany, Read-WriteMany, and ReadWriteOncePod. The access mode determines if nodes can access the PV, how many nodes can access the PV at a time, and whether they have read and/or write permission. For the exam, check to see if multiple nodes need access to the volume; that will be the key indicator of which access mode to use.
- A storage class is a way to dynamically provision storage in Kubernetes. You do not have to create a PV to use the storage class. When a question on the exam asks to use an existing storage class, you only have to create a PVC and choose which storage class to use; the volume will be created automatically.

Troubleshooting Kubernetes

As this is the biggest topic (30%) on the CKA exam, we're going to cover troubleshooting in detail in this chapter. Troubleshooting means fixing problems with applications, control plane components, worker nodes, and the underlying network. When running applications in Kubernetes, problems will arise, such as concerns with Pods, Services, and Deployments.

The troubleshooting domain

This chapter covers the troubleshooting domain of the CKA curriculum, which consists of 30% of the questions on the exam. This domain covers the techniques we use to discover and fix problems inside our Kubernetes cluster, including viewing the logs, capturing cluster events, networking problems, and application monitoring. It encompasses the following competencies.

Competency	Chapter section
Evaluate cluster and node logging.	8.1, 8.2
Understand how to monitor applications.	8.1
Manage container stdout and stderr logs.	8.1
Troubleshoot application failure.	8.1, 8.3
Troubleshoot cluster component failure.	8.2
Troubleshoot networking.	8.3

This chapter will help you understand the logs that a container might output in the process of debugging and getting the application back to a healthy state. If the problem is not the application, it may be the underlying node, the underlying operating system, or a communication problem on the network. On the exam, you'll be expected to know the differences between an application failure, a cluster-level problem, and a network problem and how to troubleshoot and determine a resolution in the shortest amount of time.

> **NOTE** The exercises in this chapter involve an action that you must take to "break" the cluster to provide something to troubleshoot. For the exam, the cluster or cluster object will already be broken so you shouldn't be too concerned about the initial action as a prerequisite for the exam.

8.1   Understanding application logs

One of the ways Kubernetes administrators find out why a problem is occurring in a cluster is by viewing the logs. Application logs help you to get more verbose information about what's going on inside a containerized application running in a Pod. Container engines (e.g., containerd) are designed to support logging and usually write all their output to standard output (stdout) and standard error (stderr) streams to a file located in the directory /var/log/containers (figure 8.1).

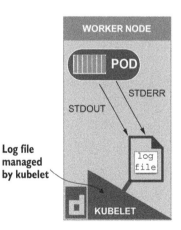

Figure 8.1   The stdout and stderr container logs are sent to a log file managed by kubelet in /var/log/ containers.

The CKA exam will test you on your ability to troubleshoot errors from within a Pod. Because Pod errors and container errors are synonymous, retrieving logs from any application in Kubernetes is simplified. An example of an exam question in this domain is as follows.

> **EXAM TASK** In cluster ik8s, in a namespace called db08328, create a Deployment
> with the kubectl command line (imperatively) named mysql, with the image
> mysql:8. List the Pods in the db08328 namespace to see if the Pod is running. If
> the Pod is not running, view the logs to determine why the Pod is not in a healthy
> state. Once you've collected the necessary log information, make changes to the
> Pod to fix it and get it back to a running, healthy state.

If you don't already have access to an existing Kubernetes cluster, you can create a
Kubernetes cluster with kind as explained in appendix A. You will only need a single-
node cluster, so follow the instructions in section A.1.1. Once you have a shell to the
control plane node using the command docker exec -it kind-control-plane bash,
set your alias for kubectl as well as tab completion, as this will help you with typos
and becoming used to using the tab completion for the exam. You can find the
instructions to do this at the end of appendix B, but here again are the commands to
run (in order):

```
apt update && apt install -y bash-completion
echo 'source <(kubectl completion bash)' >> ~/.bashrc
echo 'source /usr/share/bash-completion/bash_completion' >> ~/.bashrc
echo 'alias k=kubectl' >> ~/.bashrc
echo 'complete -o default -F __start_kubectl k' >> ~/.bashrc
source ~/.bashrc
```

On exam day, these will already be configured, so don't worry about having to memorize these commands. When you sit for the exam, you will already be able to use the k
alias and tab completion as soon as you start the exam.

   After these commands are run, create the namespace per the instructions with the
command k create ns db08328. You can follow that up by listing all namespaces with
the command k get ns. The output will look similar to this:

```
root@kind-control-plane:/# k create ns db08328
namespace/db08328 created
root@kind-control-plane:/# k get ns
NAME                STATUS   AGE
db08328             Active   4s
default             Active   11m
kube-node-lease     Active   11m
kube-public         Active   11m
kube-system         Active   11m
local-path-storage  Active   11m
```

Now that you have the correct namespace, you can change your context to the db08328
namespace, so you don't have to keep typing the namespace with every command.
You can change your context with the command k config set-context --current
--namespace db08328. The output will look like this:

```
root@kind-control-plane:/# k config set-context --current --namespace
⇢ db08328
Context "kubernetes-admin@kind" modified.
```

Now that you've set the context to the namespace in which you'll be creating the Deployment, create the Deployment named `mysql` with the command `k create deploy mysql --image mysql:8`. After this, you can list the Pods with the command `k get po`.

> **EXAM TIP** Notice that you don't have to use the `-n` option to specify your namespace each time. I will warn you that this can become confusing on the exam, as with each task you are also setting the context. So just be mindful that you'll be performing this command twice; therefore, it may be easier in some cases to type out the namespace each time, depending on how many namespaces you have to work in with each task.

The output of the Deployment creation and the listing of the Pods should look as follows:

```
root@kind-control-plane:/# k create deploy mysql --image mysql:8
deployment.apps/mysql created
root@kind-control-plane:/# k get po -w
NAME                   READY   STATUS            RESTARTS      AGE
mysql-68f7776797-w9216 0/1     CrashLoopBackOff  1 (10s ago)   7m28s
```

The result, in this case, is that the status of the Pod is in a `CrashLoopBackOff`. There are many statuses that a Pod can have, including `OOMKilled`, `ErrImagePull`, `Image-PullBackoff`, `FailedScheduling`, `NonZeroExitCode`, and `CreateContainerConfigError`. You can view the failed statuses in table 8.1.

Table 8.1 Access modes and their short form, used in the YAML for a persistent volume or persistent volume claim

Status	Meaning
CrashLoopBackOff	The Pod is trying to start, crashing, then restarting in a loop. Kubernetes will wait an increasing back-off time between restarts to give you a chance to fix the error.
ImagePullBackOff	A Pod cannot start up because it can't find the specified image locally or in the remote container registry. It will continue to try with an increasing back-off delay.
ErrImagePull	A Pod fails to start up because the image cannot be found or pulled due to authorization.
CreateContainerConfigError	A container within the Pod will not start due to missing components that are required to run.
RunContainerError	Running the container within a Pod fails due to problems with the container runtime or entry point of the container.

Table 8.1 Access modes and their short form, used in the YAML for a persistent volume or persistent volume claim *(continued)*

Status	Meaning
FailedScheduling	A Pod is unable to be scheduled to a node, either because nodes are marked as unschedulable, a taint is applied, or the node can't satisfy the requirements.
NonZeroExitCode	The container within a Pod exits unexpectedly due to an application error or missing file or directory.
OOMKilled	A Pod was scheduled, but the memory limit assigned to it has been exceeded.

A CrashLoopBackoff means that the Pod is continuing to start, crash, and restart again, and then crashing again, hence the term *crash loop*. We can see why this is happening by viewing the container logs with the command k logs mysql-68f7776797-w9216. Tab completion comes in handy here because you can start typing mysql and then quickly press the Tab key on the keyboard, and it will complete the rest for you. Tab completion will be enabled on the exam, but if you'd like to set this up in your own cluster, see appendix B. The output of the command k logs mysql-68f7776797-w9216 will look like this:

```
root@kind-control-plane:/# k logs mysql-68f7776797-w9216
2022-12-04 16:51:13+00:00 [Note] [Entrypoint]: Entrypoint script for MySQL
⮡ Server 8.0.31-1.el8 started.
2022-12-04 16:51:13+00:00 [Note] [Entrypoint]: Switching to dedicated user
⮡ 'mysql'
2022-12-04 16:51:13+00:00 [Note] [Entrypoint]: Entrypoint script for MySQL
⮡ Server 8.0.31-1.el8 started.
2022-12-04 16:51:13+00:00 [ERROR] [Entrypoint]: Database is uninitialized
⮡ and password option is not specified
    You need to specify one of the following as an environment variable:
    - MYSQL_ROOT_PASSWORD
    - MYSQL_ALLOW_EMPTY_PASSWORD
    - MYSQL_RANDOM_ROOT_PASSWORD
```

This tells us exactly what we wanted to know, which is that the database password needs to be set as an environment variable inside the container. The output even gives you the environment variable names from which to choose. If you recall in chapter 7, we created a mysql Deployment in which we set the password as an environment variable; let's refer back to it and utilize those same techniques to solve the problem that we have here. Looking back at figure 7.12 specifically, we can see that the environment variable is set inline with the name of the container image; let's apply this to our currently running Deployment with the command k edit deploy mysql. First, if you've started with a fresh kind cluster, you'll need to run the command apt update; apt install vim to edit the Deployment using the Vim text editor. Once the Deployment is open, you can make the following additions to the YAML, as you'll see depicted in figure 8.2.

Add this to the Deployment YAML.

```
spec:
  containers:
  - env:
    - name: MYSQL_ROOT_PASSWORD
      value: password
    image: mysql
    imagePullPolicy: Always
    name: mysql
    resources: {}
```

Figure 8.2 Edit the `mysql` **Deployment by adding the environment variable for a database password.**

Once you've done this, save and quit editing the `mysql` Deployment by pressing `:wq` on your keyboard. This will take you back to the command prompt, in which you can perform the command `k get po` to see if the Pod is now in a running state. The output should look like this:

```
root@kind-control-plane:/# k get po
NAME                    READY   STATUS    RESTARTS   AGE
mysql-5dcb7797f7-6spvc  1/1     Running   0          12m
```

Sure enough, the Pod now has a status of `Running`, which is exactly what we need to get the Pod back to a running, healthy state and complete the exam task.

8.1.1 Container log detail

The `k logs` command is a handy utility for viewing the stdout and stderr from a container within a Pod. If there are two containers inside of one Pod, you must add a `-c` and specify the container you'd like to access. For example, run the command `k run busybox -image busybox -command ['while true; do echo "$(date)": "I am a busybox container"; sleep 5; done] -dry-run=client -o yaml > pod.yaml` to generate the YAML for a Pod. Open the `pod.yaml` file with the command `vim pod.yaml`. We'll make a few minor changes to the YAML, first by placing the command all on one line, moving the single quotes to inside the square brackets, and then adding the following to the beginning of the line, just before the word `while`: `'sh'`, `'-c'`,. The final result should look similar to the YAML file in figure 8.3.

Open a shell.   **Run a command inside of the container.**

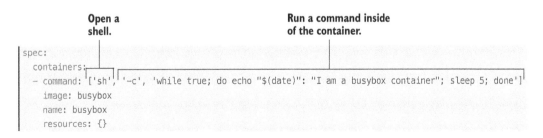

```
spec:
  containers:
  - command: ['sh', '-c', 'while true; do echo "$(date)": "I am a busybox container"; sleep 5; done']
    image: busybox
    name: busybox
    resources: {}
```

Figure 8.3 Specify in the YAML to run a command inside of a container in Kubernetes.

Now that you've made your YAML, matching the YAML line in figure 8.3, make just one more change. Copy the three lines beginning with `command`, `image`, and `name`, and paste them just below the existing three lines to specify the second container.

EXAM TIP Being able to copy and paste in Vim can save you time on the exam! Select lines by pressing Shift + V on your keyboard, followed by the up and down arrows to select. Once you've selected all the lines, press the Y key to copy and the P key to paste. This may take some practice, but it is well worth it to save time on the CKA exam!

Now that you've pasted these lines, change the name of the second container from `busybox` to `sidecar`. Also, change the sentence `I am a busybox container` to `I am a sidecar container`. Leave the rest the same. The result should look similar to the YAML in figure 8.4, which creates two different containers with different names and different commands running for each.

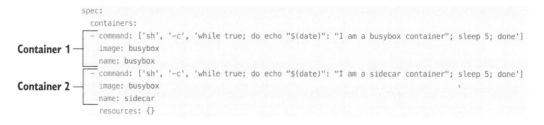

Figure 8.4 Adding a second container to a Pod YAML manifest

Now that the YAML is complete, create the Pod with the command `k apply -f pod.yaml`. If you were not able to follow along or are having trouble creating the Pod, run the command `k apply -f https://raw.githubusercontent.com/chadmcrowell/acing-the-cka-exam/main/ch_08/multi-container-pod-for-logging.yaml`. To view the Pods in the default namespace within the cluster, run the command `k get po`. The output should look similar to this:

```
root@kind-control-plane:/# k get po
NAME                     READY   STATUS    RESTARTS      AGE
busybox                  2/2     Running   0             1m
mysql-5dcb7797f7-6spvc   1/1     Running   2 (22h ago)   45h
```

To view the container logs from the first container named `busybox` within the Pod `busybox`, you can run either the command `k logs busybox` or, to be explicit, you can specify the container name as `k logs busybox -c busybox`. The output should look like this:

```
root@kind-control-plane:/# k logs busybox -c busybox
Tue Dec  6 14:36:26 UTC 2022: I am a busybox container
Tue Dec  6 14:36:31 UTC 2022: I am a busybox container
Tue Dec  6 14:36:36 UTC 2022: I am a busybox container
Tue Dec  6 14:36:41 UTC 2022: I am a busybox container
```

To view the logs from the second container named `sidecar` within the same Pod, run the command `k logs busybox -c sidecar`. The output should look like this:

```
root@kind-control-plane:/# k logs busybox -c sidecar
Tue Dec  6 14:18:59 UTC 2022: I am a sidecar container
Tue Dec  6 14:19:04 UTC 2022: I am a sidecar container
Tue Dec  6 14:19:09 UTC 2022: I am a sidecar container
```

To view the logs from both containers all at once, you can type `k logs busybox -all-containers`. The output should look similar to this:

```
root@kind-control-plane:/# k logs busybox -all-containers
Wed Dec  7 01:06:56 UTC 2022: I am a busybox container
Wed Dec  7 01:07:01 UTC 2022: I am a busybox container
Wed Dec  7 01:07:06 UTC 2022: I am a busybox container
Wed Dec  7 01:07:11 UTC 2022: I am a busybox container
Wed Dec  7 01:07:16 UTC 2022: I am a busybox container
Wed Dec  7 01:07:21 UTC 2022: I am a busybox container
Wed Dec  7 01:06:56 UTC 2022: I am a sidecar container
Wed Dec  7 01:07:01 UTC 2022: I am a sidecar container
Wed Dec  7 01:07:06 UTC 2022: I am a sidecar container
Wed Dec  7 01:07:11 UTC 2022: I am a sidecar container
Wed Dec  7 01:07:16 UTC 2022: I am a sidecar container
Wed Dec  7 01:07:21 UTC 2022: I am a sidecar container
```

If you wanted to continue to view the logs (streaming logs), you could run the command `k logs nginx -all-containers -f`. To get the prompt back, press Control-C on your keyboard.

> **EXAM TIP** The help menu can really save you during the exam. Instead of trying to memorize the commands, use the `kubectl` help menu (e.g., `k logs -help`). Best of all, the help menu contains example commands, which you can simply copy and paste!

When you run the `k logs` command, you're getting the same output as you would see in the log directory. To see the log directory, look inside the `/var/log/containers` directory on the node (where the Pod is running). For example, you can look at the `var/log/containers` directory on our control plane node and see the contents. You will see an output similar to figure 8.5.

You'll notice that the name of each log file begins with the Pod name followed by a string of unique characters (e.g., `mysql-5dcb7797…`). You can view the contents of this file to get an output similar to the `k logs` command. To view the contents of the log file, type the command `cat /var/log/containers/mysql-5dcb7797f7-6spvc_db08328_` `mysql-f9f53dc7de949452d848211d5d74aab36c2f5ae24a9d8b0b45577890d8b26ea2.log` (you can press Tab to complete the file name, so you don't have to type it all out). The output will look similar to figure 8.6.

```
root@kind-control-plane:/# ls /var/log/containers/
coredns-565d847f94-75lsz_kube-system_coredns-846396...log
etcd-kind-control-plane_kube-system_etcd-99da30be75...log
kindnet-b9f9r_kube-system_kindnet-cni-ebdb9d72af423...log
kube-apiserver-kind-control-plane_kube-system_kube-apiserver-47d...log
kube-controller-manager-kind-control-plane_kube-system_kube-controller-manager-063...log
kube-proxy-ddnwz_kube-system_kube-proxy-6d4...log
kube-scheduler-kind-control-plane_kube-system_kube-scheduler-076...log
local-path-provisioner-684...log
mysql-5dcb7797f7-6spvc_db08328_mysql-97c...log
```

Log file for each running container

Figure 8.5 An abbreviated output of each log file correlating to each running container in the /var/log/containers directory

Kubernetes Pod log directory   **Log file for Pod named mysql-5dcb7797f7-6spvc**

Figure 8.6 Looking into the log file associated with a specific Pod

What if the k logs command doesn't return any log output? Let's look at the decision tree in figure 8.7 to help us through the troubleshooting decision-making process.

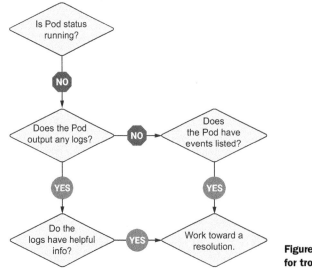

Figure 8.7 Decision-making process for troubleshooting Pod errors

This can happen from the container not starting in the first place. In this case, the next step in your troubleshooting process should be to run the k describe command to look at the events of the container. As an example, run the command k run brick --image busybox --command 'while true; do echo "$(date)"; sleep 5; done'. This will return an error. Run the command k get po to list the Pods. You should see the following output:

```
root@kind-control-plane:/# k get po
NAME                      READY   STATUS              RESTARTS      AGE
brick                     0/1     RunContainerError   1 (0s ago)    2s
busybox                   2/2     Running             0             7m57s
mysql-5dcb7797f7-6spvc    1/1     Running             2 (33h ago)   2d8h
```

When you run the command k logs brick, you don't receive any output because the container hasn't started up yet, so it hasn't had the opportunity to generate any logs. If you run the command k describe po brick, you will see the reason why this container didn't start. The output should look like this (abbreviated for context):

```
root@kind-control-plane:/# k describe po brick
Name:               brick
Namespace:          db08328
    Command:
      while true; do echo "$(date)"; sleep 5; done
    State:          Waiting
      Reason:       RunContainerError
    Last State:     Terminated
      Reason:       StartError
      Message:      failed to create containerd task: failed to create shim
➡ task: OCI runtime create failed: runc create failed: unable to start
➡ container process: exec: "while true; do echo \"$(date)\"; sleep 5;
➡ done": executable file not found in $PATH: unknown
    Exit Code:      128
    Started:        Thu, 01 Jan 1970 00:00:00 +0000
    Finished:       Wed, 07 Dec 2022 01:15:04 +0000
    Ready:          False
    Restart Count:  2
Events:
  Type      Reason      Age             From               Message
  ----      ------      ----            ----               -------
  Normal    Scheduled   19s             default-scheduler  Successfully
➡ assigned db08328/brick to kind-control-plane
  Normal    Pulled      18s             kubelet            Successfully
➡ pulled image "busybox" in 494.040497ms
  Normal    Pulled      17s             kubelet            Successfully
➡ pulled image "busybox" in 494.479219ms
  Normal    Pulling     5s (x3 over 19s) kubelet           Pulling image
➡ "busybox"
  Normal    Created     4s (x3 over 18s) kubelet           Created
➡ container brick
  Warning   Failed      4s (x3 over 18s) kubelet           Error: failed to
➡ create containerd task: failed to create shim task: OCI runtime create
➡ failed: runc create failed: unable to start container process: exec:
➡ "while true; do echo \"$(date)\"; sleep 5; done": executable file not
```

```
➥ found in $PATH: unknown
  Normal   Pulled    4s                 kubelet              Successfully
➥ pulled image "busybox" in 509.215883ms
  Warning  BackOff   3s (x3 over 17s)  kubelet              Back-off
➥ restarting failed container
```

As you see from the output of the k describe po brick command, the container failed
to start because it couldn't start the process within, which is shown in both the message and the events, all within the output of the k describe command.

8.1.2 *Troubleshooting from inside the container*

Because the network namespace is different inside a container than on the node, you
may need to troubleshoot from within the container itself. This is common in troubleshooting scenarios, as you may not be able to open a shell to a container that's in an
error state (as shown previously). Run the command k run tool --image lansible/
dnstools:latest -it -sh to create a new Pod named tool and get a shell to the container within that Pod at the same time. At this point, you will see your prompt
change. The result will look like this:

```
root@kind-control-plane:/# k run tool --image lansible/dnstools:latest -it
➥ --sh
If you don't see a command prompt, try pressing enter.
/ #
```

You can now enter various commands to troubleshoot from inside the container, in the
container's network namespace. You can run the command nslookup Kubernetes to get
back the DNS server for the Kubernetes Service. The output would look similar to this:

```
/ # nslookup kubernetes
Server:      10.96.0.10
Address:     10.96.0.10#53

** server can't find kubernetes: NXDOMAIN
```

Once you exit out of the container, you'll notice that the container is still running.

> **EXAM TIP** For the exam, if you need to troubleshoot communication to a
> Pod, use the busybox image and get a shell to it upon creation. This will keep
> the container running without having to insert a verbose command. For
> example, run the command k run busybox --image busybox -it --sh.

Because the container is still running, you can use the command k exec -it tool --sh
to get back into a shell within the container. The output will look similar to this:

```
/ # exit
Session ended, resume using 'kubectl attach tool -c tool -i -t' command
➥ when the pod is running
root@kind-control-plane:/# k exec -it tool --sh
/ #
```

Now that you have a shell again, run the command `curl -k http://10.96.0.1:443` to send a request to the Kubernetes Service. The output will look like this:

```
/ # curl -k http://10.96.0.1:443
Client sent an HTTP request to an HTTPS server.
/ #
```

Go ahead and exit out once again, and now you can run a command inside the container without getting a shell, using the command `k exec tool --cat /etc/resolv.conf`. The output should look similar to this:

```
/ # exit
root@kind-control-plane:/# k exec tool --cat /etc/resolv.conf
search kb6656.svc.cluster.local svc.cluster.local cluster.local
nameserver 10.96.0.10
options ndots:5
```

Finally, you can also get a shell to a container within a Pod, while deleting the Pod at the same time, with the command `k run curlpod --image=nicolaka/netshoot --rm -it --sh`. This will give you the same result as before, but once you exit, the Pod will be deleted because of using the `--rm` option with `kubectl run`. The output will look like this:

```
root@kind-control-plane:/# k run curlpod --image=nicolaka/netshoot --rm -it
➥ --sh
If you don't see a command prompt, try pressing enter.
~ # exit
Session ended, resume using 'kubectl attach curlpod -c curlpod -i -t'
➥ command when the pod is running
pod "curlpod" deleted
```

Practice exercises

Run the command `k run testbox --image busybox --command 'sleep 3600'` to create a new Pod named `testbox`. See if the container is running or not. Go through the decision tree to find out why, and fix the Pod so that it's running.

Create a new container named `busybox2` that uses the image `busybox:1.35.0`. Check if the container is in a running state. Find out why the container is failing, and make the corrections to the Pod YAML to get it running.

Create a new container named `curlpod2` that uses the image `nicolaka/netshoot`, while opening a shell to it upon creation. While a shell is open to the container, run `nslookup` on the Kubernetes Service. Exit out of the shell and see why the container is not running. Fix the container so that it continues to run.

8.2   *Cluster component failure*

When you run the `k describe` command, you won't always find that it's a problem with the container itself; it very well could be a problem with the control plane components that control the Pods in a Kubernetes cluster. We previously reviewed the control plane components in chapter 2 to help you understand each component's function, which helps when troubleshooting those components in the case of a failure. For example, if a Pod is in a pending state and isn't being assigned to a node, you know to investigate the scheduler, as this component is responsible for scheduling Pods to nodes. Or if the Deployment is not being scaled properly, you know to look at the controller manager because the controller manager is responsible for matching the desired state to the current state.

We know that the control plane components, such as the scheduler, controller manager, etcd, and API server, all run as Pods on the control plane node in the `kube-system` namespace. Therefore, the process for investigating these Pods is very similar to the first section of this chapter, including running the `k logs` and `k describe` commands to find the container logs and events. We also know that the YAML manifests for these control plane components are located in the `/etc/Kubernetes/manifests` directory, and any valid YAML file will automatically run here. We call this a *static Pod* because the scheduler is not aware of these Pods, so it cannot schedule them accordingly. An example question for the exam follows.

> **EXAM TASK** In cluster `ik8s`, in a namespace called `ee8881`, create a Deployment with the kubectl command line (imperatively) named `prod-app`, with the image `nginx`. List the Pods in the `ee8881` namespace to see if the Pod is running. Run the command `curl https://raw.githubusercontent.com/chadmcrowell/acing-the-cka-exam/main/ch_08/kube-scheduler.yaml --silent --output /etc/kubernetes/manifests/kube-scheduler.yaml` to make a change to the kube-scheduler, simulating a cluster component failure. Now scale the Deployment from one replica to three. List the Pods again and see if the additional two Pods in the Deployment are running. Find out why the two additional Pods are not running, and fix the scheduler so that the containers are in a running state again.

You can continue to use the same single-node cluster that we used for the previous exam task. There is no need to create a new kind Kubernetes cluster.

First, create the `ee8881` namespace with the command `k create ns ee8881`. Then, change the context to this new namespace with the command `k config set-context --current --namespace ee8881` to prevent having to type the namespace multiple times. The output should look like this:

```
root@kind-control-plane:/# k create ns ee8881
namespace/ee8881 created
root@kind-control-plane:/# k config set-context --current --namespace
```

```
⇒ ee8881
Context "kubernetes-admin@kind" modified.
```

Now that your context is in the `ee8881` namespace, you can create the Deployment named `prod-app` with the command `k create deploy prod-app --image nginx`. Immediately following, you can run `k get deploy,po` to see the Deployment running and the Pods within. The output should look like this:

```
root@kind-control-plane:/# k create deploy prod-app --image nginx
deployment.apps/prod-app created
root@kind-control-plane:/# k get deploy,po
NAME                        READY   UP-TO-DATE   AVAILABLE   AGE
deployment.apps/prod-app    1/1     1            1           9s


NAME                             READY   STATUS    RESTARTS   AGE
pod/prod-app-85c9dd4f9d-l7fmj    1/1     Running   0          9s
```

Now that the Deployment is created and the Pod within the Deployment is in a running state, run the command `curl https://raw.githubusercontent.com/chadmcrowell/ acing-the-cka-exam/main/ch_08/kube-scheduler.yaml --silent --output /etc/ kubernetes/manifests/kube-scheduler.yaml` to simulate a control plane failure. Immediately following, scale the Deployment from one replica to three with the command `k scale deploy prod-app -replicas 3`. When you look at the Pods within the Deployment with the `k get po` command, you see that the Pods are in a pending state. The output should look similar to this:

```
root@kind-control-plane:/# curl
⇒ https://raw.githubusercontent.com/chadmcrowell/acing-the-cka-
⇒ exam/main/ch_08/kube-scheduler.yaml --silent --output
⇒ /etc/kubernetes/manifests/kube-scheduler.yaml
root@kind-control-plane:/# k scale deploy prod-app --replicas 3
deployment.apps/prod-app scaled
root@kind-control-plane:/# k get po
NAME                        READY   STATUS    RESTARTS   AGE
prod-app-85c9dd4f9d-9clf1   0/1     Pending   0          7s
prod-app-85c9dd4f9d-l7fmj   1/1     Running   0          4m21s
prod-app-85c9dd4f9d-mbdk7   0/1     Pending   0          7s
```

In this case, if you run `k logs prod prod-app-85c9dd4f9d-9clf1`, you will not get any output, because the container was never able to start and generate logs. But, if you run the command `k -n kube-system logs kube-scheduler-kind-control-plane`, you'll receive useful information about why the containers aren't able to start up. As mentioned previously, knowing what the scheduler does in Kubernetes helps you find the quickest path to resolution when troubleshooting. Running the command `k -n kube-system logs kube-scheduler-kind-control-plane | tail -2` will show the last two lines of the log, which is enough for what we need to know about the error. The output should look like this:

```
root@kind-control-plane:/# k -n kube-system logs kube-scheduler-kind-
↪ control-plane | tail -2

Error: unknown flag: --kkubeconfig
```

This is a clue to the solution. If you look at the scheduler manifest in the /etc/
kubernetes/manifests/ directory with the command vim /etc/kubernetes/mani-
fests/ kube-scheduler.yaml, you will see—toward the top of the file, under the commands section of the container—the reason why the scheduler is failing (figure 8.8).

**Figure 8.8   The command that was run inside the scheduler container contains an
extra k when passing in the kubeconfig.**

To fix this, we can simply edit the file by entering insert mode (pressing I on the keyboard) and removing the additional k. Once we fix this, we can exit Vim by first pressing the Esc key on the keyboard and then typing :wq, which will get you back to the
prompt where you can see the scheduler Pod automatically repairing itself. You can
see this with the command k get po -A (or k -n kube-system get po). The output
should look like this:

```
root@kind-control-plane:/# k get po -A
NAMESPACE               NAME                                    READY
↪ STATUS               RESTARTS          AGE
db08328                 brick                                   0/1
↪ CrashLoopBackOff    21 (2m49s ago)    85m
db08328                 busybox                                 2/2
↪ Running              0                 93m
```

db08328	mysql-5dcb7797f7-6spvc	1/1
➥ Running	2 (34h ago) 2d9h	
db08328	nginx-76d6c9b8c-k22xs	1/1
➥ Running	0 48m	
db08328	nginx-76d6c9b8c-vzkmw	1/1
➥ Running	0 46m	
db08328	nginx-76d6c9b8c-w24w4	1/1
➥ Running	0 46m	
ee8881	prod-app-85c9dd4f9d-9clf1	0/1
➥ ContainerCreating	0 20m	
ee8881	prod-app-85c9dd4f9d-l7fmj	1/1
➥ Running	0 24m	
ee8881	prod-app-85c9dd4f9d-mbdk7	0/1
➥ ContainerCreating	0 20m	
kube-system	coredns-565d847f94-75lsz	1/1
➥ Running	2 (34h ago) 2d10h	
kube-system	coredns-565d847f94-8stkp	1/1
➥ Running	2 (34h ago) 2d10h	
kube-system	etcd-kind-control-plane	1/1
➥ Running	3 (34h ago) 2d10h	
kube-system	kindnet-b9f9r	1/1
➥ Running	2 (34h ago) 2d10h	
kube-system	kube-apiserver-kind-control-plane	1/1
➥ Running	3 (34h ago) 2d10h	
kube-system	kube-controller-manager-kind-control-plane	1/1
➥ Running	3 (34h ago) 2d10h	
kube-system	kube-proxy-z4qvh	1/1
➥ Running	2 (34h ago) 2d10h	
kube-system	kube-scheduler-kind-control-plane	0/1
➥ ContainerCreating	0 2s	
local-path-storage	local-path-provisioner-684f458cdd-vkbln	1/1
➥ Running	3 (34h ago) 2d10h	

By running the k get po -A command, you'll notice that the Pods from the prod-app Deployment start up at the same time, which shows that the scaling problem we had before has been resolved, and all three replicas within the prod-app Deployment are now in a running state. This satisfies the requirement for our exam task.

8.2.1   Troubleshooting cluster events

Now that we've reviewed individual Pod logs for both control plane components and other applications, we should consider an object in Kubernetes that generates events for all changes in the state of a Kubernetes resource. When a Pod goes from pending to running, or from running to failing, an event is triggered. These events—where the path to resolution isn't as clear as what we just witnessed in the last exam task—are useful for debugging. The object is different than regular log events and can tell you valuable information about the root of the problem at hand. Take a look at these events with the command k get events -A. The -A signifies all namespaces, because this object is a namespaced resource in Kubernetes. The output should look like this:

```
root@kind-control-plane:/# k get events -A
NAMESPACE    LAST SEEN    TYPE       REASON     OBJECT       MESSAGE
db08328      35s          Warning    BackOff    pod/brick    Back-off restarting
➡ failed container
```

As you can see, some valuable information is returned about the "brick" Pod that we were working with earlier, including the reason and the message.

> **EXAM TIP** For the exam, the k get events command may output too many events, including events that are "normal" messages that may not be helpful for troubleshooting. Use the command k get events --field-selector type!=Normal -A to filter out the normal events and only give you warning- and information-type events.

Keep in mind that these events are held for only 1 hour by default, so they might be different from the start of the exam to the end. You can set the --event-ttl option on the API server to change this, but I don't recommend it unless the exam task specifically tells you to do so.

The inverse of filtering certain types of logs is dumping the entire cluster information and logs of all the Pods in the cluster. To get a verbose look at the health of the cluster, you can run the command k cluster-info dump. The output will be quite large, so I have modified my command to only include the last 10 lines here:

```
root@kind-control-plane:/# k cluster-info dump | tail -10
2022/12/07 02:40:28 [notice] 1#1: nginx/1.23.2
2022/12/07 02:40:28 [notice] 1#1: built by gcc 10.2.1 20210110 (Debian
➡ 10.2.1-6)
2022/12/07 02:40:28 [notice] 1#1: OS: Linux 5.15.49-linuxkit
2022/12/07 02:40:28 [notice] 1#1: getrlimit(RLIMIT_NOFILE): 1048576:1048576
2022/12/07 02:40:28 [notice] 1#1: start worker processes
2022/12/07 02:40:28 [notice] 1#1: start worker process 32
2022/12/07 02:40:28 [notice] 1#1: start worker process 33
2022/12/07 02:40:28 [notice] 1#1: start worker process 34
2022/12/07 02:40:28 [notice] 1#1: start worker process 35
==== END logs for container nginx of pod ee8881/prod-app-85c9dd4f9d-mbdk7
➡ ====
```

You can also grep this command to look for the words *error* or *fail*, which is very effective for troubleshooting when you don't know from where the problem is originating. For example, run the command k cluster-info dump | grep error to only get lines that include the word *error*. Again, I have modified my command to shorten the output, but the command output should look like this:

```
root@kind-control-plane:/# k cluster-info dump | grep error | tail -1
E1207 20:59:46.036248       1 leaderelection.go:330] error retrieving
➡ resource lock kube-system/kube-controller-manager: Get
➡ "https://172.18.0.2:6443/apis/coordination.k8s.io/v1/namespaces/kube-
➡ system/leases/kube-controller-manager?timeout=5s": dial tcp
➡ 172.18.0.2:6443: connect: connection refused
```

8.2.2 Worker node failure

Sometimes when you're troubleshooting the nodes of a Kubernetes cluster, it can be useful to look at the status of the node to see if the kubelet service is running. Just as you would a Pod, you can run the command `k describe no kind-control-plane` to find the condition of the CPU and RAM, as well as the events at the very bottom of the output. You may find that there are no available resources or that the node is in a failed state. In addition, the metrics server will already be installed for the exam, so don't focus too much on the details of installing it in this section.

The metrics server allows you to check the CPU and memory usage in real time, and the main focus of the exam will be what commands to run to view these metrics in the provided terminal. Install the metrics server with the command `kubectl apply -f https:/ /github.com/kubernetes-sigs/metrics-server/releases/download/v0.5.0/components.yaml`. If you are following along on your own kind cluster, you'll have to apply one small patch, which you can do quite easily with the command `kubectl patch -n kube-system deployment metrics-server --type=json -p '[{"op":"add", "path":"/spec/template/spec/containers/0/args/-","value":"--kubelet-insecure -tls"}]'`. Wait just a few seconds (up to 60 seconds), and you should have a working metrics server. Test this with the command `k top no`. The output should look like this:

```
root@kind-control-plane:~# k top no
NAME                    CPU(cores)   CPU%   MEMORY(bytes)   MEMORY%
kind-control-plane      177m         4%     1735Mi          44%
```

As you can see from the output, this node is consuming 177m of CPU, which is 4% of the total CPU, and 1820 MB of memory, which is 44% of the total memory. This is a way to check if your Pods are not able to be scheduled to a node, because if they are not, they will show closer to 100% utilized using this command.

In terms of checking for available disk space, you can run the command `df -h`, which is a command to display the free disk space on a node, and the `-h` option makes the output more human readable. Here's how the output should look:

```
root@kind-control-plane:~# df -h
Filesystem      Size  Used Avail Use% Mounted on
overlay          59G   29G   27G  52% /
tmpfs            64M     0   64M   0% /dev
shm              64M     0   64M   0% /dev/shm
/dev/vda1        59G   29G   27G  52% /var
tmpfs           2.0G  139M  1.8G   8% /run
tmpfs           2.0G     0  2.0G   0% /tmp
rootfs          2.0G  333M  1.6G  17% /usr/lib/modules
tmpfs           5.0M     0  5.0M   0% /run/lock
```

You can also show the state of the node by simply running the command `k get no`, as we have done many times before in this book. Finally, to start the kubelet service on a node, run the command `systemctl start kubelet`. You can also use Journalctl to view the logs from the kubelet service. Run the command `journalctl -u kubelet` to troubleshoot any problems with the kubelet service. The output should look like figure 8.9 (abbreviated for readability).

Figure 8.9   Abbreviated output from `journalctl` utility of the kubelet logs

Another problem with the kubelet could be the kubelet configuration. In chapter 6, we modified the kubelet configuration while changing the cluster DNS. Along with the cluster DNS, some certificates are passed to the kubelet when it starts up to authenticate to the Kubernetes API; the cluster domain and the health Endpoints are also set here. On the exam, if for some reason the kubelet is not starting with the `systemctl start kubelet` command, check the `/var/lib/kubelet/config.yaml` file for misconfigurations.

Finally, in chapter 2 we talked about the kubeconfig for the kubelet, which is a file named `kubelet.conf` in the `/etc/kubernetes/` directory. This will sometimes cause problems with accessing the cluster. To properly think through this troubleshooting process, review the decision tree depicted in figure 8.10.

Sometimes the kubelet binary is missing entirely or located in a different directory. You can see where the kubelet binary is located with the command `which kubelet`. The output looks similar to this:

```
root@kind-control-plane:~# which kubelet
/usr/bin/kubelet
```

If the directory `/usr/bin/kubelet` is different than what's listed when you run `systemctl status kubelet`, then there is a problem. Check the `10-kubeadm.conf` file in the `/etc/systemd/system/kubelet.service.d/` directory to see if the `ExecStart` is set to `/usr/bin/kubelet`. When you change the kubelet configuration, keep in mind that you must reload the daemon and then start the Service. Do this with the command `systemctl daemon-reload`, and then the command `systemctl restart kubelet`, like so:

```
root@kind-control-plane:~# systemctl daemon-reload
root@kind-control-plane:~# systemctl restart kubelet
```

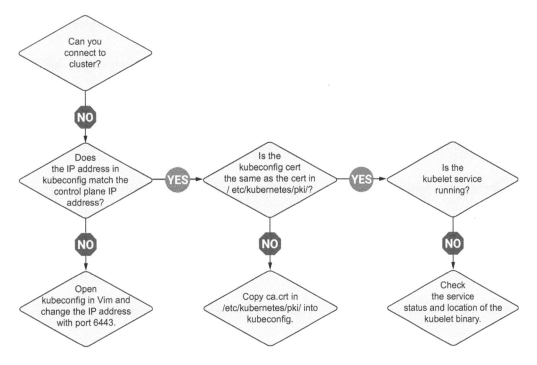

Figure 8.10   The decision process of troubleshooting access to the cluster

8.2.3   *Did you specify the right host or port?*

A common message you might receive when typing any `kubectl` command (e.g., `kubectl get po`) is "The connection to the server $SERVER:6443 was refused - did you specify the right host or port?" This message occurs either because the API is misconfigured or your kubeconfig is not set correctly. To see this message in your cluster, first run the command `curl https://raw.githubusercontent.com/chadmcrowell/acing-the-cka-exam/main/ch_08/kube-apiserver.yaml --silent --output /etc/kubernetes/manifests/kube-scheduler.yaml` to modify the API server configuration. Then run the command `k get po` immediately to try to list the Pods running in the cluster. You will see output similar to this:

```
root@kind-control-plane:~# curl
⇒ https://raw.githubusercontent.com/chadmcrowell/acing-the-cka-
⇒ exam/main/ch_08/kube-apiserver.yaml --silent --output
⇒ /etc/kubernetes/manifests/kube-apiserver.yaml
root@kind-control-plane:~# k get po
The connection to the server kind-control-plane:6443 was refused - did you
⇒ specify the right host or port?
```

If you look at the `kube-apiserver.yaml` file in the `/etc/kubernetes/manifests/` directory, you'll see the problem on line 44, where the `event-ttl` is missing an `=` sign.

EXAM TIP   Remember, the host from which you'll be taking the exam is not the same as the control plane server. You'll want to SSH to the control plane node before looking for the /etc/kubernetes/manifests/ directory.

When you put that equal sign back in, the output should look similar to figure 8.11.

```
37    - --secure-port=6443
38    - --service-account-issuer=https://kubernetes.default.svc.cluster.local
39    - --service-account-key-file=/etc/kubernetes/pki/sa.pub
40    - --service-account-signing-key-file=/etc/kubernetes/pki/sa.key
41    - --service-cluster-ip-range=10.96.0.0/16
42    - --tls-cert-file=/etc/kubernetes/pki/apiserver.crt
43    - --tls-private-key-file=/etc/kubernetes/pki/apiserver.key
44    - --event-ttl=1h0m0s
45    image: registry.k8s.io/kube-apiserver:v1.25.0-beta.0
46    imagePullPolicy: IfNotPresent
47    livenessProbe:
```

Added the equal sign back in

Figure 8.11   Part of the kube-apiserver.yaml **file that includes the correct formatting of** event-ttl

When you save and quit this file (:wq), you'll realize that the message doesn't go away.

EXAM TIP   Don't panic! You may modify the API config in a way that is unrecoverable. Along with making a backup copy of the kube-apiserver.yaml file before making a change, you can check the status of the API server Pod with crictl.

This is okay, because we can use the crictl tool to restart the container. The crictl tool is handy for when you can't use the kubectl command and want to see the state of the underlying Pods. Use the command crictl ps to view the containers, and you will see the kube-apiserver container in the list. The output will look similar to the following (this output is abbreviated) and will include different container IDs:

```
root@kind-control-plane:~# crictl ps
CONTAINER          STATE          NAME
d7b925224d332      Running        kindnet-cni
84234147eb024      Running        kube-apiserver
5dd8b3aeaa752      Running        kube-controller-manager
5228bb1f5eb7c      Running        kube-scheduler
903193dd102db      Running        coredns
97268d17eb9fd      Running        kube-proxy
f9f8ea21cb4be      Running        etcd
```

The first column in this output is the container ID. Run the command crictl stop 842 to stop the kube-apiserver container. You can use the first three characters of the container ID, as long as it's unique among all the other containers listed by crictl ps. Then immediately run the command crictl rm 842 to kill the container.

After a few seconds, you'll see another container spun up in its place. You can tell that it's a new container because after you run `crictl ps` again, it has a different container ID. Once you can view the container from `crictl` with a status of `Running`, you can run `kubectl get po` and see that it returns the list of Pods again. You will no longer see the message about the right host or port!

8.2.4 Troubleshooting kubeconfig

The other possibility when receiving the "Do you have the right host or port?" message is to check your kubeconfig to see if it's specifying the correct control plane node, if the certificate is valid, and if the `KUBECONFIG` environment variable is set correctly. When you installed `kubectl`, or within your kind cluster, a hidden directory named `.kube` was created in your home directory. This contains the server address, the certificates to authenticate to the cluster, and the user information. You can view this file just like you would any other file, with the command `cat ~/.kube/config`, but there's also a `kubectl` command for viewing the kubeconfig, which is `k config view`. The output from this command will look similar to figure 8.12.

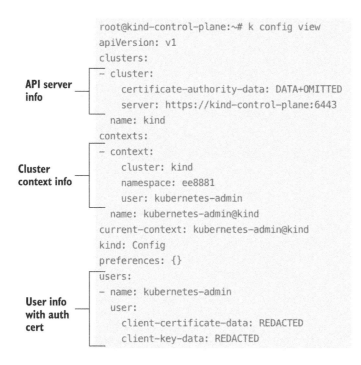

Figure 8.12   Output from the command `k config view`, which lists the API server, context, and user info

EXAM TIP The result of these two commands (`cat ~/.kube/config` and `k config view`) may not be the same on the exam. If you're tasked with fixing the context of your cluster, perhaps because you can't list the nodes, run the command `k config view --flatten > ~/.kube/config` to get them synced up. This will merge the config files and save the output to the file config in `~/.kube/config`.

It may be that on the exam this kubeconfig file is not present. Or perhaps you accidentally deleted or misconfigured it. Don't panic! There is a copy of this file stored in the `/etc/kubernetes/` directory and it's named `admin.conf`. You can use this along with the `kubectl` command by running the command `k get no --kubeconfig /etc/kubernetes/admin.conf`, for example, or you can set a special environment variable named `KUBECONFIG`. This environment variable is used with the `kubectl` command-line utility and will point your `kubectl` commands toward the config file stored in the value of this variable. Run the command `KUBECONFIG=/etc/kubernetes/admin.conf` to set the environment variable (creating a variable name in all caps is common for Linux systems), and you'll be able to access your cluster again. Or you can simply copy the file from the `/etc/Kubernetes/` directory to the `~/.kube/` directory with the command `cp /etc/kubernetes/admin.conf ~/.kube/config`. The output of these commands will look like this:

```
root@kind-control-plane:~# ls .kube/
cache
root@kind-control-plane:~# k get no --kubeconfig /etc/kubernetes/admin.conf
NAME                STATUS   ROLES          AGE     VERSION
kind-control-plane  Ready    control-plane  5d23h   v1.25.0-beta.0
root@kind-control-plane:~# KUBECONFIG=/etc/kubernetes/admin.conf
root@kind-control-plane:~# k get no
NAME                STATUS   ROLES          AGE     VERSION
kind-control-plane  Ready    control-plane  5d23h   v1.25.0-beta.0
root@kind-control-plane:~# cp /etc/kubernetes/admin.conf ~/.kube/config
root@kind-control-plane:~# ls ~/.kube
cache   config
```

You'll notice when you run the `k config view` command, as in figure 8.7, certificate data is redacted from the output. You can see the certificate data with the command `k config view -raw`. The output will look like this:

```
root@kind-control-plane:~# k config view --raw
apiVersion: v1
clusters:
- cluster:
    certificate-authority-data: LS0tLS1CRUdJTiBDRVJUSUZJQ0FURS0tLS0tCk…
    server: https://kind-control-plane:6443
  name: kind
contexts:
- context:
    cluster: kind
    namespace: ee8881
    user: kubernetes-admin
  name: kubernetes-admin@kind
current-context: kubernetes-admin@kind
```

```
kind: Config
preferences: {}
users:
- name: kubernetes-admin
  user:
    client-certificate-data: LS0tLS1CRUdJTiBDRVJUSUZJQ0FURS0tLS0tCk1JS…
    client-key-data: LS0tLS1CRUdJTiBSU0EgUFJJVkFURSBLRVktLS0tLQpNSUlFb…
```

You can do this to reveal the certificate data with which you can validate the authenticity of the certificate and match it with the `ca.crt` certificate file that's in the `/etc/Kubernetes/pki/` directory. First, run the command `k config view --raw -o jsonpath='{.clusters[0].cluster.certificate-authority-data}' | base64 -d > ca-compare.crt` to Base64 decode the certificate from the `k config view --raw` command, and store the output in a file named `ca-compare.crt`. Then, run the command `cat /etc/kubernetes/pki/ca.crt >> ca-compare.crt` to append the `ca.crt` certificate in `/etc/Kubernetes/pki/ca.crt` to the same file. Open the file and compare the two strings of text between the words BEGIN CERTIFICATE and END CERTIFICATE. The output of these commands should look as follows:

```
root@kind-control-plane:~# k config view --raw -o
➡ jsonpath='{.clusters[0].cluster.certificate-authority-data}' | base64 -
➡ d > ca-compare.crt
root@kind-control-plane:~# cat /etc/kubernetes/pki/ca.crt >> ca-compare.crt
root@kind-control-plane:~# cat ca-compare.crt
-----BEGIN CERTIFICATE-----
MIIC/jCCAeagAwIBAgIBADANBgkqhkiG9w0BAQsFADAVMRMwEQYDVQQDEwprdWJl
cm5ldGVzMB4XDTIyMTIwNDE2MjEzNVoXDTMyMTIwMTE2MjEzNVowFTETMBEGA1UE
AxMKa3ViZXJuZXRlczCCASIwDQYJKoZIhvcNAQEBBQADggEPADCCAQoCggEBAKWj
sVQRplk9WcZwoQpls2wxXbOnAFL22CLsyGQmgzQZHgMSm3M/XCnHc5RZGQpv7mQS
GVgIzMjYZrpg/gm4U4TQEgLAqXRdQ2Rd08iJfUX3/onjyc/YPnfFtzNDJ4cFHkiX
mS0LwIUoOAb2dRQzitisvGiFhnr/bWl7QALOZBq2RzyhtrNBF18rRcWVUdmrQMqb
HEHsc2ZRefCVc7HSf2x8UnqOcRbgF413VmW+0R2+lOWka3c2tFqK86GHcKky2nY3
PYF+EE/HlLOBTlwb/okbKYWIf2eKaaNZ8Ypsj/aZGTAWu6Gt23S5Bgbe4WV4W7SZ
A+juTakjkPudFpTVvmcCAwEAAaNZMFcwDgYDVR0PAQH/BAQDAgKkMA8GA1UdEwEB
/wQFMAMBAf8wHQYDVR0OBBYEFGh+GTf8f/BLCKZuEnnItDDWDk5LMBUGA1UdEQQO
MAyCCmt1YmVrbmV0ZXMwDQYJKoZIhvcNAQELBQADggEBABxG6ve/7gUzV/2nwIFl
JXPloCeFI+WeG1weKK+h98d4yYjGvVXjt9dwqCnIWGVG40KIYQvthf3kZcSpHpH0
GDNWrS4cvL8UvAzbuKH4opboGuoHAxGIs1D0YgauoPRw3ofQSxMLeUnGfDN25CP4
g0XD5DwPANaPACFR7bKEDbcIfwAvMce6TcwWJ3QfG7e/Se/Z0LiasUNb7R7FxSFp
MKd21MlcqnnjqUfuGt42n23U08pkstfyO1nddqiMzFoXefFCjCDJ26kGeunNZsMb
2c8afwHwa8iAugXzmwhZ+XiNPgq0o3YRIz9oQLkEC24ojgM9sbJ55jZyN9TAvJCO
BHM=
-----END CERTIFICATE-----
-----BEGIN CERTIFICATE-----
MIIC/jCCAeagAwIBAgIBADANBgkqhkiG9w0BAQsFADAVMRMwEQYDVQQDEwprdWJl
cm5ldGVzMB4XDTIyMTIwNDE2MjEzNVoXDTMyMTIwMTE2MjEzNVowFTETMBEGA1UE
AxMKa3ViZXJuZXRlczCCASIwDQYJKoZIhvcNAQEBBQADggEPADCCAQoCggEBAKWj
sVQRplk9WcZwoQpls2wxXbOnAFL22CLsyGQmgzQZHgMSm3M/XCnHc5RZGQpv7mQS
GVgIzMjYZrpg/gm4U4TQEgLAqXRdQ2Rd08iJfUX3/onjyc/YPnfFtzNDJ4cFHkiX
mS0LwIUoOAb2dRQzitisvGiFhnr/bWl7QALOZBq2RzyhtrNBF18rRcWVUdmrQMqb
HEHsc2ZRefCVc7HSf2x8UnqOcRbgF413VmW+0R2+lOWka3c2tFqK86GHcKky2nY3
PYF+EE/HlLOBTlwb/okbKYWIf2eKaaNZ8Ypsj/aZGTAWu6Gt23S5Bgbe4WV4W7SZ
```

A+juTakjkPudFpTVvmcCAwEAAaNZMFcwDgYDVR0PAQH/BAQDAgKkMA8GA1UdEwEB
/wQFMAMBAf8wHQYDVR0OBBYEFGh+GTf8f/BLCKZuEnnItDDWDk5LMBUGA1UdEQQO
MAyCCmt1YmVybmV0ZXMwDQYJKoZIhvcNAQELBQADggEBABxG6ve/7gUzV/2nwIFl
JXPloCeFI+WeG1weKK+h98d4yYjGvVXjt9dwqCnIWGVG40KIYQvthf3kZcSpHpH0
GDNWrS4cvL8UvAzbuKH4opboGuoHAxGIslD0YgauoPRw3ofQSxMLeUnGfDN25CP4
g0XD5DwPANaPACFR7bKEDbcIfwAvMce6TcwWJ3QfG7e/Se/Z0LiasUNb7R7FxSFp
MKd21MlcqnnjqUfuGt42n23U08pkstfyO1nddqiMzFoXefFCjCDJ26kGeunNZsMb
2c8afwHwa8iAugXzmwhZ+XiNPgqOo3YRIz9oQLkEC24ojgM9sbJ55jZyN9TAvJCO
BHM=
-----END CERTIFICATE-----

Along with the certificates, check that the server address is correct in the kubeconfig file. You can check this by comparing the output of the `k config view` command with the output of the `k cluster-info` command. Usually, the exam will use an IP address instead of the DNS name. In that case, you can check the private IP address of the control plane server (remember to first SSH to the control plane server if attempting this on the exam) by running the command `ip addr | grep eth0`. The output should look like this:

```
root@kind-control-plane:~# ip addr | grep eth0
9: eth0@if10: <BROADCAST,MULTICAST,UP,LOWER_UP> mtu 1500 qdisc noqueue
   state UP group default
    inet 172.18.0.2/16 brd 172.18.255.255 scope global eth0
22: veth0c1530f0@if4: <BROADCAST,MULTICAST,UP,LOWER_UP> mtu 1500 qdisc
   noqueue state UP group default
    inet 10.244.0.1/32 scope global veth0c1530f0
32: veth0dfc2be7@if4: <BROADCAST,MULTICAST,UP,LOWER_UP> mtu 1500 qdisc
   noqueue state UP group default
    inet 10.244.0.1/32 scope global veth0dfc2be7
```

If you take off the grep for `eth0`, you'll see the `veth` interfaces—the virtual Ethernet devices for the containers running on the control plane node—which we went over in greater detail in chapter 2 where we were investigating the virtual network interface within a container.

Exam exercises

Move the file `kube-scheduler.yaml` to the `/tmp` directory with the command `mv /etc/Kubernetes/manifests/kube-scheduler.yaml /tmp/kube-scheduler.yaml`.

Create a Pod with the command `k run nginx -image nginx`. List the Pods and see if the Pod is in a running state.

Determine why the Pod is not starting by looking at the events and the logs. Determine how to fix it and get the Pod back in a running state.

Run the command `curl https://raw.githubusercontent.com/chadmcrowell/acing-the-cka-exam/main/ch_08/10-kubeadm.conf --silent --output /etc/systemd/system/kubelet.service.d/10-kubeadm.conf; systemctl daemon-reload; systemctl restart kubelet`.

Check the status of the kubelet, and go through the troubleshooting steps to resolve the problem with the kubelet service.

8.3   Network troubleshooting

As you already know, Pod-to-Pod communication happens via CNI. If the node is not in a ready state or the containers are unable to create IP addresses, you have a problem with the network within the cluster or the container network interface. You already know from the CKA exam handbook that one of your clusters will have a loopback CNI, which may or may not require troubleshooting or fixing the CNI in some way. Regardless of which CNI is used, the exam will always give you either a YAML file with which to install the CNI or a link for where to find it. This question comes up a lot, and I want to assure you that *you will not* have to memorize the steps to install a CNI on the exam.

8.3.1   Troubleshooting the config

When trying to troubleshoot network problems, various concerns must be considered. After you've evaluated the decision tree, the resolution still might not be clear. You should pay special attention to common misspellings in the error message details. For example, a question on the exam might look like the following.

EXAM TASK In cluster `ik8s`, run the command `k replace -f https://raw .githubusercontent.com/chadmcrowell/acing-the-cka-exam/main/ch_08/kube- proxy-configmap.yaml -force` to purposely insert a bug in the cluster. Immediately after that, delete the kube-proxy Pod in the `kube-system` namespace (it will automatically recreate). List the Pods in the namespace, and see that the kube-proxy Pod is in an error state. View the logs to determine why the kube-proxy Pod is not running. Once you've collected the necessary log information, make the changes to fix the Pod and get the Pod back up in a running, healthy state.

You can continue to use the same single-node cluster that we used for the previous exam task. There is no need to create a new kind Kubernetes cluster.

First, run the command `k replace -f https://raw.githubusercontent.com/ chadmcrowell/acing-the-cka-exam/main/ch_08/kube-proxy-configmap.yaml -force` as instructed in the exam task. The output will look as follows:

```
root@kind-control-plane:/# k replace -f
➥ https://raw.githubusercontent.com/chadmcrowell/acing-the-cka-
➥ exam/main/ch_08/kube-proxy-configmap.yaml --force
configmap "kube-proxy" deleted
configmap/kube-proxy replaced
```

Delete the kube-proxy Pod with the command `k -n kube-system delete po kube-proxy-k7dt6` (the Pod name will be different for each cluster).

> **EXAM TIP**   To save time, type the `kubectl` command with the namespace first (e.g., `k -n kube-system…`). This allows you to hit the Tab key on the keyboard to autocomplete the names of resources within that namespace (e.g., Pods). This is especially useful for Deployments, where the names are usually quite long. It also prevents typos, which are a waste of time and might cost you a few points on the exam.

We can list the Pods in the `kube-system` namespace with the command `k -n kube-system get po` or `k get po -A`. The output will look similar to this:

```
root@kind-control-plane:/# k -n kube-system get po
NAME                                          READY    STATUS
⇒   RESTARTS          AGE
coredns-565d847f94-75lsz                      1/1      Running             3
⇒   (120m ago)       7d
coredns-565d847f94-8stkp                      1/1      Running             3
⇒   (120m ago)       7d
etcd-kind-control-plane                       1/1      Running             4
⇒   (120m ago)       7d
kindnet-b9f9r                                 1/1      Running             22
⇒   (120m ago)       7d
kube-apiserver-kind-control-plane             1/1      Running             1
⇒   (120m ago)       3d18h
kube-controller-manager-kind-control-plane    1/1      Running             8
⇒   (120m ago)       7d
kube-proxy-chc4w                              0/1      CrashLoopBackOff    7
⇒   (40s ago)        11m
kube-scheduler-kind-control-plane             1/1      Running             3
⇒   (120m ago)       3d18h
metrics-server-d5589cfb-4ksgb                 1/1      Running             2
⇒   (120m ago)       3d17h
```

By running this command, the Pod `kube-proxy-chc4w` is in a `CrashLoopBackOff`. Note that the Pod name will be different for each cluster; therefore, the characters after `kube-proxy-` will be different for you. Let's run the command `k -n kube-system logs kube-proxy-chc4w` to view the logs and find out why the Pod is failing. The output from this command will be similar to this:

```
root@kind-control-plane:/# k -n kube-system logs kube-proxy-chc4w
E1211 17:17:07.621228        1 server.go:500] "Error running ProxyServer"
⇒ err="stat /var/lib/kube-proxy/kubeconfigd.conf: no such file or directory"
E1211 17:17:07.621298        1 run.go:74] "command failed" err="stat
⇒ /var/lib/kube-proxy/kubeconfigd.conf: no such file or directory"
```

A lot of useful information comes from this output—in particular, the line `/var/lib/kube-proxy/kubeconfigd.conf: no such file or directory`, which tells us that there's a problem with the configuration of kube-proxy. We know this because files ending in

.conf usually coincide with configuration files on Linux systems. Also, notice that the word kubeconfig has a d at the end. To double-check if this is correct, search in the Kubernetes docs (https://kubernetes.io/docs); it autocorrects to "Did you mean kubeconfig.conf?"

We know after having read chapter 6 that the configuration for kube-proxy is stored inside of a ConfigMap in the kube-system namespace. Open it in Vim and see if you can spot if there's a line matching /var/lib/kube-proxy/kubeconfigd.conf. Most likely we'll have to make edits in this file, so we can use the command k -n kube-system edit cm kube-proxy to open the ConfigMap in Vim and make the necessary changes. The partial contents of the file are shown in figure 8.13. We see that, in fact, a line matches one of the lines from our logs; change the kubeconfigd.conf to kubeconfig .conf to see if that fixes it.

```
apiVersion: v1
data:
  config.conf: |-
    apiVersion: kubeproxy.config.k8s.io/v1alpha1
    bindAddress: 0.0.0.0
    bindAddressHardFail: false
    clientConnection:
      acceptContentTypes: ""
      burst: 0
      contentType: ""
      kubeconfig: /var/lib/kube-proxy/kubeconfigd.conf
      qps: 0
```

Change to kubeconfig.conf.

Figure 8.13   Editing the ConfigMap for kube-proxy, we notice that a line should be changed in the client connection.

After we make that change and save the file (:wq), delete the kube-proxy Pod once again so the DaemonSet can recreate it and apply the configuration changes we just made in the ConfigMap. To do this, we'll perform the command k -n kube-system delete po kube-proxy-chc4w and then immediately list the Pods in the kube-system namespace again with the command k -n kube-system get po. The output will look similar to this:

```
root@kind-control-plane:/# k -n kube-system delete po kube-proxy-chc4w
pod "kube-proxy-chc4w" deleted
root@kind-control-plane:/# k -n kube-system get po
NAME                                READY   STATUS    RESTARTS
⇒      AGE
coredns-565d847f94-75lsz            1/1     Running   3 (158m ago)
⇒      7d1h
coredns-565d847f94-8stkp            1/1     Running   3 (158m ago)
⇒      7d1h
etcd-kind-control-plane             1/1     Running   4 (158m ago)
⇒      7d1h
kindnet-b9f9r                       1/1     Running   22 (158m ago)
⇒      7d1h
```

```
kube-apiserver-kind-control-plane            1/1       Running   1 (158m ago)
⮩     3d19h
kube-controller-manager-kind-control-plane   1/1       Running   8 (158m ago)
⮩     7d1h
kube-proxy-ddnwz                             1/1       Running   0
⮩     6s
kube-scheduler-kind-control-plane            1/1       Running   3 (158m ago)
⮩     3d19h
metrics-server-d5589cfb-4ksgb                1/1       Running   2 (158m ago)
⮩     3d18h
```

We notice that the kube-proxy Pod is in a running state again. This completes our exam task, as the Pod is back in a running state once again and the function of kube-proxy is restored.

Kube-proxy is a component that may need troubleshooting on the exam, as it is responsible for creating iptables rules (firewall rules) for Pod network communication in the cluster. The kube-proxy Pod will make sure that requests to Services reach the underlying Pods associated with that Service. You can see the kube-proxy listening and monitoring the network activity with the `netstat` tool. The `netstat` tool will already be installed for the exam, but if you'd like to practice in your own cluster, run the command `netstat -plan | grep kube-proxy` to view the ports that kube-proxy is active on and listening to within the cluster. (To install `netstat`, run the command `apt update; apt install net-tools`). The output will look similar to this:

```
root@kind-control-plane:/# netstat -plan | grep kube-proxy
tcp        0      0 127.0.0.1:10249         0.0.0.0:*               LISTEN
⮩      17091/kube-proxy
tcp        0      0 172.18.0.2:35430        172.18.0.2:6443
⮩ ESTABLISHED 17091/kube-proxy
tcp6       0      0 :::10256                :::*                    LISTEN
⮩      17091/kube-proxy
```

Kube-proxy runs on each node as a DaemonSet in the Kubernetes cluster. You can list the DaemonSets in all namespaces by running the command `k get ds -A`. The output will look similar to this:

```
root@kind-control-plane:~# k get ds -A
NAMESPACE     NAME         DESIRED     CURRENT   READY   UP-TO-DATE
⮩ AVAILABLE   NODE SELECTOR            AGE
kube-system   kindnet      1           1         1       1              1
⮩             <none>                   3d11h
kube-system   kube-proxy   1           1         1       1              1
⮩             kubernetes.io/os=linux   3d11h
```

This component is installed when you first initialize the cluster. There's not a manifest for it like there is for the other cluster components, however, so some people get confused. Also, CoreDNS and kube-proxy can easily be reset (i.e., recreated) with the command `kubeadm init phase addon all`. So, if on the exam the kube-proxy Pod in the `kube-system` namespace is erroring or in a `CrashLoopBackOff`, then running the command `kubeadm init phase addon all` will be a quick way to solve your problem, as it recreates the Pod with the default configuration (as initially set when the cluster was first initialized). A Service Account and a ConfigMap are also created for kube-proxy, and they are located in the `kube-system` namespace. You can view them with the command `k -n kube-system get cm,sa | grep kube-proxy`. The output will look similar to this:

```
root@kind-control-plane:~# k -n kube-system get cm,sa | grep kube-proxy
configmap/kube-proxy                              2        3d11h
serviceaccount/kube-proxy                                  0            3d11h
```

8.3.2 Troubleshooting Services

For the exam, you may be presented with a Service that cannot reach the underlying Pods. To properly troubleshoot, check the labels and the ports that the Pods are communicating over, both on the Service and the Deployment. For example, an exam task may be as follows.

EXAM TASK In cluster `ik8s`, in a namespace called `kb6656`, run the command `k apply -f https://raw.githubusercontent.com/chadmcrowell/acing-the-cka-exam/main/ch_08/deploy-and-svc.yaml` to create a Deployment and Service in the cluster. This is an NGINX application running on port 80, so try to reach the application by using curl to reach the IP address and port of the Service. Once you realize that you cannot communicate with the application via curl, try to determine why. Make the necessary changes to reach the application using curl and return to the NGINX welcome page.

We can continue to use the same single-node cluster that we used for the previous exam task. There is no need to create a new kind Kubernetes cluster. First, we'll create the namespace with the command `k create ns kb6656`. We can switch our context to that namespace with the command `k config set-context --current --namespace kb6656`. Then, we'll run the command given to us in the exam task. That command again was `k apply -f https://raw.githubusercontent.com/chadmcrowell/acing-the-cka-exam/main/ch_08/deploy-and-svc.yaml`. This will create the Deployment and Service, and we can view them with the command `k get deploy,svc`. The output should look similar to this:

```
root@kind-control-plane:/# k create ns kb6656
namespace/kb6656 created
root@kind-control-plane:/# k config set-context --current --namespace kb6656
Context "kubernetes-admin@kind" modified.
root@kind-control-plane:/# k get po
No resources found in kb6656 namespace.
root@kind-control-plane:/# k apply -f https://raw.githubusercontent.com/
    chadmcrowell/acing-the-cka-
➥ exam/main/ch_08/deploy-and-svc.yaml
deployment.apps/nginx created
```

```
service/nginx-svc created
root@kind-control-plane:/# k get deploy
NAME    READY   UP-TO-DATE   AVAILABLE   AGE
nginx   1/1     1            1           36s
root@kind-control-plane:/# k get deploy,svc
NAME                      READY   UP-TO-DATE   AVAILABLE   AGE
deployment.apps/nginx     1/1     1            1           2m20s

NAME                  TYPE        CLUSTER-IP     EXTERNAL-IP   PORT(S)    AGE
service/nginx-svc     ClusterIP   10.96.119.24   <none>        3306/TCP
➥ 2m20s
```

Once the Deployment and Service have been created, we can reach out to the NGINX application with curl using the command `curl -k http://10.96.119.24`. The output should look like this:

```
root@kind-control-plane:/# curl -k http://10.96.119.24
curl: (7) Failed to connect to 10.96.119.24 port 80 after 4 ms: Connection
➥ refused
```

Notice that it failed to connect. You may have noticed already that when we listed the Service, the port was 3306, not 80. Let's change it to 80 and see if that fixes our problem. We can run the command `k edit svc nginx-svc` to edit the port on which our Service is exposed. This command will open the YAML in the Vim text editor and allow us to change the port from 3306 to 80. We'll save and quit (`:wq`) and then try our curl command again. The output of the command will look like this:

```
root@kind-control-plane:/# k edit svc nginx-svc
service/nginx-svc edited
root@kind-control-plane:/# curl -k http://10.96.119.24
<!DOCTYPE html>
<html>
<head>
<title>Welcome to nginx!</title>
<style>
html { color-scheme: light dark; }
body { width: 35em; margin: 0 auto;
font-family: Tahoma, Verdana, Arial, sans-serif; }
</style>
</head>
<body>
<h1>Welcome to nginx!</h1>
<p>If you see this page, the nginx web server is successfully installed and
working. Further configuration is required.</p>

<p>For online documentation and support please refer to
<a href="http://nginx.org/">nginx.org</a>.<br/>
Commercial support is available at
<a href="http://nginx.com/">nginx.com</a>.</p>

<p><em>Thank you for using nginx.</em></p>
</body>
</html>
```

Changing the port for the Service fixed our problem. This is a frequent problem that you'll be tasked with on the exam. Check that the ports of the Service match the ports of the Pod (e.g., running inside of a Deployment). Also, sometimes a label mismatch between Service and Deployment might occur. If we view the Service again with the command k get svc -o yaml, we'll see that the selector is set to direct all traffic to Pods with the label app=nginx. The output looks similar to figure 8.14.

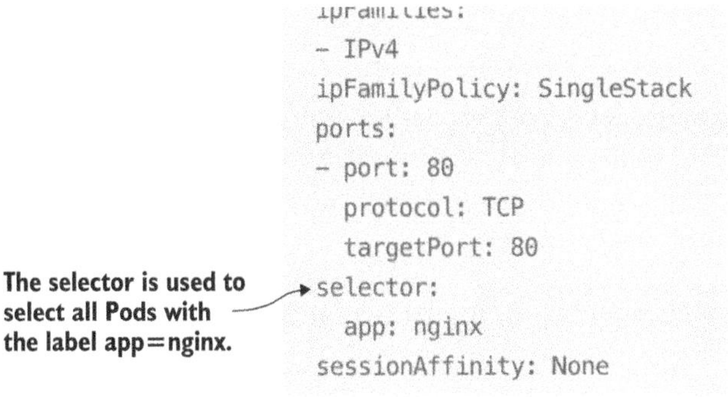

```
ipramilies:
- IPv4
ipFamilyPolicy: SingleStack
ports:
- port: 80
  protocol: TCP
  targetPort: 80
selector:
  app: nginx
sessionAffinity: None
```

The selector is used to select all Pods with the label app=nginx.

Figure 8.14   The output of k get svc -o yaml shows us the selector, which tells the Service which Pods to direct traffic to.

If we list the Pod labels with the command k get po --show-labels, we'll see that the Pod in this NGINX Deployment does in fact have the label app=nginx. The output will look similar to this:

```
root@kind-control-plane:/# k get po --show-labels
NAME                      READY   STATUS    RESTARTS   AGE    LABELS
nginx-6cdcf8f964-hdwzr    1/1     Running   0          20m    app=nginx,pod-
➥ template-hash=6cdcf8f964
```

8.3.3   Troubleshooting cluster-wide communications

In addition to incorrect ports on the Service in Kubernetes, there are other concerns to watch for that would require you to know how resources communicate with each other in Kubernetes. In general, a Deployment is connected to a Service through a label selector on the Service itself. If the Service label selector is not correct, the application will become unreachable. Also, with every Service there is at least one Endpoint, which is the Pod IP address. If there are no Endpoints for a Service, check again to see if the label selector is correct, so the Service can direct traffic to the correct Deployment or Pod.

> **EXAM TIP**   To compare what the correct label selectors are, and whether your YAML syntax is correct, run the command k create deploy nginx -image ngnix -dry-run=client -o yaml, followed by k expose deploy nginx. This will save you time, as you can just copy and paste or easily compare the two files.

Summary

- To view the logs in a Pod, we can use the `kubectl` command-line utility or look in the `/var/logs/containers` directory.

- There are many different Pod statuses, logs, and events to begin the trouble-shooting decision-making process. A Pod can be in a running state but still not accessible through the frontend.

- We can view cluster-wide events that determine from where the error is coming and what correlates to that error within the cluster.

- We can monitor the cluster metrics with the metrics server, which will already be installed within the exam environment.

- We can identify problems with our control plane components by looking within the `kube-system` namespace. Knowing what each component does will help you get to the root of the problem.

- We can identify network problems by looking at the kube-proxy, as it is the facilitator of firewalled traffic from Pod to Pod within a cluster. We can also see if a CNI is installed in our cluster to determine network problems.

- We can look for the correct ports and labels on a Service and Deployment on the exam, which will help to identify if that is at the root of why we can't connect to the application.

Taking the test

9

This chapter covers

- The most important aspects of the exam
- Preparing for exam day
- Review of the Kubernetes documentation
- Accessing your free practice exam
- Accessing a free cheat sheet for `kubectl` commands

I hope by now you are feeling prepared for the CKA exam. By going through this book, you have the best chance of acing the CKA exam. This chapter is dedicated to reviewing the book and shoring up any weak areas so that you can easily review previous chapters and bring back some of the principles and areas of study that you may have forgotten or that need further review.

9.1 Exam basics

We covered what the exam is all about in chapter 1, but this chapter points out the most important topics regarding your prep for exam day. It also reviews what is required for your technical competence, as you will be performing commands in the terminal and have to instantly remember what action to perform when presented with a specific question on the exam.

9.1.1 *Competencies condensed*

Let's review the competencies and the materials that we've covered so far so that we can properly identify the areas in which you feel strongest. Figure 9.1 shows the competencies chart.

25%	Cluster architecture and installation
✓	Create and modify RBAC.
✓	Use kubeadm to update and add to a cluster.
✓	Backup and restore etcd.
15%	**Workloads and scheduling**
✓	Scaling, updating, and rollback of Deployments.
✓	Use ConfigMaps and Secrets with apps.
✓	Deploy apps with resource requests and limits.
✓	Manage YAML manifests with templating tools.
20%	**Services and networking**
✓	Configure Linux host networking.
✓	Create and manage Services and Endpoints.
✓	Manage Ingress and Ingress controllers.
✓	Use CoreDNS and CNI.
10%	**Storage**
✓	Attach persist volumes with access modes.
✓	Create persistent volume claims and storage class.
✓	Data persistence with ephemeral Pods.
30%	**Troubleshooting**
✓	Collect container and node logs.
✓	Detect and repair clusters via monitor and logging.
✓	Detect and repair cluster networking.
✓	Monitor and troubleshoot application failure.

Figure 9.1 The CKA exam competencies to review for exam day

It's a good idea to review the competencies to check your knowledge. If you feel weak in the area of workloads and scheduling, for example, you should go back to chapters 4 and 5 to review scaling, updating and rollback of Deployments, using ConfigMaps and Secrets, deploying applications with requests and limits, and managing YAML manifests with templating tools. At the top of chapters 2–8 in this book, you can quickly review which competency relates to which chapter, so I advise you to study these. The tables at the beginning of each chapter will help you map the competencies to the chapters in which they apply.

9.1.2 Exam clusters

Once you've reviewed the competencies for the exam, you should also review the cluster configurations for the exam. There are six clusters that you'll be connecting to on exam day, for which there will be specific instructions on switching context from one cluster to another. Figure 9.2 lists the names of the clusters, the number of nodes, and the CNI used for each.

CLUSTER	NODES	CNI
k8s	1 control plane, 2 workers	Flannel
hk8s	1 control plane, 2 workers	Calico
bk8s	1 control plane, 1 worker	Flannel
wk8s	1 control plane, 2 workers	Flannel
ek8s	1 control plane, 2 workers	Flannel
ik8s	1 control plane, 1 orphaned (missing node)	Loopback

Figure 9.2 Cluster names, nodes, and CNI used for each cluster on which you are tested for the CKA exam

If you're serious about acing the exam, you'll set up at least two clusters and become familiar with changing context between the two, either by using kind Kubernetes locally or by using killercoda.com in a web browser. Review appendix A for installing a multinode cluster using kind Kubernetes. Again, changing the context is a command that's provided within the instructions for the exam task, but it's also useful to commit this to memory because time is of the essence for the 2 hours allotted to take the exam.

9.2 Chapter reviews

The following is a quick review of each chapter, beginning with chapter 2. There will be keywords discussed within each subsection that pertain to the chapter under discussion. This will help you review these terms, as they are important for the exam.

9.2.1 Quick review of chapter 2

Let's review the highlights of chapter 2, as this chapter covered the cluster architecture, cluster upgrades, etcd backup and restore, and cluster management. The reason for this quick review is to recall information that you previously read in the chapter and to encourage you to revisit the chapter if you feel the need.

The differences between the *control plane nodes* and the *worker nodes* are important to remember for the exam. They both run Pods, but the control plane node will only run system Pods (i.e., Pods that are essential to running Kubernetes itself). These system Pods are sometimes referred to as *static Pods*, which means they aren't managed by the Kubernetes scheduler.

The kubelet runs on every node in the cluster, but there is no `kubectl` command to view the kubelet because it's part of the system services on the node itself. If the kubelet is not in a running state, the Pods will not be able to run. Check out section 2.1 to see how to manage the kubelet and the possible fixes with which you'll be presented on exam day. When the data for the configuration of the cluster needs to be saved, it's stored in an *etcd datastore*, which runs as a Pod in the `kube-system` namespace.

- ☐ *Taints and tolerations*—How the control plane has a taint applied to it, and how to add tolerations for that taint. Section 2.1.3.
- ☐ *Namespaces*—How to locate the `kube-system` namespace and the Pods within, including controller manager, scheduler, API server, kube-proxy, CoreDNS, and etcd. Section 2.1.
- ☐ *Static Pods*—How to modify the system Pods via their YAML, located in the directory on the control plane `/etc/kubernetes/manifests` on the control plane node. Section 2.2.1.
- ☐ *Kubeadm*—How to upgrade the Kubernetes components, including the API server, controller manager, scheduler, kube-proxy, CoreDNS, and etcd. Section 2.1.1.
- ☐ *Kubelet*—How the kubelet runs on each node as a Linux system service (a daemon). Section 2.1.4.
- ☐ *Etcd*—How cluster configuration is stored in the etcd datastore, and how to back up etcd by taking a snapshot with the command-line tool etcdctl. Section 2.2.

9.2.2 *Quick review of chapter 3*

Let's review the highlights of chapter 3, as this chapter covered managing *role-based access control* (RBAC) and managing the cluster for high availability. If there's anything that you are unsure about in this quick review, please revisit chapter 3 to review in greater depth.

For chapter 3, it is important to remember how users and Service Accounts access the cluster via the Kubernetes API. Anything trying to access the cluster goes through RBAC to potentially create, read, update, or delete Kubernetes objects.

Section 3.1 covers "normal" users and Service Accounts, their differences, and how we can apply *Roles* and *Role bindings* to a user to lock down permissions. Cluster Roles and cluster Role bindings can be applied to a user, group, or Service Account as well. Review creating a user and Service Account in sections 3.2 and 3.3, respectively.

- ☐ `kubectl`—How to use `kubectl` to interact with the cluster via kubeconfig (copy `/etc/kubernetes/admin.conf` to `~/.kube/config`). Section 3.1.
- ☐ *RBAC*—How to access the cluster via RBAC, and the process of authentication, authorization, and access control. Section 3.1.
- ☐ *Service accounts*—How to mount Service Accounts to Pods so that Pods can access the API. Section 3.3.
- ☐ *Cluster Roles*—How to give cluster-wide permissions, and how to tie those permissions to a user, group, or Service Account. Section 3.1.1.

☐ *Roles*—How to give permissions across the namespace and tie those permissions to a user, group, or Service Account located within a given namespace. Section 3.1.1.

9.2.3 *Quick review of chapter 4*

Let's review the highlights from chapter 4, as this chapter covered ConfigMaps; Secrets; resource limits; and creating and managing Deployments in Kubernetes, including the use of templating tools. From this chapter, it is important to remember how Pods are scheduled to nodes.

The process of scheduling a Pod to only certain nodes via a *node selector* is covered in chapter 4, with an exercise in applying the node selector in your own cluster, which includes applying *labels* to nodes; however, you can use the node name as well. You can easily check what labels are applied to your nodes with the command `k get no -show-labels`. It's also helpful to know how to schedule a Pod—even if the selected node is unavailable—with *node affinity*, also covered in this chapter. What if you want to schedule a Pod to a node that already has specific Pods running on it? This is called *inter-Pod affinity* and is covered in section 4.1.2.

Using *Helm* is a competency for this exam. Helm is an easy way to package an application consisting of different Kubernetes resources and deploy it with one command using the Helm command line. An example of deploying the `metallb` application inside a cluster is used in section 4.2, as well as installing the `vault` application using Helm. Also in section 4.2, you can review how to add a Helm repo, as well as how to search for existing repos and apply templating to your manifests to be used with Helm.

Applying *resource requests* and *limits* to Pods to run on the nodes inside of your cluster is important to review for the exam. You can see an example of this in section 4.3.1, and you can review how to create multiple containers within a single Pod in section 4.3.2. ConfigMaps and Secrets are covered in section 4.3.3, which describes creating a ConfigMap for a Redis Pod as well as creating a Secret for a `busybox` Pod that is attached to the Pod via volume mount. You should be familiar with creating ConfigMaps and Secrets and the two different ways of using them with Pods by reviewing this chapter.

☐ *Node selectors*—How to use node selectors to schedule Pods to certain nodes. Section 4.1.1.

☐ *Node name*—How to run a Pod on a node by targeting its name and running that Pod on that node only. Section 4.1.1.

☐ *Node affinity*—How to configure a Pod run on a node by a specific label, and if the node(s) aren't available, still run the Pod on a different node with a different set of characteristics (e.g., operating system). Section 4.1.2.

☐ *ConfigMaps*—How to create a ConfigMap for a Redis Pod and attach it to the Pod via volume mount. Section 4.3.3.

☐ *Secrets*—How to attach a Secret to a Pod via volume mount. Section 4.3.3.

☐ *Resource limits*—How to apply resource requests and limits to Pods. Section 4.3.1.

☐ *Helm*—How to deploy applications using a Helm chart, first by searching for Helm repos locally, adding a Helm repo from a repository if necessary, and applying templating to customize a chart. Section 4.2.

9.2.4   *Quick review of chapter 5*

Let's review the highlights of chapter 5, as this chapter covered how to scale applications and what it means to roll out a new version of an application, as well as managing *Deployments* to create self-healing in Kubernetes. In a lot of ways, this is a continuation of the previous chapter; now that you know how to create a Deployment, chapter 5 shows how to maintain the Deployment after it's been running.

In Kubernetes, when we want to apply more Pods to our application for redundancy, we call this *scaling the application,* as it scales by a number of Pods within the same Deployment. Updating a running application in Kubernetes is made simple by the concept of a rollout. Commonly, there's a Service attached to a Deployment, which is covered briefly in this chapter, but you should also explore chapter 6 for complete coverage of Services.

☐ *Scale Deployments*—How to scale Deployment replicas up and down, changing the number of Pods in a given Deployment. Section 5.1.1.

☐ *ReplicaSets*—How changing the Deployment replicas affects the ReplicaSet, tracking the number of Pod replicas for each revision of the Deployment. Section 5.1.2.

☐ *Rollouts*—How to perform a rollout, checking the rollout history, which lists the revisions. Section 5.1.3.

☐ *Cordon and drain*—How to take a node down for maintenance, which includes moving all Pods of that node to another node. Section 5.2.

☐ *Adding nodes*—How to add a new node to an existing cluster. Section 5.2.2.

9.2.5   *Quick review of chapter 6*

Let's review the highlights of chapter 6, as this chapter covered networking within a Kubernetes cluster, understanding DNS and communication from Pod to Pod, the different types of Services in Kubernetes, and the container network interface plugin.

In section 6.1, the concept of cluster DNS is introduced and covered in an exercise that demonstrates changing the DNS configuration for a cluster, including the DNS service, ConfigMap, and the kubelet system service configuration. As stated in this chapter, the magic behind CoreDNS is the ability to resolve hostnames to IP addresses very quickly, decreasing the lag between applications and components running inside of a Kubernetes cluster. This is why there are multiple instances of CoreDNS running as a Deployment in the cluster.

Review how the outside world can access your application running in Kubernetes via Ingress. I highly recommend rereading the exercise of installing an Ingress controller and creating a ClusterIP Service and an Ingress resource. This will be good practice for the exam. Review additional detail on the types of Services, including ClusterIP, NodePort, and LoadBalancer Services.

☐ *CoreDNS*—How to resolve DNS names in Kubernetes, and how to change the DNS server configuration. Section 6.1.

☐ *Pod communication*—How to communicate from Pod to Pod and Service to Service in a Kubernetes cluster. Section 6.2.3.

☐ *Ingress*—How to expose a set of Pods (within a Service) to an Endpoint that's outside of the Kubernetes cluster, which includes creating an Ingress controller. Section 6.3.

☐ *Services*—How to create and use a ClusterIP, NodePort, and LoadBalancer Service type. Section 6.4.

9.2.6 *Quick review of chapter 7*

Let's review the highlights of chapter 7, as this chapter covered the many ways of configuring storage in Kubernetes, including the concept of a *persistent volume*, as well as *volume modes*, *access modes*, and *reclaim policies*. This chapter also covered storage classes and persistent volume claims for easily utilizing storage from applications running in Kubernetes, providing additional control over those volumes in terms of which Pod or Pods can access the volume as well as the type of volume, such as `ReadWriteOnce`, `ReadWriteMany`, etc., and the *filesystem* type of volume versus the *block* type of volume. Persistent volume claims reserve the volume, whatever its type, for a Pod to use. Storage classes are used to autoprovision volumes from a specific class of volume type (e.g., local or cloud storage). This chapter further provides reasoning to create temporary volumes for Pods in the creation of an `emptyDir` volume type.

☐ *Persistent volumes*—How to create a persistent volume and persistent volume claim for use from within a Pod. Section 7.1.

☐ *Volume modes*—How to set a volume mode to `Filesystem` or `Block` within a persistent volume in Kubernetes. Section 7.1.2.

☐ *Access modes*—How to give Pods read and write permissions to a persistent volume in Kubernetes. Section 7.1.3.

☐ *Storage class*—How to autoprovision volumes via persistent volume claims, which dynamically create storage for Pods. Section 7.3.

☐ `emptyDir`—How to create temporary storage for your Pod with an `emptyDir` volume type, which lives and dies by the Pod. Section 7.4.

9.2.7 *Quick review of chapter 8*

Let's review the highlights of chapter 8, as this chapter covered the many aspects of troubleshooting when encountering problems with the cluster, Pods, Services, and more. The CKA exam will test you on the ability to obtain logs from Pods running in a Kubernetes cluster.

Follow the decision tree in figure 8.7, as it's a good starting point for determining what to do when there are a lot of different types of errors leading you down different troubleshooting paths. The state of the Pod could be a clue as to resolving a particular problem with it. There are eight different Pod statuses to review in table 8.1, followed by their meanings.

There may be a problem with the control plane itself—whether it's the API server or the controller manager, there could be a misconfiguration. Pods, whether system Pods or application Pods, are not the only components that fail; the nodes themselves sometimes lead you down the troubleshooting path.

We talked about accessing the cluster in chapter 3, which may be a problem if you are not able to properly authenticate to the cluster via the kubeconfig. As it relates to Kubernetes Services, whether it be a ClusterIP, NodePort, or LoadBalancer Service type, there may be a place on the exam where the tags are mistyped or the port is missing.

- ☐ *Pod logs*—How to view the Pod logs to troubleshoot the reason for an expected failure within a containerized application. Section 8.1.
- ☐ *Network troubleshooting*—How to utilize a temporary Pod to troubleshoot DNS from Pod to Pod. Section 8.1.2.
- ☐ *Scheduler failure*—How to troubleshoot and fix a problem with the Kubernetes scheduler. Section 8.2.
- ☐ *Events*—How to analyze the overall event log from within a cluster, allowing you to gain more insight into any problems. Section 8.2.1.
- ☐ *Troubleshooting the kubeconfig*—How to determine if the kubeconfig is the reason why you're not able to access the cluster and how to fix it. Section 8.2.4.
- ☐ *Service connection concerns*—How to determine if communication is not getting to the underlying Pods, and how to check Endpoints of a Service. Section 8.3.1.

9.3 Kubernetes documentation review

You are allowed to have the documentation open in an additional tab for the exam, so why not take full advantage of this? More specifically, the URL https://kubernetes.io/docs, which contains a plethora of knowledge, can be open during the exam, and the best part is that it's searchable. First, please review the sitemap, which will give you a skeleton with which to work, and even though pages might be named similarly, you can become familiar with where the example YAML is located and what the resource name will be—so much so that you'll be able to recognize the page and scroll right down to the specific section, and you won't waste any time on the exam. Remember, you only have 2 hours, so use it wisely. You can review the sitemap in figure 9.3.

As you look at the sitemap, you'll start to make a connection between the items discussed in each chapter and the correlating documentation page. The navigation from page to page will be located on the left side of the page. Once you open a page, you'll

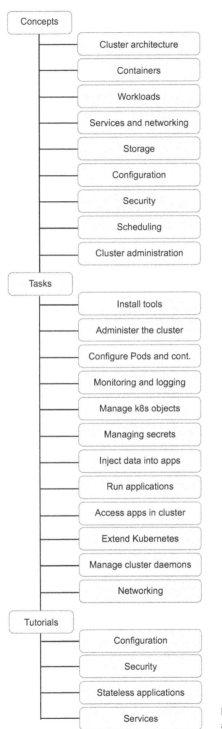

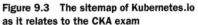

Figure 9.3   The sitemap of Kubernetes.io as it relates to the CKA exam

see another navigation on the right that will bring you to each section within the existing document. An example of the site and page navigation is shown in figure 9.4.

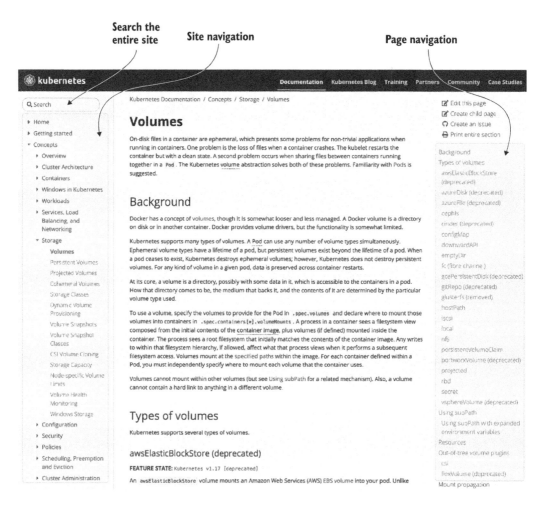

Figure 9.4   **Navigating the Kubernetes documentation to help you on the exam**

You'll also see in the Kubernetes documentation that there's a way to search the entire site. This is incredibly useful for the exam, as you can search for specific items versus having to navigate link by link. Be aware when searching the Kubernetes documentation page, you may get search results that navigate you to a completely different site, which you are not allowed to visit. You can hover over the link to see where it will take you. If it doesn't contain the prefix https://kubernetes.io/docs, then don't click it. Don't worry, however, if you do; the browser will not allow you to navigate away, and it will simply appear as if the site doesn't exist. I did this on my exam and realized that because the environment is controlled (the test is inside of a virtual machine), such firewall rules can be implemented. Also take advantage of the "find in page" feature in Firefox, which is the browser that you'll use on the exam. It allows you to quickly search the entire page so you don't have to spend extra time using the right-hand, page navigation links.

9.4 Practice exam

With every exam purchase comes a free voucher for a practice exam, provided by KLLR SHLL. Check out their website at https://killer.sh. When you sign in with your Linux Foundation credentials (the same credentials you use to purchase the exam at https://training.linuxfoundation.org/), the exam simulator will automatically appear in your dashboard. You will get two sessions in the same simulator (including a simulation of the PSI bridge); both have the same questions. I recommend treating this as a real exam, as it's presented in the same way and will prepare you for exam day. Also, the questions on the simulator are harder than the questions on the real exam, so it will make the real exam seem a little bit easier. Check out the frequently asked questions about the exam simulator at https://killer.sh/faq. Figure 9.5 shows what the exam environment looks like, which is very similar to the real exam.

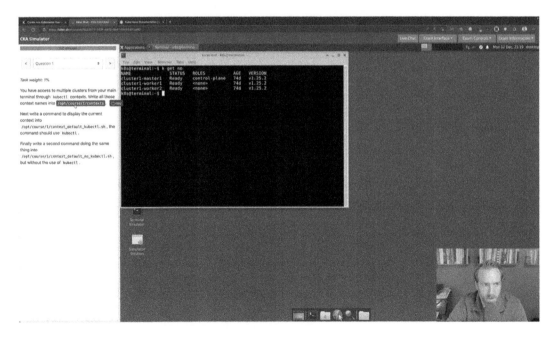

Figure 9.5   CKA exam simulator environment provided by KLLR SHLL

9.5   *Additional tips for the exam*

The more practice you get, the better you'll perform on the exam. Go through all the exercises in this book multiple times, which is the only way to cement it into memory. KLLR SHLL has a sister company named Killercoda (https://killercoda.com), which has a lot more exercises and exam-like tasks to complete for practice. You can also supplement by creating your own scenarios, which is the best way to repeat and absorb the concepts.

Have your identification ready and be prepared for somewhat strict rules on the cleanliness of the room in which you take the exam. Review more about this and the guidelines for items you can have available during the exam at http://mng.bz/d1vw, where you can also run a compatibility check of your hardware in advance. I highly recommend doing this a few days before your exam date. Be prepared for the exam proctor to ask you to pan the camera around the room to verify that you've followed these rules. On exam day, log in to the Linux Foundation portal approximately 30 minutes before your exam is scheduled to begin. You can access the Linux Foundation using the portal at https://trainingportal.linuxfoundation.org/, and you will see all exams that you've scheduled.

The results of your exam will be emailed to you 24 hours after completion of the exam. Remember, you have one free retake of the exam, so if you don't pass the first time, don't worry. You can come back and schedule your retake the very next day if you wish. Good luck!

Thank you for purchasing this book and allowing me to guide you through your best attempt at the Certified Kubernetes Administrator Exam. It was truly my pleasure to help you on this journey.

Summary

In this chapter, you've reviewed the chapters in this book, as well as been given additional tips for how to prepare when it is closer to exam day. Remember the following:

- Review the chapter highlights to truly master the content. Be sure you are ready for situations that may arise in each domain within all competencies.
- To properly prepare for the CKA exam, you must practice, practice, and then practice some more. Make it a daily habit leading up to the exam.
- Review the official Kubernetes documentation like a pro to fully take advantage of the additional open-book format of the exam.
- You will be working with multiple clusters on the exam. Even though the `kubectl` commands are given to switch context, be comfortable with how to check that you are working on the correct cluster that the exam asks.

- You have two practice exams, so it would be wise to use them. They will challenge you to accomplish harder tasks and help you become familiar with the exam environment.
- Review the handbook and all the rules for how your physical environment should look, and have everything prepared in advance.
- You have one free retake on the exam, so don't sweat it! You can do it!

appendix A
Creating a Kubernetes cluster with kind

This appendix shows you how to install a kind (Kubernetes in Docker) Kubernetes cluster with multiple nodes, where the nodes themselves are Docker containers. You will download and install kind, which will use the kubeadm tool (packaged with kind) to bootstrap your cluster. The only prerequisite for this section is Docker and kind, which we will walk through installing together.

A.1 Installing the required packages

As mentioned, the only prerequisites to creating a kind Kubernetes cluster are Docker and kind. Docker Desktop is a software suite of products by Docker that makes it easier to build, run, and share containerized applications and microservices. If you don't already have Docker Desktop installed, you can visit the following link to download it: https://docker.com/products/docker-desktop. Docker Desktop is available for Windows, macOS, and Linux operating systems. You can install kind using your operating system's package manager, or you can also download kind here: https://github.com/kubernetes-sigs/kind/releases. Kind is also available for Windows, macOS, or Linux. For this guide, we'll be using version 0.14.0.

A.1.1 Install Docker Desktop

Docker Desktop will serve as our container runtime for this practice cluster built with the kind tool. In chapter 1, I explained the purpose of the container runtime as the system service that runs underlying containers within a Pod. From this point forward, I'll just refer to Docker Desktop as Docker. Know that I'm referring to the container runtime for either Windows, macOS, or Linux. Here are the instructions to install Docker on any of these operating systems:

1 Open a web browser and go to https://www.docker.com/products/docker-desktop.
2 Download the installer that matches your operating system. You may also have to choose the chip architecture (e.g., M1 or Intel chip for macOS).
3 Run the installer (.dmg, .exe, .deb, or .rpm file extension) and accept all the defaults. (You may be prompted to restart your computer.)
4 Open the application, and you should see the whale icon in the task bar.
5 If you see the whale icon indicating that Docker is running, then you're done!

NOTE If you are on Windows and already have Docker installed, make sure you're in Linux container mode. For new installations, this is the default.

Once you've installed Docker, you can verify that it's ready to go by using the Docker CLI in the terminal (one of the tools in the Docker Desktop suite). Open a terminal or command prompt and type `docker ps`:

```
$ docker ps
CONTAINER ID   IMAGE    COMMAND   CREATED   STATUS   PORTS   NAMES
```

If you get an output like this with no errors, then you've successfully installed Docker Desktop. The command `docker ps` lists all running containers. If you're wondering why we don't see any running containers, that's because we haven't created any yet. We'll do that in the next step when we install kind.

A.1.2 Installing kind

If you thought installing Docker was easy, then prepare to be swept away! We're going to install kind with just one command. The command for macOS is `brew install kind`, the command for Windows is `choco install kind`, and the command for Linux is `curl -Lo ./kind https://kind.sigs.k8s.io/dl/v0.11.1/kind-linux-amd64 && chmod +x ./kind && sudo mv ./kind /usr/local/bin/kind`.

Now, in the terminal, just type `kind` and you'll see the following:

```
$ kind
kind creates and manages local Kubernetes clusters using Docker container
⇛ 'nodes'

Usage:
  kind [command]

Available Commands:
  build       Build one of [node-image]
  completion  Output shell completion code for the specified shell (bash,
⇛ zsh or fish)
```

```
create      Creates one of [cluster]
delete      Deletes one of [cluster]
export      Exports one of [kubeconfig, logs]
get         Gets one of [clusters, nodes, kubeconfig]
help        Help about any command
load        Loads images into nodes
version     Prints the kind CLI version

Flags:
  -h, --help               help for kind
      --loglevel string    DEPRECATED: see -v instead
  -q, --quiet              silence all stderr output
  -v, --verbosity int32    info log verbosity
      --version            version for kind

Use "kind [command] --help" for more information about a command.
```

Following this output from kind help will give you tips on creating your first cluster.

A.1.3 *Creating a kind Kubernetes cluster*

Type the following to create (bootstrap) a kind Kubernetes cluster: kind create cluster. Your output should look like this:

```
$ kind create cluster
Creating cluster "kind" ...
 ✓ Ensuring node image (kindest/node:v1.21.1) 🖼
 ✓ Preparing nodes 📦
 ✓ Writing configuration 📜
 ✓ Starting control-plane 🕹
 ✓ Installing CNI 🔌
 ✓ Installing StorageClass 💾
Set kubectl context to "kind-kind"
You can now use your cluster with:

kubectl cluster-info --context kind-kind

Have a nice day! 👋
```

That's it! Congratulations on bootstrapping your Kubernetes cluster! Now that we've created a Kubernetes cluster using kind, we can conveniently use the kubectl tool just as we would when connecting to other Kubernetes clusters created in any other way. In fact, when we created a kind cluster, kind automatically set our kubeconfig context to the cluster it just created (kind-kind). First, exec into the Docker container that is our control plane node with the command docker exec -it kind-control-plane bash, and then view which context you are in with the command kubectl config get-contexts.

Get a Bash shell inside the container
named kind-control-plane.

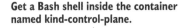

```
$ docker exec -it kind-control-plane bash
root@kind-control-plane:/# kubectl config get-contexts
CURRENT   NAME                      CLUSTER   AUTHINFO          NAMESPACE
*         kubernetes-admin@kind     kind      kubernetes-admin
```

Figure A.1 Show the current context to see which cluster you are currently accessing.

A.1.4 *Install kubectl (optional)*

kubectl is the tool that you'll be using to interface with Kubernetes during the exam. The reason why it's optional is that the Docker container that you'll exec into already has kubectl preinstalled. If you'd rather not run your commands from inside a container, then proceed to install kubectl on your local machine.

kubectl has many pronunciations. I've heard it pronounced "cube-cuttle" and "cube-eck-tell." I pronounce it "cube-C-T-L", but the "official" pronunciation is "cube-control." The first question you should ask a fellow Kubernetes administrator is, "How do you pronounce kubectl?" (kidding, of course); it'll be a good ice breaker and a fun way to talk about Kubernetes with friends.

The kubectl tool can be installed on Linux, macOS, and Windows. I will walk you through installing kubectl in this book, and you can also refer to the official installation instructions here: https://kubernetes.io/docs/tasks/tools/install-kubectl.

For macOS, you can use brew to install kubectl. Brew is a package manager for macOS, much like apt or yum for Linux. If you don't already have brew, you can install it by going to https://brew.sh. Once brew is installed, you can simply run the command brew install kubectl.

For Windows, you can use the Windows package manager called Chocolatey. If you don't already have Chocolatey installed, go to https://chocolatey.org/install. Once you've installed Chocolatey, you can simply run the command choco install kubernetes-cli.

For Linux, you can run the following command, which will download the binary and move it into your /usr/local/bin directory: curl -LO "https://dl.k8s.io/$(curl -L -s https://dl.k8s.io/release/stable.txt)/bin/linux/amd64/kubectl" && sudo chmod +x kubectl && sudo mv kubectl /usr/local/bin/kubectl.

Now that you have kubectl installed, you can verify that it's installed with the command kubectl version --client -short:

```
$ kubectl version --client --short
Client Version: v1.23.1
```

Congratulations! You have installed kubectl and can proceed to interact with your kind Kubernetes cluster.

A.2   *Creating a multinode cluster*

Now we can create a multinode cluster to simulate the exam environment and help you become more familiar with creating, accessing, and troubleshooting the components on each node, whether on the control plane or the worker nodes. This will be similar to the CKA exam, which will have mostly one control plane and two worker nodes. Just in case this changes in the future, you can access the exam documentation here: https://docs.linuxfoundation.org/tc-docs/certification/tips-cka-and-ckad#cka-and-ckad-environment.

First things first, we have to delete the kind cluster that we've already created, so let's do that with the command `kind delete cluster`. This will delete the cluster we've been working with thus far and allow us to start over and create a brand-new, three-node cluster.

To perform the three-node cluster configuration, we will use the `kind create cluster` command, in addition to adding the config parameter and a config file (also written in YAML) that specifies how many nodes to create. Let's create this cluster config file and name it `config.yaml` by copying and pasting the following into your command line (for macOS and Linux only):

```
cat << EOF | tee config.yaml
kind: Cluster
apiVersion: kind.x-k8s.io/v1alpha4
nodes:
- role: control-plane
- role: worker
- role: worker
EOF
```

If you are on Windows, use the following command to create the three-node kind cluster:

```
echo "kind: Cluster
apiVersion: kind.x-k8s.io/v1alpha4
nodes:
- role: control-plane
- role: worker
- role: worker" | tee .\config.yaml
```

Now that we have the kind configuration, we can pass that configuration to the `kind create cluster` command and create our cluster with one control plane node and two worker nodes. Do this by typing the command `kind create cluster --config config.yaml`:

```
$ kind create cluster --config config.yaml
Creating cluster "kind" ...
 ✓ Ensuring node image (kindest/node:v1.21.1) 🖼
 ✓ Preparing nodes 📦 📦 📦
 ✓ Writing configuration 📜
 ✓ Starting control-plane 🕹
```

```
✓ Installing CNI 🖋
✓ Installing StorageClass 💾
✓ Joining worker nodes 🖴
Set kubectl context to "kind-kind"
You can now use your cluster with:

kubectl cluster-info --context kind-kind

Have a question, bug, or feature request? Let us know!
📧 https://kind.sigs.k8s.io/#community ☺
```

Once the cluster has been created, we can verify that we now have three nodes total with the command `kubectl get no`:

```
$ kubectl get no
NAME                 STATUS   ROLES                  AGE    VERSION
kind-control-plane   Ready    control-plane,master   98s    v1.21.1
kind-worker          Ready    <none>                 70s    v1.21.1
kind-worker2         Ready    <none>                 70s    v1.21.1
```

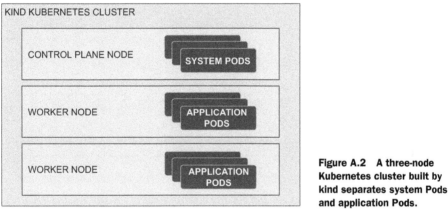

Figure A.2   A three-node Kubernetes cluster built by kind separates system Pods and application Pods.

Congratulations, you have now created a three-node Kubernetes cluster!

A.3   Advanced configuration for kind

To follow some of the examples in this book, you'll need to set up your kind cluster with a more advanced configuration. The following example creates a single-node kind cluster with a label applied to a node as well as port 80 exposed. We create a `config2.yaml` file, similar to how we created one in the previous section, but we add a few extra lines. Let's create the cluster config file named `config2.yaml` by copying and pasting the following into your terminal (for macOS and Linux only):

```
cat << EOF | tee config2.yaml
kind: Cluster
apiVersion: kind.x-k8s.io/v1alpha4
nodes:
```

```
 - role: control-plane
   extraPortMappings:
   - containerPort: 80
     hostPort: 80
   labels:
     ingress-ready: true
EOF
```

If you are on Windows, use the following command to create the config2.yaml file:

```
echo "kind: Cluster
apiVersion: kind.x-k8s.io/v1alpha4
nodes:
- role: control-plane
  extraPortMappings:
  - containerPort: 80
    hostPort: 80
  labels:
    ingress-ready:true" | tee .\config.yaml
```

Now that we've created the config2.yaml file, like we did in the previous section, we can pass that file to the kind create cluster command and create our cluster with those additional node labels and ports. Let's run the command kind create cluster --config config2.yaml:

```
$ kind create cluster --config config2.yaml
Creating cluster "kind" ...
 ✓ Ensuring node image (kindest/node:v1.21.1) 📦
 ✓ Preparing nodes 📦
 ✓ Writing configuration 📜
 ✓ Starting control-plane 🕹️
 ✓ Installing CNI 🔌
 ✓ Installing StorageClass 💾
 ✓ Joining worker nodes 🚜
Set kubectl context to "kind-kind"
You can now use your cluster with:

kubectl cluster-info --context kind-kind

Have a question, bug, or feature request? Let us know! https://
    kind.sigs.k8s.io/#community ☺
```

Once the cluster has been created, we can verify that we now have a label on the node with the command kubectl get no --show-labels. We can also verify that the port on the node is exposed with the command docker port kind-control-plane. You should get an output similar to this:

```
$ kubectl get no --show-labels && docker port kind-control-plane        [20:03:30]
NAME                STATUS   ROLES          AGE    VERSION   LABELS
kind-control-plane  Ready    control-plane  105s   v1.27.0   beta.kubernetes.io/
    arch=amd64,beta.kubernetes.io/os=linux,ingress-ready=true,kubernetes.io/
    arch=amd64,kubernetes.io/hostname=kind-control-plane,kubernetes.io/
```

```
    os=linux,node-role.kubernetes.io/control-plane=,node.kubernetes.io/exclude-
    from-external-load-balancers=
6443/tcp -> 127.0.0.1:55726
80/tcp -> 0.0.0.0:80
```

We now have a single-node cluster that can accept traffic over port 80 and for a Pod to select a node based on its label `"ingress-ready=true"`.

> **NOTE** If you already have a kind cluster running, to create a second cluster, you must give the new cluster a name other than `kind`. To give your kind cluster a custom name, append `--name` to the end of the `kind create` command. For example, if I wanted to name my cluster `cka` and use the `config2.yaml` file, I would run the command `kind create cluster --config config2.yaml --name cka`.

appendix B
Setting the context
for a kind cluster

This appendix shows you how to set the context in a Kubernetes cluster with multiple kubeconfig files. You will learn how to use `kubectl config` to determine which context you are currently in and how to switch to a different context, which should help you to become comfortable accessing multiple clusters for the CKA exam.

B.1 Setting the context with kubeconfig

As you learned in chapter 3, you can have multiple kubeconfig files that pertain to different clusters, or you can merge all the cluster-access information into one kubeconfig file. You can now read the individual kubeconfig file and its contents. This kubeconfig file (named `admin.conf`) is located in the `/etc/kubernetes/` directory. During the bootstrap process, the file is copied, renamed to `config`, and placed into the `~/.kube/` directory. Why is this? Well, `/etc` is a system directory, which requires root privilege to access. Because you're running `kubectl` commands as a regular user (not root), copying it to your home directory allows full ownership of the file. Simply running the command `kind get kubeconfig --name "kind"` will allow you to view the contents of that kubeconfig file(`~/.kube/config`). Similarly, you can view the contents of the kubeconfig file with the command `kubectl config view --minify`.

Alternatively, you can use a kubeconfig file that's in a different location that can be set with the `KUBECONFIG` environment variable. If you get a shell inside the

236

kind-control-plane container again, you'll see the environment variable is already set.
You can echo the environment variable with the command echo $KUBECONFIG:

```
$ docker exec -it kind-control-plane bash
root@kind-control-plane:/# echo $KUBECONFIG
/etc/kubernetes/admin.conf
```

Let's say you have an additional kubeconfig file named config2. This file is in the
~/Downloads directory, but you still want kubectl to use it to access your Kubernetes
cluster. You can tell kubectl to use that kubeconfig file to authenticate to your cluster
by typing export KUBECONFIG=~/Downloads/config2, and from that point forward, it will
access the cluster using that config2 kubeconfig file. If you want to use two different
kubeconfig files, both of which are located in different directories, you can type
export KUBECONFIG=~/.kube/config:~/Downloads/config2 and use both. To access each
cluster, you can switch contexts by using the command kubectl config use-context:

```
$ export KUBECONFIG=~/Downloads/config2:~/.kube/config
$ kubectl config get-contexts
CURRENT   NAME              CLUSTER           AUTHINFO          NAMESPACE
          docker-desktop    docker-desktop    docker-desktop
*         k8s               k8s               k8s
          kind-kind         kind-kind         kind-kind
$ kubectl config use-context kind-kind
Switched to context "kind-kind".
$ kubectl config get-contexts
CURRENT   NAME              CLUSTER           AUTHINFO          NAMESPACE
          docker-desktop    docker-desktop    docker-desktop
          k8s               k8s               k8s
*         kind-kind         kind-kind         kind-kind
```

You will need to know how to switch contexts for the exam; however, the exam instructions will tell you how to do it. There will be multiple contexts on the exam because
each question will contain one or more tasks to perform on different clusters. You will
need to switch to a new context each time the exam prompts you to do so to proceed
with completing the given task.

B.2   Setting an alias for kubectl

You can set an abbreviated name for kubectl, as it might be time-consuming to type
kubectl over and over again. This is called an alias, and the most common alias is k.
For example, instead of typing kubectl get no, you can type k get no with the alias set to
k. To set the alias, type the command alias k=kubectl from within the control plane
Bash shell (e.g., docker exec -it kind-control-plane bash). Then type the command
k get no to verify that the alias was set correctly. The output should look similar to this:

```
root@kind-control-plane:/# k get no
NAME                STATUS   ROLES           AGE   VERSION
kind-control-plane  Ready    control-plane   23h   v1.25.0-beta.0
```

If you want the setting to persist after you exit the shell and reenter, you can add it to the .bashrc file in your home folder. An easy way to do this is by typing the command echo 'alias k=kubectl' >> ~/.bashrc from a Bash shell to the control plane node. Then type source ~/.bashrc to have this implemented immediately, or simply log out and back in again. The output should look similar to this:

```
root@cka-control-plane:/# echo 'alias k=kubectl' >> ~/.bashrc
root@cka-control-plane:/# source ~/.bashrc
root@cka-control-plane:/# k get no
NAME                STATUS    ROLES           AGE    VERSION
cka-control-plane   Ready     control-plane   19m    v1.25.0-beta.0
```

B.3   *Setting kubectl autocomplete*

Setting autocomplete is important for the exam because Kubernetes resources contain complex names that are prone to typos. Always use copy and paste when you can, and also use autocomplete when you are using kubectl to navigate namespaces and resource names. For example, typing k -n c10 followed by pressing the Tab key will autocomplete the name of the namespace as k -n c103832034. Using autocomplete will save you time on the exam and also help prevent typos.

Setting the autocomplete parameters in kind is a matter of running the following commands in this order:

```
apt update && apt install -y bash-completion
echo 'source <(kubectl completion bash)' >> ~/.bashrc
echo 'source /usr/share/bash-completion/bash_completion' >> ~/.bashrc
echo 'alias k=kubectl' >> ~/.bashrc
echo 'complete -o default -F __start_kubectl k' >> ~/.bashrc
source ~/.bashrc
```

Run these one by one in the command line, inside of a shell to the control plane node (i.e., docker exec -it kind-control-plane bash).

appendix C
Installing a CNI
in a kind cluster

This appendix shows how to install a new CNI in your kind cluster. We'll install Flannel and Calico, which are both used for the CKA exam, going through the process step by step on how to do this within a kind cluster. This involves creating the kind cluster without a CNI, installing the bridge CNI plugin, and then installing either Flannel or Calico.

C.1 Creating a kind cluster without CNI

Before we create a kind Kubernetes cluster, we must first create a YAML file that we can use as an input with the `kind create` command. Create a file named `config.yaml` and paste it in the contents like this:

```
kind: Cluster
apiVersion: kind.x-k8s.io/v1alpha4
networking:
  disableDefaultCNI: true
nodes:
role: control-plane
role: worker
```

Now run the command `kind create cluster --image kindest/node:v1.25.0-beta.0 --config config.yaml` to create a kind cluster according to the configuration we specified in the `config.yaml` file. The output will look similar to this:

```
$ kind create cluster --image kindest/node:v1.25.0-beta.0 --config
➥ config.yaml
 [21:44:59]
Creating cluster "kind" ...
 ✓ Ensuring node image (kindest/node:v1.25.0-beta.0) 🖼
 ✓ Preparing nodes 📦 📦
 ✓ Writing configuration 📜
 ✓ Starting control-plane 🕹
 ✓ Installing StorageClass 💾
 ✓ Joining worker nodes 🚜
Set kubectl context to "kind-kind"
You can now use your cluster with:

kubectl cluster-info --context kind-kind

Have a question, bug, or feature request? Let us know!
➥ https://kind.sigs.k8s.io/#community ☺
```

C.2 *Installing a bridge CNI plugin*

Now that our cluster is created, let's get a shell to both of the node containers, one at
a time, with the commands docker exec -it kind-control-plane bash and docker exec
-it kind-worker bash. Once you have a Bash shell, go ahead and run the command apt
update; apt install wget on both kind-control-plane and kind-worker. This will install
wget, a command-line tool that we can use to download files from the web, which is what
we'll do with the command wget https://github.com/containernetworking/plugins/
releases/download/v1.1.1/cni-plugins-linux-amd64-v1.1.1.tgz. Because this file is a
tarball, you'll have to untar it with the command tar -xvf cni-plugins-linux-amd64-
v1.1.1.tgz. The output will look similar to this:

```
root@kind-control-plane:/# tar -xvf cni-plugins-linux-amd64-v1.1.1.tgz
./
./macvlan
./static
./vlan
./portmap
./host-local
./vrf
./bridge
./tuning
./firewall
./host-device
./sbr
./loopback
./dhcp
./ptp
./ipvlan
./bandwidth
```

The bridge file is the one that's most important for our case, as this will provide the
necessary plugin for Kubernetes to use Flannel as a CNI. This file also needs to be in a

specific directory to be picked up for the cluster. That directory is `/opt/cni/bin/`, so we'll move the file bridge to that directory with the command `mv bridge /opt/cni/bin/`.

C.3   Installing Flannel CNI

Now that we've installed the bridge CNI plugin on both `kind-control-plane` and `kind-worker`, we can install Flannel CNI by creating the Flannel Kubernetes objects inside our cluster while inside of a shell on the control plane node with the command `kubectl apply -f https://raw.githubusercontent.com/flannel-io/flannel/master/Documentation/kube-flannel.yml`. You can verify that the nodes are now in a ready state with the command `kubectl get no`. The output will look similar to this:

```
root@kind-control-plane:/# kubectl get no
NAME                STATUS    ROLES            AGE    VERSION
kind-control-plane  Ready     control-plane    16m    v1.25.0-beta.0
kind-worker         Ready     <none>           16m    v1.25.0-beta.0
```

We can also verify that the CoreDNS Pods are running, as well as the Flannel Pods created and running, with the command `kubectl get po -A`. The output will look similar to this:

```
root@kind-control-plane:/# k get po -A
NAMESPACE           NAME                                        READY
⮕ STATUS
kube-flannel        kube-flannel-ds-d6v6t                       1/1
⮕ Running
kube-flannel        kube-flannel-ds-h7b5v                       1/1
⮕ Running
kube-system         coredns-565d847f94-txdvw                    1/1
⮕ Running
kube-system         coredns-565d847f94-vb4kg                    1/1
⮕ Running
kube-system         etcd-kind-control-plane                     1/1
⮕ Running
kube-system         kube-apiserver-kind-control-plane           1/1
⮕ Running
kube-system         kube-controller-manager-kind-control-plane  1/1
⮕ Running
kube-system         kube-proxy-9hsvk                            1/1
⮕ Running
kube-system         kube-proxy-gkvrz                            1/1
⮕ Running
kube-system         kube-scheduler-kind-control-plane           1/1
⮕ Running
local-path-storage  local-path-provisioner-684f458cdd-8bwkh     1/1
⮕ Running
```

This will complete the setup of installing Flannel.

C.4   Creating a new kind cluster

Installing the Calico CNI is very similar to installing Flannel, except for the YAML that's used to create the Kubernetes objects. So, go through sections C.1 and C.2 again, and let's proceed from there. If you already have a kind cluster running, you can either perform the command `kind delete cluster` to delete the existing cluster or you can create a new cluster named `cka` alongside the existing cluster with the command `kind create cluster --image kindest/node:v1.25.0-beta.0 --config config.yaml --name cka`. You will see an output similar to this:

```
$ kind create cluster --image kindest/node:v1.25.0-beta.0 --config
➥ config.yaml
--name cka
➥ [9:39:37]
Creating cluster "cka" ...
 ✓ Ensuring node image (kindest/node:v1.25.0-beta.0) 🖼
 ✓ Preparing nodes 📦 📦
 ✓ Writing configuration 📜
 ✓ Starting control-plane 🕹
 ✓ Installing StorageClass 💾
 ✓ Joining worker nodes 🚜
Set kubectl context to "kind-cka"
You can now use your cluster with:

kubectl cluster-info --context kind-cka

Thanks for using kind! 😊
```

If you chose to install a new cluster alongside the one you already have to get a shell to the nodes, you have to address them by the correct prefix (e.g., `cka`). For example, if you are following along and chose `cka` as the name for your cluster, to get a shell to the control plane node you would type `docker exec -it cka-control-plane bash`. To get a shell to the worker node, you would type `docker exec -it cka-worker bash`. Now that we're caught up, let's go through the process of installing Calico as our CNI.

C.5   Installing the Calico CNI

Picking up from section C.2 where you installed the bridge CNI plugin, let's install the Kubernetes objects required to implement the Calico CNI. While in a shell to your control plane (e.g., `docker exec -it cka-control-plane bash`), you can create those Kubernetes objects with the command `kubectl apply -f https://raw.githubusercontent .com/projectcalico/calico/v3.25.0/manifests/calico.yaml`. You will see a similar output to the following:

```
root@cka-control-plane:/# kubectl apply -f https://docs.projectcalico.org/
    manifests/calico.yaml
poddisruptionbudget.policy/calico-kube-controllers created
serviceaccount/calico-kube-controllers created
serviceaccount/calico-node created
configmap/calico-config created
```

```
customresourcedefinition.apiextensions.k8s.io/bgpconfigurations.crd.project
↪ calico.org created
customresourcedefinition.apiextensions.k8s.io/bgppeers.crd.projectcalico.or
↪ g created
customresourcedefinition.apiextensions.k8s.io/blockaffinities.crd.
↪ projectcalico.org created
customresourcedefinition.apiextensions.k8s.io/caliconodestatuses.crd.
↪ projectcalico.org created
customresourcedefinition.apiextensions.k8s.io/clusterinformations.crd.
↪ projectcalico.org created
customresourcedefinition.apiextensions.k8s.io/felixconfigurations.crd.
↪ projectcalico.org created
customresourcedefinition.apiextensions.k8s.io/globalnetworkpolicies.crd.
↪ projectcalico.org created
customresourcedefinition.apiextensions.k8s.io/globalnetworksets.crd.
↪ projectcalico.org created
customresourcedefinition.apiextensions.k8s.io/hostendpoints.crd.
↪ projectcalico.org created
customresourcedefinition.apiextensions.k8s.io/ipamblocks.crd.projectcalico.
↪ org created
customresourcedefinition.apiextensions.k8s.io/ipamconfigs.crd.
↪ projectcalico.org created
customresourcedefinition.apiextensions.k8s.io/ipamhandles.crd.projectcalico
↪ .org created
customresourcedefinition.apiextensions.k8s.io/ippools.crd.projectcalico.org
↪ created
customresourcedefinition.apiextensions.k8s.io/ipreservations.crd.
↪ projectcalico.org created
customresourcedefinition.apiextensions.k8s.io/kubecontrollersconfigurations
↪ .crd.projectcalico.org created
customresourcedefinition.apiextensions.k8s.io/networkpolicies.crd.
↪ projectcalico.org created
customresourcedefinition.apiextensions.k8s.io/networksets.crd.
↪ projectcalico.org created
clusterrole.rbac.authorization.k8s.io/calico-kube-controllers created
clusterrole.rbac.authorization.k8s.io/calico-node created
clusterrolebinding.rbac.authorization.k8s.io/calico-kube-controllers created
clusterrolebinding.rbac.authorization.k8s.io/calico-node created
daemonset.apps/calico-node created
deployment.apps/calico-kube-controllers created
```

Now that you've installed the Kubernetes objects necessary to install the Calico CNI, you can verify that the nodes are in a ready status with the command `kubectl get no`. You'll see output similar to the following:

```
root@cka-control-plane:/# kubectl get no
NAME                STATUS   ROLES           AGE   VERSION
cka-control-plane   Ready    control-plane   61m   v1.25.0-beta.0
cka-worker          Ready    <none>          61m   v1.25.0-beta.0
```

You can also see that the CoreDNS Pods, as well as the Calico Pods, are now up and running in the `kube-system` namespace by using the command `kubectl get po -A`. The output will look similar to the following:

```
root@cka-control-plane:/# kubectl get po -A
NAMESPACE              NAME                                              READY
    STATUS
kube-system            calico-kube-controllers-58dbc876ff-l9w9t          1/1
    Running
kube-system            calico-node-g5h7s                                 1/1
    Running
kube-system            calico-node-j8g9r                                 1/1
    Running
kube-system            coredns-565d847f94-b6jv4                          1/1
    Running
kube-system            coredns-565d847f94-mb554                          1/1
    Running
kube-system            etcd-cka-control-plane                            1/1
    Running
kube-system            kube-apiserver-cka-control-plane                  1/1
    Running
kube-system            kube-controller-manager-cka-control-plane         1/1
    Running
kube-system            kube-proxy-9ss5r                                  1/1
    Running
kube-system            kube-proxy-dlp2x                                  1/1
    Running
kube-system            kube-scheduler-cka-control-plane                  1/1
    Running
local-path-storage     local-path-provisioner-684f458cdd-vbskp           1/1
    Running
```

This completes installing the Calico CNI.

appendix D
Solving the exam
practice exercises

This appendix will walk you through the methods to solve the exam practice exercises, organized by chapter, starting with chapter 1. This will get you in the right frame of mind to initiate possible solutions for tasks on the CKA exam. If you've read the book, the solutions should be apparent, but this appendix will not simply present you with the answers right away, with the intention being to prepare you for exam day.

D.1   Chapter 1 exam exercises

There are fewer exam exercises in this chapter than in the other chapters, as this was an introductory chapter. The exercises are more exploratory, and we'll review them here.

D.1.1   Listing API resources

When listing API resources from within the cluster, you should first consider using the kubectl command-line utility. This is by far the easiest method. If you don't know the command off hand, you can always use the help menu by simply typing kubectl, which will provide some clues. The output of the help menu should look similar to this (abbreviated):

```
root@kind-control-plane:/# kubectl
kubectl controls the Kubernetes cluster manager.
```

```
Find more information at: https://kubernetes.io/docs/reference/kubectl/

Basic Commands (Beginner):
  create          Create a resource from a file or from stdin
  run             Run a particular image on the cluster
  set             Set specific features on objects

...

Other Commands:
  alpha           Commands for features in alpha
  api-resources   Print the supported API resources on the server
  api-versions    Print the supported API versions on the server, in the
➥ form of "group/version"
  config          Modify kubeconfig files
  plugin          Provides utilities for interacting with plugins
  version         Print the client and server version information

Usage:
  kubectl [flags] [options]
```

If you look in the section of the help menu that says Other Commands, you'll see that the command to "Print the supported API resources on the server" is `api-resources`. Therefore, the command to solve this exercise is `kubectl api-resources`.

D.1.2   *Listing services*

Listing the services in your cluster on a Linux operating system was covered in section 1.7 and is different from the Kubernetes Services that we talk about in chapter 7. Whenever you see the terms *Linux, daemon,* or *system service,* you should think about the system components on the node itself, whereas in the context of Kubernetes, Services are a completely different resource. To list the Services that are related to Kubernetes on the node, we run the command `systemctl list-unit-files --type service --all`, and then we can use the grep feature in Linux to further search through the results of the `list-unit-files` command. The complete command will look similar to the following:

```
root@kind-control-plane:/# systemctl list-unit-files --type service --all |
➥ grep kube
kubelet.service                        enabled        enabled
```

A lot of system services exist, which is why we use the grep function to list only the one we need, which is kubelet. In the context of the CKA exam, kubelet is the only system service located on the node itself. To send the output to a file named `services.csv`, we can add a `> services.csv` to the existing command. Therefore, the complete command will be `systemctl list-unit-files --type service --all | grep kubelet > services.csv`.

D.1.3   *The status of the kubelet service*

For this exam exercise, the same rules apply as in the previous exercise. The kubelet service will be the only system service that's running on the node itself. When you think about doing anything with the kubelet Service, think `systemctl`. You saw it used in the previous exercise as well. `systemctl` is the standard utility tool for controlling systemd, which is the overarching system service that controls them all. The command to obtain the status of any systemd service is `systemctl status`. You can find a hint for this in the help menu, so don't be concerned if you completely forget this during the exam. (Let the help menu be your friend with the command `systemd -h`.) So, the complete command is `systemctl status kubelet`. Using the same method from the last exercise, we'll output that to a file named `kubelet-status.txt` with the complete command `systemctl status kubelet > kubelet-status.txt`.

D.1.4   *Using declarative syntax*

As we learned about in section 1.8, declarative syntax helps retain a history of our Kubernetes configurations. As opposed to imperative, which is one command after another in sequence, declarative lets us define the configuration's end state, and the Kubernetes controller will make it so. To create a YAML file with the specifications for a Pod, we can use the Vim text editor.

Create and open the file in Vim with the command `vim chap1-pod.yaml`. Once the file is open in Vim, you can write the YAML. As an alternative, and something that I've recommended you do many times in the book to save you time on the exam, you can let the `kubectl` command line write the YAML for you with the command `k run pod --image nginx --dry-run=client -o yaml > chap1-pod.yaml`. The result will be the following:

```
apiVersion: v1
kind: Pod
metadata:
  creationTimestamp: null
  labels:
    run: pod
  name: pod
spec:
  containers:
  - image: nginx
    name: pod
    resources: {}
  dnsPolicy: ClusterFirst
  restartPolicy: Always
status: {}
```

Whichever way you'd like to complete this exercise is fine, but just know that the latter is a shortcut that I recommend using on the exam.

D.1.5   Listing Kubernetes services

This is where we make the distinction between system services (as a part of Linux on the node) and what we call Kubernetes services. As the exercise mentioned, list the services created in your Kubernetes cluster, where "created in your Kubernetes cluster" are the keywords that lead you down the path of using the kubectl tool, as opposed to the systemctl tool.

To list the Services, we can use the kubectl help menu to find the correct command. As with many other operations that would list a Kubernetes resource, think about this like a GET request to the API. We're listing what's in the API, and we're using the kubectl tool to do so. The way we list everything in our cluster is by tacking on the --all-namespaces or -A for short. So the complete command is kubectl get svc -A, or it could be another answer that is kubectl get services --all-namespaces. The output will look similar to the following:

```
root@kind-control-plane:~# kubectl get svc -A
NAMESPACE       NAME            TYPE        CLUSTER-IP      EXTERNAL-IP
╰▸ PORT(S)                      AGE
default         kubernetes      ClusterIP   10.96.0.1       <none>
╰▸ 443/TCP                      56d
kube-system     kube-dns        ClusterIP   10.96.0.10      <none>
╰▸ 53/UDP,53/TCP,9153/TCP  56d
```

D.2   Chapter 2 exam exercises

These are the exam exercises located at the end of chapter 2. There are approximately the same amount of exercises as in the previous chapter, so we'll go through these with the same intentions.

D.2.1   Shortening the kubectl command

We talked about this briefly in chapter 1, but the alias will already be set for you on the exam. This is an exercise that you'll need to practice for the local cluster that you'll use (and clusters that you'll use on the job). Setting the alias is fairly straightforward; however, there are two ways to do it because performing the command alias k=kubectl is correct; this will reset itself once you log out of your current Bash session. To make this persistent, we can add it to your Bash profile with the command echo "alias k=kubectl" >> ~/.bashrc. This is the more permanent command, as you can log out and log back into your machine, and the alias will persist.

D.2.2   Listing running Pods

We've reached the point where we'll be using the kubectl command-line tool, and you should become very familiar with this tool. You will use it in almost every task that you attempt to solve on the exam. To list the running Pods in the kube-system namespace, you should be thinking of the keyword get, as it's the common word that comes after kubectl (or alias k) in listing most Kubernetes resources. In addition, this exercise asks us to show the Pod IP addresses, so we're looking for a verbose output. In showing the IP addresses of Pods and nodes, think "output wide." When you put this all together, the complete command is k get po -n kube-system -o wide. The output should look similar to the following:

```
root@kind-control-plane:~# k get po -n kube-system -o wide
NAME                                           READY   STATUS    RESTARTS
⇨ AGE    IP             NODE
coredns-565d847f94-75lsz                       1/1     Running   7 (28h ago)
⇨ 56d    10.244.0.11    kind-control-plane
coredns-565d847f94-8stkp                       1/1     Running   7 (28h ago)
⇨ 56d    10.244.0.7     kind-control-plane
etcd-kind-control-plane                        1/1     Running   8 (28h ago)
⇨ 56d    172.18.0.2     kind-control-plane
kindnet-b9f9r                                  1/1     Running   27 (28h ago)
⇨ 56d    172.18.0.2     kind-control-plane
kube-apiserver-kind-control-plane              1/1     Running   5 (28h ago)
⇨ 52d    172.18.0.2     kind-control-plane
kube-controller-manager-kind-control-plane     1/1     Running   19 (67m ago)
⇨ 56d    172.18.0.2     kind-control-plane
kube-proxy-ddnwz                               1/1     Running   4 (28h ago)
⇨ 49d    172.18.0.2     kind-control-plane
kube-scheduler-kind-control-plane              1/1     Running   14 (67m ago)
⇨ 52d    172.18.0.2     kind-control-plane
metrics-server-d5589cfb-4ksgb                  1/1     Running   8 (28h ago)
⇨ 52d    10.244.0.10    kind-control-plane
```

Now that you have the output, you can save it to a file named pod-ip-output.txt, with the command k get po -n kube-system -o wide > pod-ip-output.txt.

D.2.3 *Viewing the kubelet client certificate*

We learned in this chapter that every component within Kubernetes has a certificate authority and either a client certificate or a server certificate. This is how a client–server model works, with the most common example being the World Wide Web.

When you think of certificates, you should always think of the /etc/kubernetes directory, as it stores all the certificate files and configurations. Whether it's in /etc/kubernetes/pki or /etc/kubernetes/pki/etcd, you will find the appropriate certificate file, as they are all properly labeled. In this case, from the control plane node, we can change the directory to /etc/kubernetes/pki with the command cd /etc/Kubernetes/pki. If we then list the contents with the ls command, we'll get an output similar to the following:

```
root@kind-control-plane:/# cd /etc/kubernetes/pki
root@kind-control-plane:/etc/kubernetes/pki# ls
apiserver-etcd-client.crt  apiserver-kubelet-client.crt  apiserver.crt
⇨ ca.crt  etcd               front-proxy-ca.key       front-proxy-
⇨ client.key  sa.pub
apiserver-etcd-client.key  apiserver-kubelet-client.key  apiserver.key
⇨ ca.key  front-proxy-ca.crt  front-proxy-client.crt  sa.key
```

The result, as you can decipher, is the location of the kubelet client certificate, which you can output to a file named `kubelet-config.txt` with the command `echo "/etc/kubernetes/pki" > kubelet-config.txt`.

D.2.4 *Backing up etcd*

As we know from reading chapter 2, etcd is a datastore for all the configurations of the cluster. It's what keeps track of the Pods running in the `kube-system` namespace, and it also retains the data about the kubelet configuration. It maintains its own server certificate, as the API server must authenticate to it to access the data within. This is an important component of Kubernetes and, therefore, proves why we need to back it up.

To interface with the etcd datastore, we use a tool called `etcdctl`, which also has a help menu—in case you find yourself blanking on the exam. Type the command `etcdctl -h` to get a list of possible commands we can run to back up the etcd datastore.

> **NOTE** You won't have to do this on the exam, but if you're doing this exercise in your lab at home (e.g., using kind Kubernetes), run the command `apt update; apt install -y etcd-client; export ETCDCTL_API=3` to install the `etcdctl` command-line tool, and set to version 3.

When the version is set to 3, the help menu includes the command `snapshot save`. Furthermore, if you view the help page of `snapshot save` with the command `etcdctl snapshot save -h`, you'll see the description "stores an etcd node backend snapshot to a given file." Following help pages like this is, in a lot of ways, a great resource when you forget the command on exam day, which is why I'm going into detail about it here.

As mentioned in the previous paragraph (and in chapter 2), the etcd datastore has its own server certificate, meaning you must authenticate to it to access the data within. This means we must pass the certificate authority (CA), client certificate, and key along with our request to back up etcd. Luckily, we already know that all certificates are located in the `/etc/Kubernetes/pki/etcd` directory. Therefore, we can point to them in their existing locations after the global options `--cacert`, `--cert`, and `--key` (we're able to see the global options from the help page as well). The final command is `etcdctl snapshot save etcdbackup1 --cacert /etc/kubernetes/pki/etcd/ca.crt --cert /etc/kubernetes/pki/etcd/server.crt --key /etc/kubernetes/pki/etcd/server.key`. Once backed up, we can run the command `etcdctl snapshot status etcdbackup1 > snapshot-status.txt` to get the status of the backup and redirect it to a file. The result of these commands will look similar to the following:

```
root@kind-control-plane:~# etcdctl snapshot save etcdbackup1 --cacert
↪ /etc/kubernetes/pki/etcd/ca.crt --cert /etc/kubernetes/pki/etcd/server.crt
↪ --key /etc/kubernetes/pki/etcd/server.key
2023-01-30 17:41:32.602411 I | clientv3: opened snapshot stream;
↪ downloading
2023-01-30 17:41:32.624918 I | clientv3: completed snapshot read; closing
Snapshot saved at etcdbackup1
```

```
root@kind-control-plane:~# etcdctl snapshot status etcdbackup1
9ec8949e, 1662, 807, 1.7 MB
root@kind-control-plane:~# etcdctl snapshot status etcdbackup1 > snapshot-
➥ status.txt
```

D.2.5   *Restoring etcd*

If you haven't done the previous exercise, the following exercise will not work, as it continues from the point at which you conducted a backup. So now that we have the snapshot named `etcdbackup1`, we can restore using the `etcdctl` command-line tool, with an option to restore instead of backing up. Again, if we can run the command `etcdctl snapshot -h`, we'll see the available commands are `restore`, `save`, and `status`. Choose the `restore` command, and run the command `etcdctl snapshot restore -h` to get more information. From the output of the help menu, it looks like we can specify a data directory. This will allow us to restore to a directory that etcd has already accessed. We know that the directory for the current etcd data directory is `/var/lib`. We know this because of the manifest for etcd, which is located in the `/etc/kuberne-tes/manifests` directory. We can run the command `cat /etc/kubernetes/manifests/etcd.yaml | tail -10`. The output will look similar to this:

```
root@kind-control-plane:~# cat /etc/kubernetes/manifests/etcd.yaml |
➥ tail -10
  volumes:
  - hostPath:
      path: /etc/kubernetes/pki/etcd
      type: DirectoryOrCreate
    name: etcd-certs
  - hostPath:
      path: /var/lib/etcd
      type: DirectoryOrCreate
    name: etcd-data
status: {}
```

This means that we can specify a similar directory, let's say `/var/lib/etcd-restore`. The complete command is `etcdctl snapshot restore snapshotdb --data-dir /var/lib/etcd-restore`.

D.2.6   *Upgrading the control plane*

Whenever you see the word `upgrade` for the exam, think kubeadm. It would be a good habit to practice using kubeadm to upgrade multiple times before taking the exam. I always like using the help menu to find my way around, so again, let's run the command `kubeadm -h` to see what options we have available to us for the upgrade. From the output, among the available options is the command `upgrade`. If we drill down one more level in the help pages with the command `kubeadm upgrade -h`, we can surmise that `plan` will check our cluster for the available version to choose. Let's try it, with the command `kubeadm upgrade plan`. The output will be very long, but the important part will look like this:

```
Upgrade to the latest version in the v1.24 series:

COMPONENT                    CURRENT    TARGET
kube-apiserver               v1.24.7    v1.24.10
kube-controller-manager      v1.24.7    v1.24.10
kube-scheduler               v1.24.7    v1.24.10
kube-proxy                   v1.24.7    v1.24.10
CoreDNS                      v1.8.6     v1.8.6
etcd                         3.5.3-0    3.5.3-0

You can now apply the upgrade by executing the following command:

    kubeadm upgrade apply v1.24.10
```

If we compare the versions, we see that we can upgrade from v1.24.7 to v1.24.10. The output even gave us the exact command to run, which is very convenient! Let's run the command kubeadm upgrade apply v1.24.10.

> **NOTE** You may get the error message "Specified version to upgrade 'v1.24.10' is higher than the kubeadm version 'v1.24.7.'" You can fix this message by running the command apt update; apt install -y kubeadm=1.24.10-00.

D.3   *Chapter 3 exam exercises*

These exercises are intertwined, so I advise you to do all of the exam exercises from chapter 3 at one time. This will give you the best practice for the CKA exam.

D.3.1   *Creating a Role*

To create a Role in Kubernetes, we use the kubectl command-line utility. Make sure to utilize the help menu, as there are usually examples that you can copy and paste directly into your terminal for the exam. For example, if you run the command k create role -h, you will get several examples, as in the following:

```
Examples:
  # Create a role named "pod-reader" that allows user to perform "get",
➥ "watch" and "list" on pods
  kubectl create role pod-reader --verb=get --verb=list --verb=watch -
➥ resource=pods

  # Create a role named "pod-reader" with ResourceName specified
  kubectl create role pod-reader --verb=get --resource=pods --resource-
➥ name=readablepod --resource-name=anotherpod

  # Create a role named "foo" with API Group specified
  kubectl create role foo --verb=get,list,watch --resource=rs.extensions

  # Create a role named "foo" with SubResource specified
  kubectl create role foo --verb=get,list,watch --resource=pods,pods/status
```

This is not a trick; you can copy and paste these into the terminal for the exam, and I advise you to do so. For this exercise, as it will allow the create verb for Service

Accounts, we will copy the first example from the help menu and change it to be
`kubectl create role sa-creator --verb=create --resource=sa`.

This will give us a new Role that will allow us to create Service Accounts. We can
see that this Role exists with the proper permissions with the command `k get role
sa-creator -o yaml`. The output will look similar to this:

```
root@kind-control-plane:~# k get role sa-creator -o yaml
apiVersion: rbac.authorization.k8s.io/v1
kind: Role
metadata:
  creationTimestamp: "2023-02-17T02:54:46Z"
  name: sa-creator2
  namespace: default
  resourceVersion: "190882"
  uid: 2517a9db-0a1c-4b3b-bf40-59fa799b5fd8
rules:
- apiGroups:
  - ""
  resources:
  - serviceaccounts
  verbs:
  - create
```

D.3.2   Create a role binding

The following exercise can only be completed if you already created the `sa-creator`
Role. If you haven't already, complete the first exam exercise in this chapter. Much
like creating a Role, we can use the help menu to find the right command. Let's run
the command `k create rolebinding -h`, and we'll see a helpful example to use and
modify to our liking. The examples from the output should look like this:

```
Examples:
  # Create a role binding for user1, user2, and group1 using the admin
➥ cluster role
  kubectl create rolebinding admin --clusterrole=admin --user=user1 -
➥ user=user2 --group=group1
```

Let's copy and paste that example and modify it to be `kubectl create rolebinding sa-
creator-binding --role=sa-creator --user=sandra`. Once the role binding is created,
you can verify the settings with the command `k get rolebinding sa-creator-binding -o
yaml`. The output should look similar to this:

```
root@kind-control-plane:~# k get rolebinding sa-creator-binding -o yaml
apiVersion: rbac.authorization.k8s.io/v1
kind: RoleBinding
metadata:
  creationTimestamp: "2023-02-17T03:03:28Z"
  name: sa-creator-binding
  namespace: default
  resourceVersion: "191629"
  uid: 0191d224-654b-44fb-8824-2b4e68028fef
```

```
roleRef:
  apiGroup: rbac.authorization.k8s.io
  kind: Role
  name: sa-creator
subjects:
- apiGroup: rbac.authorization.k8s.io
  kind: User
  name: sandra
 Using auth can-i
```

Again, we'll use the help menu to give us clues as to the correct command to run. The output of the command k auth can-i -h will give you the following examples:

```
Examples:
  # Check to see if I can create pods in any namespace
  kubectl auth can-i create pods --all-namespaces

  # Check to see if I can list deployments in my current namespace
  kubectl auth can-i list deployments.apps

  # Check to see if I can do everything in my current namespace ("*" means
⇒ all)
  kubectl auth can-i '*' '*'

  # Check to see if I can get the job named "bar" in namespace "foo"
  kubectl auth can-i list jobs.batch/bar -n foo

  # Check to see if I can read pod logs
  kubectl auth can-i get pods --subresource=log

  # Check to see if I can access the URL /logs/
  kubectl auth can-i get /logs/

  # List all allowed actions in namespace "foo"
  kubectl auth can-i --list --namespace=foo
```

We can deduce that the command to run is kubectl auth can-i create sa --as sandra. The result of running that command will look as follows:

```
root@kind-control-plane:~# k auth can-i create sa --as sandra
yes
```

D.3.3 *Creating a new user*

From reading chapter 3, you get the idea that a user is just a construct, not an actual user in a user database. This means that even though we create the user Sandra, we are simply creating a certificate, where the common name is Sandra. Kubernetes does not have this concept of users but can integrate with other identity providers. For the exam, you'll have to know how to generate this certificate, so I advise you to perform this exercise multiple times, as there are no straightforward answers in the Kubernetes documentation (which you can have open during the exam). Let's start by using the openssl command-line tool, which will be available to you (installed) for the exam and comes with all Linux systems, including the one that you're using for your practice lab. Let's generate a private key using 2048-bit encryption with the command openssl genrsa -out sandra.key 2048. The output will look like this:

```
root@kind-control-plane:/# openssl genrsa -out sandra.key 2048
Generating RSA private key, 2048 bit long modulus (2 primes)
.....................................................+++++
.........................+++++
e is 65537 (0x010001)
```

Now let's make a certificate-signing request file using the private key we just created, which we'll eventually give to the Kubernetes API. It's important here that we specify the user Sandra in the common name of the certificate-signing request with the command openssl req -new -key carol.key -subj "/CN=sandra" -out sandra.csr:

```
root@kind-control-plane:/# openssl req -new -key carol.key -subj
➥ "/CN=carol/O=developers" -out carol.csr
root@kind-control-plane:/# ls | grep carol
carol.csr
carol.key
```

Next, store the CSR file in an environment variable, as we'll need it later. To do this, use the command export REQUEST=$(cat sandra.csr | base64 -w 0) to store the Base64-encoded version of the CSR file in an environment variable named REQUEST.

Then, create the CSR resource from that request with the following multiline command:

```
cat <<EOF | kubectl apply -f -
apiVersion: certificates.k8s.io/v1
kind: CertificateSigningRequest
metadata:
  name: sandra
spec:
  groups:
  - developers
  request: $REQUEST
  signerName: kubernetes.io/kube-apiserver-client
  usages:
  - client auth
EOF
```

This will create the resource and input the request all in one command. You can view the request with the command k get csr. The output will look like this:

```
root@kind-control-plane:/# kubectl get csr
NAME     AGE    SIGNERNAME                              REQUESTOR
➥ CONDITION
sandra   4s     kubernetes.io/kube-apiserver-client     kubernetes-admin
➥ Pending
```

You can approve the request with the command `kubectl certificate approve Sandra`, and you'll see the condition change from `pending` to `Approved,Issued`:

```
root@kind-control-plane:/# kubectl certificate approve sandra
certificatesigningrequest.certificates.k8s.io/sandra approved
root@kind-control-plane:/# kubectl get csr
NAME     AGE      SIGNERNAME                              REQUESTOR
↪ CONDITION
sandra   2m12s    kubernetes.io/kube-apiserver-client     kubernetes-admin
↪ Approved,Issued
```

Now that it's been approved, you can extract the client certificate from the signed certificate, Base64-decode it, and store it in a file named `sandra.crt` with the command `kubectl get csr sandra -o jsonpath='{.status.certificate}' | base64 -d > carol.crt`:

```
root@kind-control-plane:/# kubectl get csr sandra -o
↪ jsonpath='{.status.certificate}' | base64 -d > sandra.crt
```

D.3.4   *Adding Sandra to kubeconfig*

If you want to assume the Role of Sandra, you must add the user, along with the certificate (which is the important part) to the kubeconfig file (the file we use to run `kubectl`). To add the user Sandra to our context, we'll run the command `kubectl config set-context carol --user=sandra --cluster=kind`. Once you run this command, you'll notice that that the context has been added by running the command `kubectl config get-contexts`. You will see an output similar to this:

```
root@kind-control-plane:/# kubectl config set-context sandra --user=sandra
↪ --cluster=kind
Context "carol" created.
root@kind-control-plane:/# kubectl config get-contexts
CURRENT   NAME                     CLUSTER   AUTHINFO            NAMESPACE
          sandra                   kind      sandra
*         kubernetes-admin@kind    kind      kubernetes-admin
```

The star in the `current` column on the left indicates which context we are currently using. Therefore, to switch contexts, run the command `kubectl config use-context sandra`. You'll notice the asterisk changed the current context to `Sandra`.

D.3.5   *Creating a new Service Account*

As we know from reading chapter 3, tokens of Service Accounts are mounted to a Pod automatically, and it takes a special configuration setting to prevent the mounting of that token. The first step is to view the help menu. I always start with the help menu because, in the heat of the moment (on the exam), you'll sometimes lose your train of thought and perhaps forget what command to use or the order of commands and options. It happens to the best of us! Don't worry, and remember that the help menu is there if you need it. It's there for a reason. For example, you can run the command k create -h and see a list of available commands, and wouldn't you know, serviceaccount is listed as one of the available commands. Let's run the command k create serviceaccount -h and see what options exist for Service Accounts specifically. The output will give us a lot more options, but most notably, it will present the following example:

```
Examples:
  # Create a new service account named my-service-account
  kubectl create serviceaccount my-service-account
```

We can copy and paste this example and change it to kubectl create serviceaccount secure-sa, which will create the Service Account we need for this exercise. Then, to make sure the token is not exposed to the Pod, we can run the command k get sa secure-sa -o yaml > secure-sa.yaml and then the command echo "automountService-AccountToken: false" >> secure-sa.yaml to ensure that the token doesn't automount to a Pod. To apply the change, run the command k apply -f secure-sa.yaml, which will apply the configuration change to disable automounting the token for all Pods using this Service Account.

D.3.6 *Creating a new cluster role*

We created a Role in the first exercise of this chapter; now we're going to create a cluster role in a similar way. I hope you are familiar with using the help menu by now to find excellent examples of kubectl commands for creating a cluster role. I'm going to take the first example from the command k create clusterrole -h and change it to be kubectl create clusterrole acme-corp-role --verb=create --resource=deploy,rs,ds. Next, we'll create a role binding (notice how it didn't say cluster role binding), which we'll call acme-corp-role-binding, bind it to the secure-sa Service Account, and make sure the Service Account can only create Deployments, ReplicaSets, and DaemonSets in the default namespace (and not the kube-system namespace). We'll use the example from the command k create rolebinding -h and change it to kubectl create rolebinding acme-corp-role-binding --clusterrole=acme-corp-role --serviceaccount=default:secure-sa. Then, we'll check the Role with the command kubectl -n kube-system auth can-i create deploy --as system:serviceaccount:default:nomount-sa. You should get the response no.

D.4 *Chapter 4 exam exercises*

Chapter 4 exam exercises revolve around scheduling Deployments or Pods in Kubernetes. You won't have to deploy a StatefulSet for the exam, as it's not listed as an objective for the exam criteria. When you think of scheduling, just think of creating a Pod—whether in a Deployment or not—and placing it on a node. Throughout this chapter, there are ways to control which node the Pod is placed on, and that's where we'll focus for the exercises.

D.4.1   *Applying a label and creating a Pod*

This exercise simply involves applying a label to a node. If you have no idea where to begin, there's a help menu for that! Let's run the command `kubectl -h | grep label` to see if there's a `label` under available commands. The output will look similar to this:

```
root@kind-control-plane:~# k -h | grep label
  delete          Delete resources by file names, stdin, resources and
➥ names, or by resources and label selector
  label           Update the labels on a resource
```

To label the node `kind-worker`, we can run the command `k label no kind-worker disk=ssd`. We can then show the labels on our nodes with the command `k get no -show-labels`. The output will look similar to the following:

```
root@kind-control-plane:~# k get no --show-labels
NAME                STATUS   ROLES          AGE    VERSION    LABELS
kind-control-plane  Ready    control-plane  8d     v1.24.7
➥ beta.kubernetes.io/arch=amd64,beta.kubernetes.io/os=linux,ingress-
➥ ready=true,kubernetes.io/arch=amd64,kubernetes.io/hostname=kind-
➥ control-plane,kubernetes.io/os=linux,node-role.kubernetes.io/control-
➥ plane=,node.kubernetes.io/exclude-from-external-load-balancers=
kind-worker         Ready    <none>         8d     v1.24.7
➥ beta.kubernetes.io/arch=amd64,beta.kubernetes.io/os=linux,disk=ssd,kube
➥ rnetes.io/arch=amd64,kubernetes.io/hostname=kind-
➥ worker,kubernetes.io/os=linux
```

We can see that the label was successfully applied, and now we can create the YAML for a Pod with the command `k run fast --image nginx -dry-run=client -o yaml > fast.yaml`. Let's open the file and change two lines that will schedule the Pod to that node with the label `disk=ssd`. At the very end of the file, just above the word `status`, in line with `restartPolicy`, we'll add the following lines:

```
nodeSelector:
  disk: ssd
```

Save your changes and close the file. Now that you have the YAML file, you can create the Pod with the command `k create -f fast.yaml`. Make sure that it was scheduled to the correct node with the command `k get po -o wide`. The output will look similar to this:

```
root@kind-control-plane:~# k get po -o wide
NAME                        READY    STATUS    RESTARTS       AGE
➥ IP              NODE          NOMINATED NODE    READINESS GATES
fast                        1/1      Running   1 (36h ago)    8d
➥ 10.244.162.144  kind-worker   <none>            <none>
```

D.4.2   *Editing a running Pod*

When you edit a running Pod with the `k edit po` command, you can only change certain fields within the YAML. This is normal behavior, and even though you can't change it directly, Kubernetes will save a copy of the Pod YAML in a file in the `/tmp/` directory. Let's go ahead and see what that looks like by running the command `k edit po fast`, which will open the Pod YAML in a Vim editor. You can search for `nodeSelector` by pressing the slash (/) key on the keyboard followed by the word `nodeSelector` (e.g., type `/nodeSelector` in Vim) and press Enter. The Vim text editor will first highlight the word `nodeSelector` in the annotations, so press the N key to go to the next result, which will be the one we're looking for. You can then press the I key on the keyboard to go into insert mode. Change the text from `disk: ssd` to `disk: slow`. The portion of the YAML that you must change for this exercise will look like the following when you are done:

```
nodeName: kind-worker
nodeSelector:
  disk: slow
preemptionPolicy: PreemptLowerPriority
```

Now that you've changed the YAML, you can save and quit the file; however, you'll get a warning message indicating that the Pod updates may not change fields other than `spec.containers[*].image`. This is fine, as you will continue to quit the file. Only then will the file be saved to the `/tmp` directory. The message that you'll receive when you quit the file will look similar to this:

```
root@kind-control-plane:~# k edit po fast
error: pods "fast" is invalid
A copy of your changes has been stored to "/tmp/kubectl-edit-
➥ 589741394.yaml"
error: Edit cancelled, no valid changes were saved.
```

This is still okay, even though we received an error. This is the part where we apply the YAML that was stored in the `/tmp` directory and force the Pod to restart. The command to do this is `k replace -f /tmp/kubectl-edit-589741394.yaml --force` (the name of the YAML file will be different for you). This will result in the currently running Pod being deleted and a new Pod (with a new name) being created. The output will look similar to this:

```
root@kind-control-plane:~# k replace -f /tmp/kubectl-edit-589741394.yaml -
➥ force
pod "fast" deleted
pod/fast replaced
```

Once this is achieved, you can check if the Pod is running with the new config, using the command `k get po fast; k get po fast -o yaml | grep disk`.

```
root@kind-control-plane:~# k get po fast; k get po fast -o yaml | grep disk:
NAME    READY    STATUS        RESTARTS    AGE
fast    1/1      Running       0           4m39s
    disk: slow
```

D.4.3 *Using node affinity for a new Pod*

Node affinity, as we know from reading chapter 4, is scheduling a Pod to a node based on certain preferences for nodes with a specific label. For example, in this exercise, we're saying that the Pod should be scheduled to a node that has the label disk=ssd as its first preference. It has a backup plan, however, in case there are no available nodes that have the disk=ssd label. The backup plan is to schedule to nodes that have the label Kubernetes.io/os=linux.

Let's start by creating the YAML for a Pod with the command k run ssd-pod -image nginx -dry-run=client -o yaml > ssd-pod.yaml. Now open the file ssd-pod.yaml and insert the node affinity configuration. For the exam, here's where I would utilize the Kubernetes docs, which you can have open during the exam. So, with the site https:// kubernetes.io/docs open in a web browser, type node selector in the search bar and press Enter. Select the first link, named Assigning Pods to Nodes, and click the link Affinity and Anti-affinity from the right side of the page. You will see the YAML listed on this page, which you can copy and paste right into your existing ssd-pod.yaml file. The part that you need to copy will be the entire affinity section below spec:. We'll modify it slightly to look like the following:

```
affinity:
  nodeAffinity:
    requiredDuringSchedulingIgnoredDuringExecution:
      nodeSelectorTerms:
      - matchExpressions:
        - key: kubernetes.io/os
          operator: In
          values:
          - linux
    preferredDuringSchedulingIgnoredDuringExecution:
    - weight: 1
      preference:
        matchExpressions:
        - key: disk
          operator: In
          values:
          - ssd
```

Once you have this pasted into the file ssd-pod.yaml you can save and quit. You can create the Pod with the command k apply -f ssd-pod.yaml. Check if the Pod has been successfully scheduled to the correct node with the command k get po -o wide. The output should look similar to this:

```
root@kind-control-plane:~# k apply -f ssd-pod.yaml
pod/ssd-pod created
```

```
root@kind-control-plane:~# k get po -o wide
NAME                          READY    STATUS    RESTARTS       AGE
⇒ IP                 NODE             NOMINATED NODE    READINESS GATES
ssd-pod                       1/1      Running   0              16s
⇒ 10.244.162.152    kind-worker      <none>            <none>
```

D.5   *Chapter 5 exam exercises*

These are different than the last set of exercises because they have more to do with the maintenance of currently running Deployments and Pods. These exercises will deal with scaling, updating images, and viewing the rollouts of a Deployment. This is helpful for the exam because you'll be asked to roll out to a new version of an application running on Kubernetes, or you may be asked to roll back to a previous version.

D.5.1   *Scaling replicas in a Deployment*

Most likely for the exam, there will be a Deployment already running, but to simulate this in our practice lab, we'll have to create one ourselves. The most important part of this exercise is the scaling operation, not so much creating the Deployment. Let's start by running the command k create deploy apache --image httpd:latest. This will create the Deployment, and the Deployment will be created with one replica because we didn't specify within the imperative command. You can verify that the Pod within the Deployment has been created with the command k get deploy,po. The output will look like this:

```
root@kind-control-plane:~# k get deploy,po
NAME                          READY    UP-TO-DATE    AVAILABLE    AGE
deployment.apps/apache        1/1      1             1            3m30s

NAME                              READY    STATUS    RESTARTS    AGE
pod/apache-67984dc457-5mcvj       1/1      Running   0           3m30s
```

Now that the Pod is up and running, we can scale the Deployment from one replica to five replicas. The command to scale the replicas is k scale deploy apache -replias 5. Once we run that command, we'll see four more Pods have been started. To verify that this is happening, run the command k get deploy,po again. The output will now look like this:

```
root@kind-control-plane:~# k scale deploy apache --replicas=5
deployment.apps/apache scaled
root@kind-control-plane:~# k get deploy,po
NAME                          READY    UP-TO-DATE    AVAILABLE    AGE
deployment.apps/apache        3/5      5             3            5m57s

NAME                              READY    STATUS           RESTARTS
⇒ AGE
pod/apache-67984dc457-5mcvj       1/1      Running          0
⇒ 5m57s
pod/apache-67984dc457-bcs6q       1/1      Running          0
⇒ 3s
```

```
pod/apache-67984dc457-dwzl9    0/1    ContainerCreating    0
↳ 3s
pod/apache-67984dc457-kl7rq    0/1    ContainerCreating    0
↳ 3s
pod/apache-67984dc457-rdgh5    1/1    Running              0
↳ 3s
```

D.5.2   *Updating the image*

In the previous exercise, we created a Deployment named `apache`, and we'll continue in this exercise with the same Deployment. If you haven't yet completed the previous exercise, please do so before starting this one. Updating the image within a Deployment, as we know from reading chapter 5, causes Kubernetes to create a new ReplicaSet and record this action as a new rollout. We can update the image with the command `k set image deploy apache httpd=httpd:latest httpd=httpd:2.4.54`. You can verify that the Deployment contains the correct image with the command `k get deploy apache -o yaml | grep image`. The output will look similar to this:

```
root@kind-control-plane:~# k get deploy apache -o yaml | grep image
    - image: httpd:2.4.54
      imagePullPolicy: Always
```

D.5.3   *Viewing ReplicaSet events*

Every time you change the image, along with other characteristics of the Deployment, there's a new ReplicaSet that is created. This is because the Pods change configuration; therefore, the old Pods are terminated and new Pods are created. As we know by reading chapter 5, this is all handled by the ReplicaSet, which is the controller to help with rolling out new versions of the Deployment. We can view the events by running the command `k describe rs apache-67984dc457`. Note that the name of the ReplicaSet will be different for you. The output contains a lot of information, but the important part is at the end, in the events section, which should look similar to this:

```
Events:
  Type     Reason            Age     From                    Message
  ----     ------            ----    ----                    -------
  Normal   SuccessfulCreate  58m     replicaset-controller   Created pod:
↳ apache-67984dc457-kl7rq
  Normal   SuccessfulCreate  58m     replicaset-controller   Created pod:
↳ apache-67984dc457-rdgh5
  Normal   SuccessfulCreate  58m     replicaset-controller   Created pod:
↳ apache-67984dc457-dwzl9
  Normal   SuccessfulCreate  58m     replicaset-controller   Created pod:
↳ apache-67984dc457-bcs6q
  Normal   SuccessfulDelete  7m59s   replicaset-controller   Deleted pod:
↳ apache-67984dc457-rdgh5
  Normal   SuccessfulDelete  6m45s   replicaset-controller   Deleted pod:
↳ apache-67984dc457-bcs6q
  Normal   SuccessfulDelete  6m44s   replicaset-controller   Deleted pod:
↳ apache-67984dc457-5mcvj
```

```
   Normal   SuccessfulDelete   6m43s   replicaset-controller   Deleted pod:
➡ apache-67984dc457-dwzl9
   Normal   SuccessfulDelete   6m43s   replicaset-controller   Deleted pod:
➡ apache-67984dc457-kl7rq
```

D.5.4 *Rolling back to a previous app version*

Now that we've successfully rolled out to a new version (by changing the Deployment image), we can easily roll back to the previous version, with the previous image, by performing the command k rollout undo deploy apache. You can now see from running the command k rollout status deploy apache, followed by k rollout history deploy apache, what revision we are on.

```
root@kind-control-plane:~# k rollout undo deploy apache
deployment.apps/apache rolled back
root@kind-control-plane:~# k rollout status deploy apache
Waiting for deployment "apache" rollout to finish: 1 old replicas are
➡ pending termination...
Waiting for deployment "apache" rollout to finish: 1 old replicas are
➡ pending termination...
Waiting for deployment "apache" rollout to finish: 1 old replicas are
➡ pending termination...
Waiting for deployment "apache" rollout to finish: 4 of 5 updated replicas
➡ are available...
deployment "apache" successfully rolled out
root@kind-control-plane:~# k rollout history deploy apache
deployment.apps/apache
REVISION   CHANGE-CAUSE
2          <none>
3          <none>
```

D.5.5 *Changing the rollout strategy*

To change the rollout strategy, we have to modify the Deployment YAML. We can easily do this by running the command k edit deploy apache. This will open the Deployment YAML in a Vim text editor. We can go down to the line that starts with strategy and change the type to Recreate. The rest of the YAML under strategy can be deleted. The final result will look like this:

```
    app: apache
  strategy:
    type: Recreate
  template:
```

Once you've changed the strategy from RollingUpdate to Recreate, you can save and quit the file. The Deployment will be updated automatically. No rollout will occur, as this will only take effect in the next rollout phase. The result after exiting the Deployment YAML will look like this:

```
root@kind-control-plane:~# k edit deploy apache
deployment.apps/apache edited
```

For extra credit, you can perform the previous exercise again and see that all Pods are terminated before the new Pods are created, as this is the rollout strategy that we intended to change.

D.5.6 *Cordoning and uncordoning a node*

For this exercise, we'll first create a three-node cluster. See appendix A on how to create a multinode cluster using kind Kubernetes. When the three-node cluster is up and running, and you've run the command `docker exec -it kind-control-plane` to gain access to the control-plane node (where `kubectl` is already installed), you can continue with this task.

Cordoning a node means that we're marking it as unschedulable. This doesn't necessarily evict the Pods from the node. You'll have to run the drain command to do this. To cordon a node, run the command `k cordon kind-worker`. You can verify that scheduling has been disabled on this node by running the command `k get no`. The output will look similar to the following:

```
root@kind-control-plane:/# k cordon kind-worker
node/kind-worker cordoned
root@kind-control-plane:/# k get no
NAME                     STATUS                    ROLES           AGE
⇛ VERSION
kind-control-plane       Ready                     control-plane   58s
⇛ v1.26.0
kind-worker              Ready,SchedulingDisabled  <none>          38s
⇛ v1.26.0
kind-worker2             Ready                     <none>          38s
⇛ v1.26.0
```

Now we can schedule a Pod, and it should go to the node `kind-worker2` because we've just cordoned the node `kind-worker`. To schedule a Pod, let's run the command `k run nginx --image nginx`. Then, we can check that the Pod was scheduled to the correct node with the command `k get po -o wide`. The output should look similar to this:

```
root@kind-control-plane:/# k run nginx --image nginx
pod/nginx created
root@kind-control-plane:/# k get po -o wide
NAME      READY    STATUS            RESTARTS    AGE    IP        NODE
⇛ NOMINATED NODE    READINESS GATES
nginx     0/1      ContainerCreating 0           5s     <none>    kind-worker2
⇛ <none>             <none>
```

Next, we'll uncordon the node `kind-worker` with the command `k uncordon kind-worker`. Now that the node is uncordoned, we can schedule Pods to it again. Go ahead and move the Pod from the node `kind-worker2` to the node `kind-worker` by adding a node selector. We'll add the node selector in the Pod YAML using the command `k edit po nginx` (you may need to run the command `apt update; apt install -y vim` to install Vim again on your new kind cluster). This will open the YAML in a Vim text editor. In the file, locate the line starting with nodeName (line 29). Change the line from nodeName: kind-worker2 to nodeName: kind-worker. Save and quit the file. This will prompt you with a message indicating that the Pod updates may not change fields other than spec.containers[*].image, which is fine, as you will continue to quit the file. Once you quit the file, you'll notice that it stored a copy of the YAML in the /tmp directory. You can run the command k replace -f /tmp/kubectl-edit-3840075995.yaml --force to terminate the old nginx Pod, which will create a new Pod and schedule it to the node kind-worker. We can verify this by running the command k get po -o wide.

```
root@kind-control-plane:/# k edit po nginx
error: pods "nginx" is invalid
A copy of your changes has been stored to "/tmp/kubectl-edit-
⇨ 3840075995.yaml"
error: Edit cancelled, no valid changes were saved.
root@kind-control-plane:/# k replace -f /tmp/kubectl-edit-3840075995.yaml
⇨ --force
pod "nginx" deleted
pod/nginx replaced
root@kind-control-plane:/# k get po -o wide
NAME    READY   STATUS    RESTARTS   AGE     IP           NODE
⇨ NOMINATED NODE   READINESS GATES
nginx   1/1     Running   0          4m17s   10.244.1.2   kind-worker
⇨ <none>           <none>
```

We can see that, in fact, it was scheduled to the node kind-worker.

D.5.7 *Removing a taint from a node*

The exam will most likely already have a Deployment running, but for your practice lab environment, you may not, so we'll first create a Deployment to simulate this exam-like scenario. We can use the same cluster that we used in the previous exercise.

We'll start by creating a Deployment named nginx, using the nginx image with the command k create deploy nginx -image nginx. Then, we'll remove the taint from the control-plane node with the command k taint no kind-control-plane node-role.kubernetes.io/control-plane:NoSchedule-. Now that the taint has been removed, we can schedule Pods to it without including a toleration for the taint. Let's go ahead and do this, but first, we'll have to modify the Deployment YAML. We can do this with the command k edit deploy nginx, which will open the Deployment YAML in a Vim text editor. We can add a node selector to the YAML by inserting the following to the Pod spec:

```
spec:
  containers:
  - image: nginx
    imagePullPolicy: Always
    name: nginx
    resources: {}
    terminationMessagePath: /dev/termination-log
    terminationMessagePolicy: File
```

```
dnsPolicy: ClusterFirst
nodeSelector:
  kubernetes.io/hostname: kind-control-plane
restartPolicy: Always
schedulerName: default-scheduler
securityContext: {}
terminationGracePeriodSeconds: 30
```

As soon as we add the node selector line, the new configuration will be applied automatically, as the Deployment controller will recognize the change and reschedule the Pod to the control plane node. We can verify that this took place by using the command k get po -o wide. The output will look similar to the following:

```
root@kind-control-plane:/# k edit deploy nginx
deployment.apps/nginx edited
root@kind-control-plane:/# k get po -o wide
NAME                      READY   STATUS    RESTARTS    AGE     IP
➥ NODE                   NOMINATED NODE    READINESS GATES
nginx                     1/1     Running   0           27m     10.244.1.2
➥ kind-worker            <none>            <none>
nginx-cd5574b4f-qbz9z     1/1     Running   0           3m46s   10.244.0.5
➥ kind-control-plane     <none>            <none>
```

D.6   *Chapter 6 exam exercises*

The exam exercises in chapter 6 become slightly more complex, as we start to deal with DNS and communication within the cluster. These exercises go together, so I would advise you to start at the first and continue to the second, third, and so on. If you try to start in the middle of the exercises, you won't be able to proceed without having done the prior exercises. We will cover all the details here as to how to solve these exercises, so you can be best prepared for the exam.

D.6.1   *exec-ing into a Pod*

For the exam, you'll have the Pod already created, but to practice in your own personal lab environment (e.g., kind Kubernetes), go ahead and create the Pod as a prerequisite. If you are continuing from the chapter 5 exercises, you can use the Pod named nginx that we created. If you are starting from scratch, you can run the command k run nginx -image nginx to create a Pod. Once you created the Pod, you can check that it's up and running using a command inside the container. To obtain the IP address of the DNS server that the Pod uses to resolve domain names (that's injected into each Pod at run time), we can run the command k exec -it nginx --cat / etc/resolv.conf. The output of the command will look like this:

```
root@kind-control-plane:/# k exec -it nginx --cat /etc/resolv.conf
search default.svc.cluster.local svc.cluster.local cluster.local
nameserver 10.96.0.10
options ndots:5
```

D.6.2   Changing the DNS service

To change the DNS service IP address, first change the CIDR range in the API server YAML configuration. We can do this by changing the YAML file located in /etc/ kubernetes/manifests, which is named kube-apiserver.yaml. Let's open it and modify the service-cluster-ip value in the YAML. We'll run the command vim /etc/kubernetes/ manifests/kube-apiserver.yaml, which will open the file in a Vim text editor, then we can change the CIDR from 10.96.0.0/6 to 100.96.0.0/6. Once we've made that change, we can save and quit, and the changes will apply automatically. You may have to wait up to 5 minutes for the API server Pod to be recreated in the kube-system namespace. Now, locate the DNS service, which will always reside in the kube-system namespace. Let's run the command k -n kube-system get svc to see the service. The output of the command will look like this:

```
root@kind-control-plane:/# k -n kube-system get svc
NAME           TYPE        CLUSTER-IP     EXTERNAL-IP   PORT(S)
⇒ AGE
kube-dns       ClusterIP   10.96.0.10     <none>        53/UDP,53/TCP,9153/TCP
⇒ 107m
```

The cluster IP is 10.96.0.10, and for this exercise, we're going to change it to 100.96.0.10. We can change the Service IP address with the command k -n kube-system edit svc kube-dns, which will open the YAML for the Service in a Vim text editor. Once the YAML is open, we can change the two values just below the spec. We'll change 10.96.0.10 to 100.96.0.10 for the two instances of that IP address. Once we've made the changes, we can save and quit. We should expect to see the warning message that you may not change this value. You can continue to quit the file (!q), and a copy of the YAML file will be stored in the /tmp directory. The output will look similar to this:

```
root@kind-control-plane:/# k -n kube-system edit svc kube-dns
error: services "kube-dns" is invalid
A copy of your changes has been stored to "/tmp/kubectl-edit-
⇒ 2356510614.yaml"
error: Edit cancelled, no valid changes were saved.
```

Let's run a replace of this YAML, which will terminate the Service and create a new Service with our new IP address for DNS in its place. To do this, we'll run the command k replace -f /tmp/kubectl-edit-2356510614.yaml --force to replace the instance of the Service.

D.6.3   Changing the kubelet configuration

Now that we've modified the kube-dns Service, we need to modify the kubelet configuration for the Pods to get the new DNS IP information. This can be done by modifying the file named config.yaml in the /var/lib/kubelet/ directory. Let's open the file in Vim with the command vim /var/lib/kubelet/config.yaml. Once the file is open in Vim, we can change the value for clusterDNS from 10.96.0.10 to 100.96.0.10. Once you've done this, you can save and quit the file. Now that we've changed the Service configuration, we'll have to reload the kubelet daemon with the commands `systemctl daemon-reload` and `systemctl restart kubelet` to restart the kubelet service on the node. Finally, we'll verify that the service is active and running with the command `systemctl status kubelet`. The output will contain a lot of information, but the important part is that the service is active and running, which can be located at the beginning of the output here:

```
root@kind-control-plane:/# systemctl status kubelet
  kubelet.service - kubelet: The Kubernetes Node Agent
     Loaded: loaded (/etc/systemd/system/kubelet.service; enabled; vendor
➥ preset: enabled)
    Drop-In: /etc/systemd/system/kubelet.service.d
             └─10-kubeadm.conf
     Active: active (running) since Sat 2023-02-18 19:04:20 UTC; 1min 20s
➥ ago
       Docs: http://kubernetes.io/docs/
```

D.6.4   *Editing the kubelet ConfigMap*

To locate the ConfigMap, which, similar to the Service, is located in the kube-system namespace, we can run the command `k -n kube-system get cm`. The output will look like this:

```
root@kind-control-plane:/# k -n kube-system get cm
NAME                                   DATA   AGE
coredns                                1      134m
extension-apiserver-authentication     6      134m
kube-proxy                             2      134m
kube-root-ca.crt                       1      133m
kubeadm-config                         1      134m
kubelet-config                         1      134m
```

The ConfigMap that we're looking at specifically for this exercise is named `kubelet-config`. We can edit the ConfigMap with the command `k -n kube-system edit cm kubelet-config`. This will open the YAML for the ConfigMap in a Vim text editor. Go down to the line that starts with `clusterDNS` and change the value underneath from `10.96.0.10` to `100.96.0.10`. We can save and quit the file to have the changes applied automatically. The output will look like this:

```
root@kind-control-plane:/# k -n kube-system edit cm kubelet-config
configmap/kubelet-config edited
```

Now that we've upgraded the node, because the kubelet is a daemon that's currently running on the node, we must update the node of this configuration, as well as reload the daemon and restart the kubelet service on the node. First, to update the kubelet configuration on the node, perform the command `kubeadm upgrade node phase kubelet-config`. The output will look like this:

```
root@kind-control-plane:/# kubeadm upgrade node phase kubelet-config
[upgrade] Reading configuration from the cluster...
[upgrade] FYI: You can look at this config file with 'kubectl -n kube-
➡ system get cm kubeadm-config -o yaml'
W0914 17:44:33.203828    3618 utils.go:69] The recommended value for
➡ "clusterDNS" in "KubeletConfiguration" is: [10.96.0.10]; the provided
➡ value is: [100.96.0.10]
[kubelet-start] Writing kubelet configuration to file
➡ "/var/lib/kubelet/config.yaml"
[upgrade] The configuration for this node was successfully updated!
[upgrade] Now you should go ahead and upgrade the kubelet package using
➡ your package manager.
```

Now that we've upgraded the kubelet configuration for the node, we can reload the daemon with the command `systemctl daemon-reload` and restart the service with the command `systemctl restart kubelet`. You will not receive an output; you will just return to the command prompt, so as long as there are no error messages, you have successfully restarted the kubelet service.

D.6.5 Scaling the CoreDNS Deployment

The DNS service in Kubernetes is running as a Deployment. To scale this Deployment, we'll run the same command that we run to scale any other Deployment, which is `k -n kube-system scale deploy coredns -replicas 3`. You can then check if the replicas scaled with the command `k -n kube-system` are deployed. The output will look similar to the following:

```
root@kind-control-plane:/# k -n kube-system scale deploy coredns --replicas
➡ 3
deployment.apps/coredns scaled
root@kind-control-plane:/# k -n kube-system get deploy
NAME      READY   UP-TO-DATE   AVAILABLE   AGE
coredns   3/3     3            3           141m
```

D.6.6 Verifying DNS changes from a Pod

Now that we've made these changes to DNS, we'll verify that new Pods are also receiving these changes as they are created. The command to create a Pod named `netshoot` with the netshoot image is `kubectl run netshoot --image=nicolaka/netshoot --command sleep --command "3600"`. We run the two commands `sleep` and `3600` so that the Pod will remain in a running state (for 3,600 seconds, or 60 minutes). We can check if the Pod is in a running state with the command `k get po`. The output should look similar to this:

```
root@kind-control-plane:/# kubectl run netshoot --image=nicolaka/netshoot -
➡ -command sleep --command "3600"
pod/netshoot created
root@kind-control-plane:/# k get po
NAME       READY   STATUS    RESTARTS   AGE
netshoot   1/1     Running   0          40s
```

The Pod is running, so now you can get a Bash shell to the container. To do this, perform the command `k exec -it netshoot -bash`. You will notice that your prompt changes, which means you have successfully entered the container within the Pod. The output should look like this:

```
root@kind-control-plane:/# k exec -it netshoot --bash
bash-5.1#
```

Now that you have a Bash shell open in the container, you can run the command `cat /etc/resolv.conf` to check that the correct DNS IP address is listed. The output should be similar to this:

```
root@kind-control-plane:/# k exec -it netshoot --bash
bash-5.1# cat /etc/resolv.conf
search default.svc.cluster.local svc.cluster.local cluster.local
nameserver 100.96.0.10
options ndots:5
```

This means that the DNS is correctly configured; therefore, Pods are able to resolve DNS names using CoreDNS in the cluster. You can check that this Pod is able to resolve a DNS query to example.com with the command `nslookup example.com`. Nslookup is a DNS utility that allows you to query name servers. The output should look like this:

```
bash-5.1# nslookup example.com
Server:     100.96.0.10
Address:    100.96.0.10#53

Non-authoritative answer:
Name:    example.com
Address: 93.184.216.34
Name:    example.com
Address: 2606:2800:220:1:248:1893:25c8:1946
```

D.6.7   Creating a Deployment and Service

To create a Deployment named `hello` using the image `nginxdemos/hello:plain-text`, you can run the command `k create deploy hello --image nginxdemos/hello:plain-text`. We can then expose the Deployment with the command `k expose deploy hello --name hello-svc --port 80`. To verify that we've created the Service correctly, we'll run the command `k get svc`. The output of the previous commands will look like the following:

```
root@kind-control-plane:/# k create deploy hello --image
➥ nginxdemos/hello:plain-text
deployment.apps/hello created
root@kind-control-plane:/# k expose deploy hello --name hello-svc --port 80
service/hello-svc exposed
root@kind-control-plane:/# k get svc
NAME            TYPE        CLUSTER-IP       EXTERNAL-IP   PORT(S)   AGE
hello-svc       ClusterIP   100.96.226.92    <none>        80/TCP    2s
kubernetes      ClusterIP   10.96.0.1        <none>        443/TCP   153m
```

D.6.8   *Changing the ClusterIP Service to NodePort*

To change the Service type, we can run the command `k edit svc hello-svc`, which will open the YAML in a Vim text editor. Under the spec, we can change the line that starts with `type` (line 32) from `type: ClusterIP` to `type: NodePort`. Then, we can add `nodePort: 3000` under the list of ports (directly under `port: 80`). The final YAML after the changes will look like the following:

```
ipFamilyPolicy: SingleStack
ports:
- nodePort: 30000
  port: 80
  protocol: TCP
  targetPort: 80
selector:
  app: hello
sessionAffinity: None
type: NodePort
status:
  loadBalancer: {}
```

When you save and quit the file, the changes will be applied automatically. We can view the Service again with the command `k get svc`. The output will look like the following:

```
root@kind-control-plane:/# k get svc
NAME         TYPE        CLUSTER-IP      EXTERNAL-IP   PORT(S)        AGE
hello-svc    NodePort    100.96.226.92   <none>        80:30000/TCP   5m5s
kubernetes   ClusterIP   10.96.0.1       <none>        443/TCP        159m
```

To access the application through the Service over the node port, we have to retrieve both the location of the Pod (which node it's on) and the IP address of the node. We can view this with the command `k get po -o wide; k get no -o wide`. The output will look like this:

```
root@kind-control-plane:/# k get po -o wide; k get no -o wide
NAME                     READY   STATUS    RESTARTS   AGE    IP
⇨  NODE                  NOMINATED NODE    READINESS GATES
hello-5dc6ddf4c4-qrwq4   1/1     Running   0          12m    10.244.2.7
⇨  kind-worker2          <none>            <none>
nginx                    1/1     Running   0          62m    10.244.1.3
⇨  kind-worker           <none>            <none>
nginx-cd5574b4f-qbz9z    1/1     Running   0          130m   10.244.0.5
⇨  kind-control-plane    <none>            <none>
NAME                STATUS   ROLES           AGE     VERSION   INTERNAL-IP
⇨  EXTERNAL-IP      OS-IMAGE              KERNEL-VERSION    CONTAINER-RUNTIME
kind-control-plane  Ready    control-plane   166m    v1.26.0   172.18.0.7
⇨  <none>           Ubuntu 22.04.1 LTS    5.15.49-linuxkit   containerd://1.6.12
kind-worker         Ready    <none>          165m    v1.26.0   172.18.0.3
⇨  <none>           Ubuntu 22.04.1 LTS    5.15.49-linuxkit   containerd://1.6.12
kind-worker2        Ready    <none>          165m    v1.26.0   172.18.0.2
⇨  <none>           Ubuntu 22.04.1 LTS    5.15.49-linuxkit   containerd://1.6.12
```

We can see that the Pod resides on `kind-worker2` and the IP address is 172.18.0.2. Let's use curl now to access the application with the command `curl 172.18.0.2:30000`. The output will look like the following:

```
root@kind-control-plane:/# curl 172.18.0.2:30000
Server address: 10.244.2.7:80
Server name: hello-5dc6ddf4c4-qrwq4
Date: 18/Feb/2023:19:47:09 +0000
URI: /
Request ID: fb4b47a4fe62ed734b2c023d802bf46e
```

D.6.9   *Installing Ingress controller and Ingress resource*

Let's install the Ingress controller, according to the instructions for this exercise, with the command `k apply -f https://raw.githubusercontent.com/chadmcrowell/acing-the-cka-exam/main/ch_06/nginx-ingress-controller.yaml`. Once the Ingress controller has been installed, we can change the `hello-svc` Service back to a ClusterIP Service with the command `k edit svc hello-svc`. This will open the Service in a Vim text editor, where we can change the type back to `ClusterIP` from `NodePort` and then make sure to remove the line that has the node port number (nodeport: 30000). The final YAML will look like the following:

```
ports:
- port: 80
  protocol: TCP
  targetPort: 80
selector:
  app: hello
sessionAffinity: None
type: ClusterIP
```

Now we can create an Ingress resource, which is where I would take advantage of having the Kubernetes documentation open during the exam. From the site https://kubernetes.io/docs, open a browser, type `ingress` in the search bar, and press Enter. Click the first link, which is named Ingress, and on the right side of the page, click The Ingress Resource. You can copy and paste directly from the page into your terminal. Let's create a file named `ingress.yaml` with the command `vim ingress.yaml`, change the YAML slightly from what's in the documentation, and paste it as follows:

```
apiVersion: networking.k8s.io/v1
kind: Ingress
metadata:
  name: hello
  annotations:
    nginx.ingress.kubernetes.io/rewrite-target: /
spec:
  rules:
  - host: hello.com
    http:
      paths:
```

```
     - path: /
       pathType: Prefix
       backend:
         service:
           name: hello-svc
           port:
             number: 80
```

Once you have the YAML set, you can apply the YAML with the command k apply -f ingress.yaml. Then run the command k get ing to list the hello Ingress resource. The output will be similar to the following:

```
root@kind-control-plane:/# k apply -f ingress.yaml
ingress.networking.k8s.io/hello created
root@kind-control-plane:/# k get ing
NAME    CLASS    HOSTS       ADDRESS    PORTS    AGE
hello   <none>   hello.com              80       2s
```

D.6.10 *Installing a container network interface (CNI)*

To install a kind Kubernetes cluster without a CNI, see appendix C. Once you've created the cluster and run the Docker exec -it kind-control-plane command to access the control plane node (which has kubectl already installed), let's continue with this exercise.

To install a bridge CNI, let's first make sure we have wget installed. Let's install it on both the control plane and the worker node with the command apt update; apt install wget. Once wget is installed, we'll run the command wget https://github.com/ containernetworking/plugins/releases/download/v1.1.1/cni-plugins-linux-amd64- v1.1.1.tgz to download the CNI plugins. We'll untar the file with the command tar - xvf cni-plugins-linux-amd64-v1.1.1.tgz and then run the command mv bridge /opt/ cni/bin/ to move the file into the bin directory. Now we can install the Calico CNI with the command kubectl apply -f https://raw.githubusercontent.com/projectcalico/ calico/v3.25.0/manifests/calico.yaml. When you run the command k get no, you will see the status of the nodes goes from Not Ready to Ready. The output will look similar to this:

```
root@kind-control-plane:/# k get no
NAME                 STATUS    ROLES            AGE    VERSION
kind-control-plane   Ready     control-plane    11m    v1.25.0-beta.0
kind-worker          Ready     <none>           10m    v1.25.0-beta.0
```

D.7   *Chapter 7 exam exercises*

The following exam exercises are based on storage and much like the previous chapters will need to be done sequentially. You will not be able to complete the second exercise before the first. Having a good understanding of persistent volumes, persistent volume claims, and storage classes are crucial for the exam.

D.7.1   Creating a persistent volume

To create a persistent volume claim (PVC), we can refer to the Kubernetes documentation, which we can keep open during the exam. This will allow us to copy and paste directly from the page to our terminal, which will best utilize the limited time you have for the exam. Go to https://kubernetes.io/docs and use the search bar on the left side of the screen to search for the term *use a persistent volume*. Click on the link that says Configure a Pod to Use a PersistentVolume for Storage | Kubernetes and scroll down to the section Create a Persistent Volume. The full URL of the page is https://kubernetes.io/docs/tasks/configure-pod-container/configure-persistent-volume -storage/#create-a-persistentvolume. Copy and paste the YAML from this page into a new file named pv.yaml.

We'll change the name of the persistent volume from `task-pv-volume` to `vol-store308` and change the storage from `10Gi` to `22Mi`. Save the file pv.yaml and create the persistent volume with the command `k create -f pv.yaml`. If you perform the command `k get pv`, you will see an output similar to the following:

```
root@kind-control-plane:/# k get pv
NAME            CAPACITY    ACCESS MODES    RECLAIM POLICY    STATUS      CLAIM
⇥ STORAGECLASS
volstore308  100Mi       RWO             Retain            Available
⇥ manual
```

D.7.2   Creating a persistent volume claim

To create a PVC, we'll reference the same page in the documentation mentioned previously, so hopefully you still have it open. If not, here's the link: https://kubernetes .io/docs/tasks/configure-pod-container/configure-persistent-volume-storage/#create -a-persistentvolumeclaim. Copy and paste the YAML into a file named pvc.yaml (use the command `vim pvc.yaml`).

We'll change the name of the PVC from `task-pv-claim` to `pv-claim-vol` and change storage from `3Gi` to `90Mi`. Create the PVC with the command `k apply -f pvc.yaml`. Once the resource is created, you can view the PVC with the command `k get pvc`, and you can also view the persistent volume (PV) with the command `k get pv`. The output of the command will look like this:

```
root@kind-control-plane:/# k get pvc
NAME            STATUS    VOLUME    CAPACITY    ACCESS MODES    STORAGECLASS
⇥ AGE
pv-claim-vol  Bound     vol02833  100Mi       RWO             manual
⇥ 4m
```

D.7.3   Creating a Pod to use the claim

To create the YAML for a Pod named `pod-access` with the `centos:7` image, we'll run the command `k run pod-access --image centos:7 --dry-run -o yaml > pod-access.yaml`. Once the file has been saved, we can open it in the Vim text editor with the command `vim pod-access.yaml`. Once the file is open, we can add the section that will attach the volume via the claim we just created in the previous exercise. Under `containers:`, add `volumeMounts:` inline with the container name and image. Under `volumeMounts:`, add the name as `- name: vol` and `mountPath: /tmp/persistence` just below. To keep the container alive, we can add the sleep command just below with `- command:` followed by `- sleep` and `- "3600"`. The result will look like this:

```
containers:
- command:
  - sleep
  - "3600"
  image: centos:7
  name: pod-access
  resources: {}
  volumeMounts:
  - name: vol
    mountPath: /tmp/persistence
volumes:
- name: vol
  persistentVolumeClaim:
    claimName: pv-claim-vol
```

You can create the Pod with the command `k apply -f pod-access.yaml`.

D.7.4 Creating a storage class

To create a storage class named `node-local`, we can refer again to the Kubernetes documentation. From https://kubernetes.io/docs, let's search storage class in the search bar. Click on the first result, which is named Storage Classes, and click Local from the right side of the page. Copy and paste the YAML from the page right into your terminal. We'll paste it exactly as it is and change the name to `node-local` into a new file named `sc.yaml`. The final result will be the following:

```
apiVersion: storage.k8s.io/v1
kind: StorageClass
metadata:
  name: node-local
provisioner: kubernetes.io/no-provisioner
volumeBindingMode: WaitForFirstConsumer
```

The storage class can be created with the command `k apply -f sc.yaml`. We can view the storage class with the command `k get sc`.

D.7.5 Creating a persistent volume claim for a storage class

To create a PVC for a storage class named `claim-sc`, we'll use the previously created PVC and modify it. Let's copy that file with the command `cp pvc.yaml pvc-sc.yaml`. We'll change the name of the PVC to `claim-sc`, change the claim to `39Mi`, and change the access mode to `ReadWriteOnce`. The final YAML for this PVC should look like the following:

```
apiVersion: v1
kind: PersistentVolumeClaim
metadata:
  name: claim-sc
spec:
  storageClassName: claim-sc
  accessModes:
    - ReadWriteOnce
  resources:
    requests:
      storage: 39Mi
```

We can create the PVC with the command k apply -f pvc-sc.yaml.

D.7.6   *Creating a Pod from a storage class*

To create a Pod named pod-sc with the nginx image, we can run the command k run
pod-sc --image nginx --dry-run=client -o yaml > pod-sc.yaml. Once the file has been
saved, we can open it in the Vim text editor with the command vim pod-sc.yaml. Once
the file is open, we can add the section that will attach the volume via the claim we just
created in the previous exercise. Under containers:, add the volumeMounts: inline with
the container name and image. Under volumeMounts:, add the name as - name: vol and
mountPath: /tmp/persistence just below that. To keep the container alive, we can add
the sleep command just below with command: followed by - sleep and - "3600". The
result will look like this:

```
containers:
  image: nginx
  name: pod-sc
  resources: {}
  volumeMounts:
  - name: vol
    mountPath: /tmp/persistence
    command:
      - sleep
      - "3600"
volumes:
- name: vol
  persistentVolumeClaim:
    claimName: claim-sc
```

You can create the Pod with the command k apply -f pod-sc.yaml.

D.8   *Chapter 8 exam exercises*

Chapter 8 is all about troubleshooting, so a lot of these exercises will require you to
simulate something being "broken" in the cluster. Just know that for the exam, these
will probably be staged in a way that the component is already broken, whereas here
in our practice lab environment, we'll need to set up the scenario, which may take a
few extra steps.

D.8.1   Fixing the Pod YAML

Run the command in the exercise, which is `k run testbox --image busybox --command 'sleep 3600'`. When you do this, you'll see that the status is `RunContainerError`. The first step in troubleshooting is to check the logs with the command `k logs testbox`. But the result will not return any logs, so we must go through the decision tree and describe the Pod. To do this, we can run the command `k describe po testbox`. We can see the events from the `describe` command, which look like this:

```
Events:
  Type      Reason     Age            From                Message
  ----      ------     ----           ----                -------
  Normal    Scheduled  119s           default-scheduler   Successfully
⇒ assigned default/testbox to kind-worker
  Normal    Pulled     116s           kubelet             Successfully
⇒ pulled image "busybox" in 2.754916379s
  Normal    Pulled     114s           kubelet             Successfully
⇒ pulled image "busybox" in 622.019612ms
  Normal    Pulled     98s            kubelet             Successfully
⇒ pulled image "busybox" in 710.339798ms
  Normal    Created    73s (x4 over 116s) kubelet         Created
⇒ container testbox
  Warning   Failed     73s (x4 over 116s) kubelet         Error: failed
⇒ to create containerd task: failed to create shim task: OCI runtime
⇒ create failed: runc create failed: unable to start container process:
⇒ exec: "sleep 3600": executable file not found in $PATH: unknown
  Normal    Pulled     73s            kubelet             Successfully
⇒ pulled image "busybox" in 526.759076ms
  Warning   BackOff    45s (x7 over 114s) kubelet         Back-off
⇒ restarting failed container
  Normal    Pulling    33s (x5 over 118s) kubelet         Pulling image
⇒ "busybox"
  Normal    Pulled     32s            kubelet             Successfully
⇒ pulled image "busybox" in 497.474074ms
```

The error is "failed to create containerd task," which means that we need to modify the YAML before we start the container again. We can edit the Pod with the command `k edit po testbox` and change the YAML at the line that starts with the word `command`. Instead of the term `sleep 3600`, put the `3600` on the next line and surround it with quotes and another dash. The final result of the YAML should be like this:

```
containers:
- command:
  - sleep
  - "3600"
  image: busybox
```

When you try to save and quit, you'll get an error message, but you can simply quit and ignore the message. You'll see that a copy of the file has been saved in the `/tmp` directory. You can replace the Pod YAML with the command `k replace -f /tmp/`

kubectl-edit-8848373.yaml. Note that the name of the YAML file will be different from the one here. This will create a new Pod, and you will see now that the Pod is running.

```
root@kind-control-plane:/# k replace -f /tmp/kubectl-edit-4023269864.yaml -
➥ -force
pod "testbox" deleted
pod/testbox replaced
root@kind-control-plane:/# k get po
NAME       READY   STATUS    RESTARTS   AGE
testbox    1/1     Running   0          2s
```

D.8.2 Fixing the Pod image

To create a new container named busybox2 that uses the busybox:1.35.0 image, run the command k run busybox2 -image busybox:1.35.0. You will see the following result by running the command k get po:

```
root@kind-control-plane:/# k get po
NAME       READY   STATUS      RESTARTS     AGE
busybox2   0/1     Completed   2 (20s ago)  23s
```

We can follow the decision tree by first trying to obtain the logs, but there are no logs for this container. We'll then describe the Pod with the command k describe po busybox2. The events in the Pod description don't tell us much, so it seems to be operating correctly. We can perform a trick in one simple command to prevent the container from completing. Let's run the command k run busybox2 --image busybox:1.35.0 -it -sh, which will open a shell to the container. When we exit the shell, we can run k get po and see that the container is running.

D.8.3 Fixing a completed Pod

To create a new container named curlpod2 with the nicolaka/netshoot image, we'll run the command k run curlpod --image nicolaka/netshoot -it --sh. This will open a shell to the container within. Let's run the command nslookup kubernetes and exit out of the shell. We see again that the Pod has completed. This is because it doesn't have the commands within the container image to keep it running. We can add this with the command kubectl run curlpod --image=nicolaka/netshoot --command sleep --command "3600".

D.8.4 Fixing the Kubernetes scheduler

Move the file kube-scheduler.yaml to back it up. This is always a good idea, especially for the exam when you can't simply rebuild the cluster. Let's run the command cp /etc/Kubernetes/manifests/kube-scheduler.yaml /tmp/kube-scheduler.yaml. We can then modify the existing file by running the command vim /etc/Kubernetes/manifests/kube-scheduler.yaml. Once we have that open in our Vim text editor, add an extra r to the end of the word kube-scheduler so that it becomes kube-schedulerr. Save and quit the file.

Now that the scheduler configuration has been modified, let's see if a Pod can be scheduled with the command `k run nginx -image nginx` and check the status of the Pod by running the command `k get po`. The output will look like the following:

```
root@kind-control-plane:/# k run nginx --image nginx
pod/nginx created
root@kind-control-plane:/# k get po
NAME       READY   STATUS    RESTARTS        AGE
curlpod    1/1     Running   1 (6m37s ago)   8m1s
nginx      0/1     Pending   0               1s
```

This is one of those cases where we know the problem, but let's pretend we don't. Look at the events with the command `k -n kube-system describe po kube-scheduler-kind-control-plane`. The events will look like this:

```
Events:
  Type     Reason   Age                     From      Message
  ----     ------   ----                    ----      -------
  Normal   Created  3m22s (x4 over 4m7s)    kubelet   Created container kube-
⮡ scheduler
  Warning  Failed   3m22s (x4 over 4m6s)    kubelet   Error: failed to create
⮡ containerd task: failed to create shim task: OCI runtime create failed:
⮡ runc create failed: unable to start container process: exec: "kube-
⮡ schedulerr": executable file not found in $PATH: unknown
  Warning  BackOff  2m53s (x12 over 4m5s)   kubelet   Back-off restarting
⮡ failed container
  Normal   Pulled   2m41s (x5 over 4m7s)    kubelet   Container image
⮡ "registry.k8s.io/kube-scheduler:v1.25.0-beta.0" already present on machine
```

You'll also notice that the Pod is in a `crashloopbackoff` state. You can see the error "unable to start container process."

D.8.5 *Fixing the kubelet*

Let's run the command `curl https://raw.githubusercontent.com/chadmcrowell/acing-the-cka-exam/main/ch_08/10-kubeadm.conf --silent --output /etc/systemd/system/kubelet.service.d/10-kubeadm.conf; systemctl daemon-reload; systemctl restart kubelet`. This will break the cluster in a way that affects the kubelet. Let's check the status of the kubelet service with the command `systemctl status kubelet`. We notice that the service is inactive and see that the process has an error. Let's check the file in `/etc/systemd/system/kubelet.service.d`, which is named `10-kubeadm.conf`. We'll notice that the file has an incorrect `bin` directory, which is `/usr/local/bin` as opposed to `usr/bin`. Let's change the file to `/usr/bin` and see if that fixes it. Open the file with the command `vim /etc/systemd/system/kubelet.service.d/10-kubeadm.conf`. Once we have the file open, we can change the contents as follows:

```
# This eventually leads to kubelet failing to start, see:
⮡ https://github.com/kubernetes-sigs/kind/issues/2323
ExecStartPre=/bin/sh -euc "if [ ! -f /sys/fs/cgroup/cgroup.controllers ] &&
⮡ [ ! -d /sys/fs/cgroup/systemd/kubelet ]; then mkdir -p
```

```
➥ /sys/fs/cgroup/systemd/kubelet; fi"
ExecStart=
ExecStart=/usr/bin/kubelet $KUBELET_KUBECONFIG_ARGS $KUBELET_CONFIG_ARGS
➥ $KUBELET_KUBEADM_ARGS $KUBELET_EXTRA_ARGS --cgroup-root=/kubelet
```

Once your file looks like this, save and quit the file. Then reload the daemon with the command `systemctl daemon-reload`, followed by restarting the kubelet service with the command `systemctl restart kubelet`. Check the status of the kubelet service with the command `systemctl status kubelet`, and the service should be active and running now.

index